THE BOOK OF PILLS
FOR MEN AND WOMEN
OVER 4

WITH AN INTRODUCTION BY

DR. ROBERT DANOFF

INFORMATION SUPPLIED BY

FIRST DATABANK

ibooks

New York
www.ibooks.net
DISTRIBUTED BY SIMON & SCHUSTER, INC.

A Publication of ibooks, Inc.

Copyright © 2003 ibooks
Information supplied by First Databank, Inc. Copyright © 2003 First Databank

An ibooks, Inc. Book

Distributed by Simon & Schuster, Inc.
1230 Avenue of the Americas, New York, NY 10020

ibooks, Inc.
24 West 25th Street
New York, NY 10010

The ibooks World Wide Web Site Address is:
http://www.ibooks.net

ISBN 0-7434-5885-0
First ibooks, Inc. printing August 2003
10 9 8 7 6 5 4 3 2 1

Cover design by j vita

Printed in the U.S.A.

Important Note: This book was written to provide selected information to the public concerning frequently prescribed medications. Research about prescription drugs is an ongoing process; side effects and adverse reactions to particular drugs sometimes continue to be reported to the FDA after a drug has been approved for use in the general market. While every effort has been made to include the most up-to-date information in this book, there can be no guarantee that such information won't change with time and further research. The reader should also keep in mind that we have included information on open questions, debates, and controversies regarding drug use and safety that have been reported in medical journals and major periodicals. Our aim here is simply to report that these concerns exist, not to take a position on the scientific validity of any one position. Readers should bear in mind that this book is not intended to be used for self-diagnosis or self-treatment; they should consult their doctors about any and all medical problems. Readers should never stop taking a prescription drug or alter the dosage or dosing schedule without first consulting their physicians. Neither the publisher nor the author take any responsibility for any possible consequences from any treatment, action or application of medicine or preparation by any person reading or following the information in this book.

The following information is intended to suppliment, not substitute for, the expertise and judgement of your physician, pharmacist or other healthcare professional. It should not be construed to indicate that the use of the drug is safe, appropriate, or effective for you. Consult your healthcare professional before taking this drug.

The information in these monographs is not indended to cover all possible uses, directions, precautions, drug interactions, or adverse effects. This information is generalized and is not intended as specific medical advice. If you have questions about the medicines you are taking or would like more information, check with your doctor, pharmacist, or nurse.

Target Audience: This book is intended for use by those approaching middle age or older. If you are younger than forty, and especially if you are pregnant or breast-feeding, it is strongly advised that you use this book only as the first part of your research. The selection of the medications and specific precautions primarily address older adults.

INTRODUCTION

A s a family doctor, I have the privilege of helping patients with their health concerns. People of all different backgrounds and ages are confronted by health problems at some time or another. Perhaps you or a loved one is ill or has a condition of some kind and you want to do all you can to facilitate a speedy recovery with as little pain as possible. In times like these it is natural for you to wonder what medication to take. This is often the case with many of my patients. They might read about a medication which may help their condition before they even come into the office. This scenario is especially true for the highly informed, health conscious, "baby-boomer" generation–my generation. As a generation we are staying healthier longer.

My grandmother used to say to me "Robby, it's no good getting old. There are lots of pills to remember to take and just too many doctors' appointments to make." She would also wonder whether taking all her medications at once was safe.

In her wisdom, my grandmother's insights were on-target. I spent tens of thousands of dollars in medical school to learn a single word that sums up this concern: polypharmacy, or literally "many medications." Nowadays polypharmacy is a common occurrence. As our population gets older we tend to take more and more medications in order to maintain our health–or as Anna, a wonderful woman 91-years-young calls it, to keep the "giddy-up a-going strong."

MEDICATING IS A SERIOUS BUSINESS   In order to reach long life we need to medicate safely. That's where *The Book of Pills for Men and Women Over 40* is a very useful tool. Let me give you some numbers to illustrate why I feel so strongly about the importance of this book. In the year 2002 the elderly (65 and above) made up more than 14 percent of the population of the United States. However, when it comes to prescription medications, this small group of our population accounted for nearly 40 percent of all prescription-medication users. This is a huge number and a big concern. As we get older, we tend to be at a higher risk for having a drug-induced adverse reaction, especially since older Americans tend to have more than one medical condition at a time, such as diabetes and high cholesterol.

Multiple medical conditions often result in multiple prescription medications, and the more drugs a person is taking, the greater the risk of a drug-drug interaction. There is no getting around it: polypharmacy in the older adult is almost always a problem.

THE DANGEROUS ROAD   What can you do to reduce your risk of an adverse reaction to a prescription medication? There is a lot you can do. Here is a situation that might sound familiar: You leave the physician's office with a prescription, thinking you remember the name of the medication you're supposed to take. You get in the car or board the bus and try to read the writing on the prescription. The writing is nearly illegible! You move the piece of paper this way and that, then hold it up to the light while moving your head in all directions. In an attempt to get your own second opinion, you ask a family member or the local handwriting specialist to try to decipher the writing. Is the difficult-to-read letter an "e" or an "a;" a "v" or an "o;" or an "l" or a "t"?

When you thought you were able to figure out the wording on the prescription, the name of the medication seems to be different from what you thought you heard in the office. You hand the prescription to the pharmacist. The pharmacist reads the prescription as Celexa (for depression)—but it could be Celebrex (for pain), or Cephalexin (an antibiotic). I have heard of a patient who was supposed to be on Allegra (for allergies), but was given Viagra. This sounds difficult to believe, but it happened. In fact, the Food and Drug Administration gets at least 75 reports per month of mix-ups due to similarly named drugs and difficult-to-read handwriting.

When you pick up the medication you may not read the label, you may have difficulty reading the label because of the small type used, or you may read it but figure the name differs from the one your physician told you because your insurance plan only pays for generic medications. You might figure the different name on the label "must be a generic!" So you go home and take the medication you thought was for allergies, and other results may occur, including some dangerous side effects.

REDUCING THE RISKS   How can we reduce the chances of the medication mix-ups? We all have to take responsibility. First, it would be helpful if the pharmaceutical companies didn't use similar names for drugs with different actions. For example, the drug Micronor (used for oral contraception) sounds like the medication Midamor (a diuretic). When poorly written, Desowen (a steroid cream) may look like Desogen (for contraception); only the "w" and "g" are different in those names.

Next, we as physicians need to write our prescriptions much more clearly, and to take the time to speak with our patients regarding the name and use of the medication we have prescribed. At the pharmacy, it would be helpful if the pharmacist would speak with the person getting the medication to ensure that it is the right one for the condition the person is being treated.

Most important, remember that you are the CEO of your own healthcare. You as the patient or as the caregiver to a loved one must take an active role in your health treatment plan. When you are at your doctor's office, make sure you tell the doctor any medications whatsoever you are taking, even herbal or non-herbal preparations. Bring them with you and ask if they will interact with the prescription medication(s) you are about to take.

A SAFE JOURNEY   Ask your doctor to write down the brand name(s) and generic name(s) of the medication(s) you are about to take, to state what they are for, and to tell you how often you should use them. Take a good look at the prescription to make sure you can read the handwriting. After those questions are answered, get complete information from your your pharmacist or physician before you take those pills.

What to ask your doctor or pharmacist about your prescription:

- what the pill looks like, so you know you are getting the right one
- the best time to take the medication
- whether the medication should be taken with or without food
- whether certain foods or juices (such as grapefruit juice) interfere with the medication
- the length of time the medication will need to be taken
- possible side effects and what to do if side effects occur
- what to do if a dose is missed
- possible interactions with any other medications you are taking
- whether the current medication replaces something else you were taking
- where and how to store the medication

I know many of you may sometimes feel that you are bothering your healthcare professional by asking questions. Please don't feel that way. Your health depends upon good communication, and good communication is a two-way street. *The Book of Pills for Men and Women Over 40* may just be the road map you need to find your way to a healthy destination.

Peace and good health to you.
DR. ROBERT DANOFF

HOW TO USE THIS BOOK

The prescription medications within this book are presented alphabetically by generic name in a large-print, easy-to-follow format. An index at the end of the book lists all brand names and generics. Each listing includes the following:

Generic Name

The generic name of a drug is its common name not associated with any brand name or trademark. The generic name is usually identified by the primary ingredient that has been approved by the Food and Drug Administration. Prescription-drug medications might have more than one brand name but only one generic name. Your doctor may indicate to the pharmacist that the prescription may be filled by a medication's generic equivalent. In this case, the medication will have the same effect and will most likely cost much less than its brand-name.

Common Brand Names

The prescription medication listings in this book include the most common brand name(s) associated with a generic drug. Each generic drug might have more than one brand name associated with it. The listings are by no means exhaustive and are meant to include only the most widely-available brands. If you don't see your brand name listed, ask your health-care practitioner for the name of its generic and look under that listing.

Uses

This entry gives an overview of the conditions and diseases for which a medication is prescribed.

How to Use

This listing indicates method, time of day, and frequency with which a medication is normally taken.

Side Effects

Symptoms of discomfort that may be associated with a particular prescription drug.

Also included are more serious symptoms that require medical consultation (by telephone) or attention (with a visit to a doctor's office).

Precautions
A listing, if applicable, of any specific conditions that might preclude the taking of the medication. If you have been prescribed a medication for which you see a precaution that applies to you, it would be wise to consult with your health-care practitioner just to make sure that he or she is aware of the condition.

Drug Interactions
Notes on any specific drug groups with which the prescribed medication does not interact well.

Notes
Specific activities to avoid or speed with which the medication should take effect are listed here as a gauge of what seems on-target, and what might require a doctor's attention.

Missed Dose
When and how to resume taking a prescribed medication if you should happen to miss a dose.

Storage
Any special information about storage temperature and when a medication must be refrigerated.

IF YOU DO NOT KNOW THE GENERIC NAME OF YOUR MEDICATION

If you want to read about a certain medication and only know its brand name, here is a listing by brand name, cross-referenced by its generic.

Brand Name	Generic Name	Page
Cleocin	Clindamycin	73
Codeine	Promethazine / Codeine	276
Colsalide	Colchicine	81
Combivent	Ipratropium/Albuterol	171
Comtan	Entacapone	103
Concerta	Methylphenidate	212
Cordarone	Amiodarone	13
Cotrim	Trimeth/Sulfameth	345
Coumadin	Warfarin	358
Covera-HS	Verapamil	356
Cozaar	Losartan	199
Cycrin	Medroxyprogesterone	206
Darvocet	Propoxyphene with Acetaminophen (APAP)	278
Deltasone	Prednisone	271
Desyrel	Trazodone	337
Detrol	Tolterodine	333
Dia Beta	Glyburide	143
Diflucan	Fluconazole	117
Digitek	Digoxin	93
Dilantin	Phenytoin	261
Diovan	Valsartan	349
Diovan HCT	Valsartan/HCTZ	351
Ditropan	Oxybutynin	246
Dizac	Diazepam Common	89
Doryx	Doxycycline	99
Dyazide	Triamterene/HCTZ	343
Effexor	Venlafaxine	354
Elavil	Amitriptyline	15

Brand Name	Generic Name	Page
Theolair	Theophylline	331
Tiazac	Diltiazem	95
Toprol XL	Metoprolol	219
Tricor	Fenofibrate	111
Trimox	Amoxicillin	21
Tylenol #3	Acetaminophen with Codeine	1
Tylox	Oxycodone/APAP	250
Ultram	Tramadol	335
Uniphyl	Theophylline	331
Valium	Diazepam Common	89
Valtrex	Valacyclovir	347
Vasotec	Enalapril	101
Veetids	Penicillin VK	257
Ventolin	Albuterol Sulfate	5
Verapamil HCL	Verapamil	356
Verelan	Verapamil	356
Viagra	Sildenafil Citrate	313
Vibramycin	Doxycycline	99
Vicodin	Hydrocodone with APAP	159
Vicoprofen	Hydrocodone/Ibuprofen	156
Vioxx	Rofecoxib	296
Vistaril	Hydroxyzine	161
Voltaren	Diclofenac	91
Wellbutrin	Bupropion HCL	45
Xalatan	Latanoprost	181
Xanax	Alprazolam	11
Zantac	Ranitidine	290
Zestoretic	Lisinopril/HCTZ	191

WHAT TO DO
IF THERE IS AN EMERGENCY

As we get older, it is important to create a network of family, friends, and neighbors with whom to check in on a regular basis and to whom we can turn when there is trouble. Older adults especially may be more susceptible to falls in the home; may experience an unexpected reaction to a medication; or may inadvertently follow a dosing schedule incorrectly.

Be prepared for any situation by having important phone numbers— your doctor, a local poison control center, or a neighbor—readily at hand or on the speed-dial function of your telephone.

If there is an actual emergency situation, such as a possible overdose, accidental poisoning, or severe adverse side-effect from taking a prescription-drug medication, it is important to remain calm and try to get help as quickly as possible.

If you are alone, dial "911" for immediate assistance and keep your prescription bottle(s) available to show to the emergency medical personnel and to take to the hospital with you. If you are allergic to any medications, make that information available as well.

If you have called for emergency medical attention or have called a poison control center, the dispatcher will most likely instruct you as to what to do. In some cases of poisoning, you might be instructed to drink a glass of water or take something to force you to vomit. Follow the instructions closely and try to answer all questions as calmly as you can.

If you are with someone who needs medical attention, call for medical help immediately and then make sure that the person is comfortable. If the person is breathing, loosen the collar or belt. If the person is not breathing, lay the person on his or her back and push the neck gently upward to open the airway between the mouth and lungs.

If the person is not breathing, begin mouth-to-mouth resuscitation.

If the person is having convulsions or is unconscious, try to lie him on his stomach with his head to one side so that if he vomits, he will not choke.

Other Safety Tips Take a class in CPR or emergency first-aid at a local "Y" or adult-education center. If this is not possible, then perhaps a neighbor, family member, or caregiver can go.

Store your medication in the container in which it came.

Always keep your prescription bottles in the same place so that you will be able to find them when it is time to take your medication.

Keep a pair of glasses near your prescription bottles so that you can always make sure you are taking the proper dose of the proper medication.

Read the label in plenty of available light. Do not go by memory as to what the dose should be.

When you have finished with a prescription, dispose of any unusued medicine by flushing it down the toilet. Do not give unused medicine to others.

Get to know your pharmacist so that you will feel comfortable asking any questions you may have about your medication.

Try to get your prescriptions filled at the same pharmacy so that any possible adverse drug interactions can be caught by the pharmacist or the store's computerized back-up system.

ACETAMINOPHEN WITH CODEINE

Common Brand Name: Tylenol # 3

Uses
This medication is used to relieve moderate-to-severe pain.

How to Use
Take this medication by mouth, exactly as prescribed. To prevent upset stomach, take with food or milk.

Pain medications work best in preventing pain before it occurs. Once the pain becomes intense, the medication is not as effective in relieving it.

Use this medication exactly as directed by your doctor. Do not increase your dose, take it more frequently, or use it for a longer period of time than prescribed because this drug can be habit-forming. Also, if used for an extended period of time, do not suddenly stop using this drug without your doctor's approval.

When used for extended periods, this drug may not work as well and may require different dosing. Talk with your doctor if this medication stops working well.

Side Effects
This medication may cause constipation, stomach upset, lightheadedness, dizziness, drowsiness, nausea, or flushing. If any of these effects persist or worsen, contact your doctor or pharmacist promptly.

Tell your doctor immediately if you have any of these unlikely but serious side effects: loss of coordination, confusion, irregular heartbeat, slow/irregular breathing, anxiety, tremors.

An allergic reaction to this drug is unlikely, but seek immediate medical attention if it occurs. Symptoms of an allergic reaction include: rash, itching, swelling, severe dizziness, trouble breathing.

If you notice other effects not listed above, contact your doctor or pharmacist.

Precautions
Tell your doctor your medical history, especially if you have: liver or kidney conditions, history of alcohol use, heart problems, abdominal/stomach problems,

1

breathing problems, seizure disorders, drug dependency, severe diarrhea, drug allergies.

Avoid alcoholic beverages, because they may increase certain side effects of this drug. Use caution when performing tasks requiring alertness such as driving or using heavy machinery.

This product contains acetaminophen, which may cause liver damage. Daily use of alcohol, especially when combined with acetaminophen, may increase your risk for liver damage. Check with your doctor or pharmacist for more information.

Caution is advised when prescribing or using this drug with older people or very young since they may be more sensitive to the effects of this medication.

Drug Interactions

Tell your doctor of all prescription andnonprescription drugs you use, including: MAO inhibitors (e.g., furazolidone, linezolid, phenelzine, selegiline, tranylcypromine), psychiatric drugs, tranquilizers, sleep medications, rifampin, other narcotic pain relievers, barbiturates, anti-seizure drugs, drowsiness-causing antihistamines (e.g., diphenhydramine), isoniazid, zidovudine, sulfinpyrazone, cimetidine.

Before taking pain relievers, cough-and-cold medicines or allergy products, read their labels to be sure that they do not also contain acetaminophen. An overdose of acetaminophen can be harmful. If you are uncertain your medicines contain acetaminophen, ask your pharmacist.

Do not start or stop any medicine without first consulting your doctor or pharmacist.

Notes

To prevent constipation, increase your intake of fiber, drink plenty of water and exercise.

This medication has been prescribed for your current condition only. Do not use it later for another condition unless told to do so by your doctor. A different medication may be necessary in those cases. Do not share this medication with others.

Missed Dose

If you miss a dose, take it as soon as you remember. If it is near the time of the next dose, skip the missed dose and resume your usual dosing schedule. Do not double the dose to catch up.

Storage

Store at room temperature away from light and moisture.

ACYCLOVIR

Common Brand Name: Zovirax

Uses
This medication is used to treat herpes infections of the skin, mouth, mucous membranes, genital herpes, herpes zoster (shingles), and chickenpox in some individuals. This medication does not cure herpes, but relieves the pain and may make the infection clear faster.

How to Use
Begin taking this medication as soon as symptoms appear.

Take this medication as directed. Consult your doctor or pharmacist if you have any questions. Try to take the medication at evenly spaced intervals throughout the day and night. This will ensure a constant blood level of the medication and is most effective.

Side Effects
This medication may cause stomach upset, loss of appetite, nausea, vomiting, diarrhea, headache, dizziness or weakness. These effects should disappear in a few days as your body adjusts to the medication. If they persist or become worse, inform your doctor.

Notify your doctor if you experience: numbness or tingling of the hands or feet, leg pain, sore throat, skin rash, change in the amount of urine.

An allergic reaction to this drug is unlikely, but seek immediate medical attention if it occurs. Symptoms of an allergic reaction include: rash, itching, swelling, dizziness, trouble breathing.

If you notice other effects not listed above, contact your doctor or pharmacist.

Precautions
There are no special precautions for the older adult.

Drug Interactions
Inform your doctor about all the medicines you use (both prescription and nonprescription).

Do not start or stop any medicine without first consulting your doctor or pharmacist.

Notes
Avoid sexual activity while signs and symptoms of genital herpes are present to prevent infecting your partner.

Inform your doctor if this medication does not appear to decrease the frequency or severity of recurrent infections. This medication needs to be dosed as per the patients kidney function.

Missed Dose
If you miss a dose, take it as soon as you remember. If it is near the time of the next dose, skip the missed dose and resume your usual dosing schedule. Do not double the dose to catch up.

Storage
Store at room temperature away from sunlight and moisture.

ALBUTEROL SULFATE

Common Brand Names: Proventil, Ventolin

Uses
This drug relaxes the smooth muscle in the lungs and dilates airways to improve breathing. It is used in the treatment of asthma, chronic bronchitis, emphysema, or chronic obstructive lung disease.

How to Use
Take this medication exactly as prescribed. Do not take it more frequently without your doctor's approval. Excessive use may result in increased side effects.

Side Effects
Dizziness, headache, lightheadedness, heartburn, loss of appetite, altered taste sensation, restlessness, anxiety, nervousness, trembling or sweating may occur but should subside as your body adjust to the medication. If these symptoms persist or worsen, inform your doctor.

Notify your doctor if you experience: chest pain, palpitations, vomiting, breathing difficulties.

If you notice other effects not listed above, contact your doctor or pharmacist.

Precautions
Tell your doctor if you have blood pressure, an overactive thyroid gland, epilepsy, diabetes.

Tell your doctor if you ever had a bad reaction to bitolterol, ephedrine, epinephrine, metaproterenol, phenylephrine, phenylpropanolamine, pseudoephedrine, or terbutaline. Many nonprescription products contain these drugs (e.g., diet pills and medication for colds and asthma), so check the labels carefully. Do not take any of these medications without consulting your doctor (even if you never had a problem taking them before).

Drug Interactions
Tell your doctor of all prescription and nonprescription drugs you may use, especially

if you have: drugs used for asthma, antidepressants, cold medications, beta-blockers (e.g., atenolol, propranolol).

Do not start or stop any medicine without first consulting your doctor or pharmacist.

Notes
If symptoms do not improve or worsen after taking this medication, call your doctor immediately.

Missed Dose
If you miss a dose, take it as soon as you remember. If it is near the time of the next dose, skip the missed dose and resume your usual dosing schedule. Do not double the dose to catch up.

Storage
Store at room temperature away from sunlight and moisture. Some products may require refrigeration. See packaging for exact storage directions, or check with your pharmacist.

ALENDRONATE

Common Brand Name: Fosamax

Uses
Alendronate is used to treat certain cases of osteoporosis (brittle bones) and Paget's disease (a bone weakening disorder).

How to Use
Take this medication with 6 to 8 ounces (180ml-240ml) of plain water once daily. Swallow the tablets whole. Do not suck or chew them.

This medication must be taken on an empty stomach at least 30 minutes before eating or drinking anything other than water, (including other medicines or vitamins).

Do not lie down for at least 30 minutes after taking it. This will help decrease the chance of irritation to your esophagus.

Side Effects
The most common side effect is stomach pain. Other less common side effects are nausea, vomiting, heartburn, stomach fullness, gas, constipation, diarrhea, headache or altered taste.

Notify your doctor if you notice: an increase in muscle or bone pain, severe heartburn, chest pain, black or tarry stools.

If you notice other effects not listed above, contact your doctor or pharmacist.

Precautions
This medication should not be used by patients with kidney disease, low blood calcium levels, or if allergic to biphosphonates.

Tell your doctor your medical history, especially if you have: trouble swallowing, ulcers or other gastrointestinal problems.

It is also important to not smoke and to limit the amount of alcohol used as these can increase the risk of osteoporosis.

Drug Interactions

Tell your doctor of all prescription and nonprescription drugs you may use, especially if you have: estrogens, aspirin, other arthritis medications.

Do not start or stop any medicine without first consulting your doctor or pharmacist.

Notes

It is very important to not take this medication with anything other than water. Even juice and coffee have been found to interfere with its absorption from the stomach . Exercising regularly and acquiring calcium in the diet via eating well-balanced meals can help reduce the risk of osteoporosis. Your doctor will advise you if you should take supplemental calcium as well as vitamin D.

Missed Dose

If you miss a dose, take it as soon as you remember. If it is near the time of the next dose, skip the missed dose and resume your usual dosing schedule. Do not double the dose to catch up.

Storage

Store this medication between 58 and 86 degrees F (15-30 degrees C) away from moisture. Do not store in the bathroom.

ALLOPURINOL

Common Brand Name: Zyloprim

Uses
This medication is used in the treatment of gout. It is also used in the management of certain types of kidney stones and to reduce elevated uric acid levels in the blood caused by certain illnesses.

How to Use
This drug is best taken with food or milk to prevent an upset stomach.

It is advisable to drink a full glass of water with each dose and to drink at least 8 glasses (8 ounces each) of water a day while taking this drug, in order to prevent the formation of kidney stones (unless you require fluid restrictions). Consult your doctor or pharmacist.

Large doses of Vitamin C should be avoided while taking this medicine as it can increase the risk of kidney stone formation.

Side Effects
Allopurinol may cause drowsiness especially during the first few days. Use caution if engaging in activities that require alertness.

Stomach upset, nausea, diarrhea, vomiting, and headache may also occur as your body adjusts to the medication.

Notify your doctor if you develop: yellowing of the eyes or skin, sore throat, easy bruising or bleeding, muscle aches, numbness or tingling of legs and arms, fatigue, rash or itchy skin.

In the unlikely event you have an allergic reaction to this drug, seek immediate medical attention. Symptoms of an allergic reaction include: rash, itching, swelling, dizziness, trouble breathing.

If you notice other effects not listed above, contact your doctor or pharmacist.

Precautions
Before using this drug, tell your doctor your medical history especially if you have: kidney or liver disease, high blood pressure, diabetes, drug allergies.

Drug Interactions
Tell your doctor of any over-the-counter or prescription drugs you are taking, particularly: amoxicillin, ampicillin, azathioprine, chlorpropamide, cyclophospham-ide, diuretics ("water pills"), mercaptopurine.

Alcohol can decrease the effectiveness of allopurinol. Ask your doctor for advice on drinking alcoholic beverages with this medicine.

Do not start or stop any medicine without first consulting your doctor or pharmacist.

Notes
There are no special instructions for this drug.

Missed Dose
If you miss a dose, take it as soon as you remember. If it is near the time of the next dose, skip the missed dose and resume your usual dosing schedule. Do not double the dose to catch up.

Storage
Store at room temperature between 59 and 86 degrees F (between 15 and 30 degrees C) away from moisture and sunlight. Do not store in the bathroom.

ALPRAZOLAM

Common Brand Name: Xanax

Uses
This medication has a calming effect. It is used to relieve anxiety, nervousness and tension in the treatment of anxiety disorders and panic disorders.

How to Use
Take this medication by mouth exactly as prescribed.

Do not take this more often, increase your dose or take this longer than directed without consulting your doctor.

Do not suddenly stop taking this medication if you have been taking this regularly for several weeks. Your dose will need to be gradually decreased before it is stopped completely.

Side Effects
Drowsiness, incoordination, headache, fatigue, change in sex drive, change in appetite, change in weight, difficulty urinating or stomach upset may occur the first few days as your body adjusts to the medication. If any of these effects continue or become bothersome, inform your doctor.

To relieve dry mouth, suck on (sugarless) hard candy or ice chips, chew (sugarless) gum, drink water or use saliva substitute.

Notify your doctor if you develop: rapid/pounding/irregular heartbeat, skin rash, changes in vision, slurred speech, confusion, depression, behavioral changes.

If you notice other effects not listed above, contact your doctor or pharmacist.

Precautions
Tell your doctor if you have liver disease, glaucoma, muscle weakness, history of drug dependence, any allergies.

This medication may cause drowsiness or dizziness. Use caution operating machinery or engaging in activities requiring alertness.

Limit intake of alcohol while taking this medication since it may aggravate drowsiness and dizziness.

11

Older adults may be more sensitive to the effects of this medication and should use this medication carefully.

Drug Interactions
Tell your doctor of any over-the-counter or prescription medication you take, including: anti-seizure drugs, antidepressants, narcotic pain relievers, erythromycin-like antibiotics, erythromycin, clarithromycin cimetidine, sleeping pills, tranquilizers, azole antifungals (e.g., fluconazole, itraconazole, ketoconazole).

Do not start or stop any medicine without first consulting your doctor or pharmacist.

This medication can worsen drowsiness caused by other medicines that can make you sleepy.

Notes
This medication when used in high doses or for prolonged periods of time can lead to physical and psychological dependence. Therefore, it is important to follow your dosing instructions closely.

Missed Dose
If you miss a dose, take it as soon as you remember. If it is near the time of the next dose, skip the missed dose and resume your usual dosing schedule. Do not double the dose to catch up.

Storage
Store this medication at room temperature between 59 and 86 degrees F (15 to 30 degrees C) away from heat, light and moisture. Do not store in the bathroom. Keep this and all medications out of the reach of children.

AMIODARONE

Common Brand Name: Cordarone

Uses
This medication is used to treat irregular heart rhythms (arrhythmias) and maintain a normal heart rate.

How to Use
This is best taken with food. However, it is most important to take amiodarone under the same conditions, consistently, for each dose. Ask your pharmacist for additional information.

This medication works best when there is a constant level of the drug in your body. To do this, take each dose exactly as prescribed at evenly spaced intervals throughout the day and night. Try to take each dose at the same time each day.

Do not stop taking this medication or change the dose without first consulting your doctor.

Side Effects
Constipation, loss of appetite, bitter taste in mouth, dizziness, headache, nausea, vomiting, flushing of face or decreased sexual interest may occur as your body adjusts to the medication. If these effects persist or worsen, inform your doctor.

Report immediately if you develop: painful breathing, shortness of breath, cough, slight fever, blue-gray coloring of skin, coldness, sweating, irregular pulse, yellowing eyes or skin, vision changes, easy bruising/bleeding, persistent sore throat.

In the unlikely event you have an allergic reaction to this drug, seek immediate medical attention. Symptoms of an allergic reaction include: rash, itching, swelling, dizziness, trouble breathing.

If you notice other effects not listed above, contact your doctor or pharmacist.

Precautions
Tell your doctor your complete medical history, especially if you have: liver disease, heart problems, kidney problems, lung diseases, thyroid problems, allergies (especially drug allergies).

This medication may make you more sensitive to the sun. Avoid prolonged sun exposure; use a sunscreen with a sun protection factor of at least 15 and wear protective clothing when outdoors.

Drug Interactions
Inform your doctor about all the medicines you use (both prescription and nonprescription), especially if you have: all heart drugs, beta-blockers (e.g. metroprlol), digoxin, phenytoin, simvastatin, calcium channel blockers (e.g. diltazem) theophylline.

Avoid eating grapefruit or drinking grapefruit juice while using this medication unless your doctor instructs you otherwise.

Do not start or stop any medicine without first consulting your doctor or pharmacist.

Grapefruit juice may affect the amount of amiodarone that is absorbed into your body.

Notes
Your doctor may want you to check your pulse rate every day while you take this medication. Learn how to monitor your pulse.

Eye exams and periodic tests of thyroid function are required with this drug. Any skin coloration cause by this dug is reversable.

To evaluate the effectiveness of this medication, your doctor may periodically take a blood sample to measure the amount of the drug in your body. Chest X-rays or electrocardiogram (EKG) may also be done. Keep all appointments with your doctor.

Missed Dose
If you miss a dose, take it as soon as you remember. If it is near the time of the next dose, skip the missed dose and resume your usual dosing schedule. Do not double the dose to catch up.

Storage
Store at room temperature away from moisture and sunlight. Do not store in the bathroom.

AMITRIPTYLINE

Common Brand Name: Elavil

Uses
This medication is used to treat depression, obsessive-compulsive disorders, and certain types of chronic pain problems.

How to Use
Use this as prescribed. Try to use each dose at the same time(s) each day so you remember to routinely use it.

It may take 2 to 3 weeks before the full benefit of this medication becomes apparent.

Do not stop using this medication without your doctor's approval. Nausea, headache or fatigue can occur if the drug is suddenly stopped.

Side Effects
May cause drowsiness, dizziness, increased sun sensitivity or blurred vision.

May initially cause dizziness and lightheadedness when rising too quickly from a sitting or lying position.

Other side effects include heartburn, loss of appetite, dry mouth, strange taste in mouth, anxiety, restlessness or sweating.

If any side effects persist or worsen, notify your doctor.

Report promptly: chest pain, rapid or irregular heartbeat, difficulty urinating, nightmares, ringing in the ears, excessive drowsiness, uncoordinated movements, fainting.

Taking this medication at bedtime may help minimize side effects. Talk to your doctor about this.

In the unlikely event you have an allergic reaction to this drug, seek medical attention immediately. Symptoms of an allergic reaction include: rash, itching, swelling, dizziness, trouble breathing.

If you notice other effects not listed above, contact your doctor or pharmacist.

Precautions

Before using this drug tell your doctor your medical history, especially if you have: glaucoma, prostate problems, decreased urine output, thyroid disease, breathing problems, seizure problems, alcohol use, heart disease, mental/emotional problems, liver or kidney disease, any drug allergies.

Use caution when engaging in tasks requiring alertness such as driving or operating machinery.

Limit alcohol consumption as it may increase the drowsiness and dizziness effects of this drug.

Limit exposure to hot weather as it may lead to heat stroke.

Older adults may be more sensitive to the effects of the drug.

Drug Interactions

Inform your doctor about the medicines you take, especially if you take: clonidine, guanadrel, guanethidine, monoamine oxidase inhibitors (e.g., furazolidone, linezolid, phenelzine, selegiline, tranylcypromine), cimetidine, SSRIs (e.g., fluoxetine, sertraline), warfarin, carbamazepine, certain diet pills (e.g., phentermine, fenfluramine), adrenaline-type drugs (e.g., dopamine, ephedrine, epinephrine, pseudoephedrine, phenylephrine, isoproterenol- some of which may be found in cough-and-cold or asthma products), narcotic pain medications (e.g., codeine), cisapride, St John's wort, any other prescription or nonprescription drugs you take.

Do not start or stop any medicine without first consulting your doctor or pharmacist.

Notes

Do not allow anyone else to use this medication.

Missed Dose

If you miss a dose, take it as soon as you remember. If it is near the time of the next dose, skip the missed dose and resume your usual dosing schedule. Do not double the dose to catch up.

Storage

Store at room temperature away from moisture and sunlight. Do not store in the bathroom. Do not freeze liquid forms of this medication.

AMLODIPINE

Common Brand Name: Norvasc

Uses

This drug is a calcium channel blocker. Calcium is involved in blood vessel contraction. By blocking calcium movement into the cells of the heart and blood vessels.

Amlodipine relaxes and widens the blood vessels. It is used to treat high blood pressure or chest pain (angina).

Ask your doctor or pharmacist about possible problems related to use of short-acting calcium channel blockers.

How to Use

This medication should be swallowed whole without regard to meals unless your doctor directs you otherwise.

This drug must be taken as directed if used to prevent chest pain. It is not effective if taken only when chest pain occurs.

Do not stop taking this medication suddenly without your doctor's permission. Chest pain or high blood pressure can occur if the medication is stopped too fast. Your dose may need to be gradually decreased before stopping the medicine completely.

Side Effects

This drug may cause dizziness and lightheadedness especially during the first few days. Avoid activities requiring alertness until you get used to the medication. When you sit or lie down for a while, get up slowly to allow your body to adjust and minimize dizziness.

You may also experience fatigue or weakness, nausea, swelling of ankles or feet, heartburn, muscle cramps, headache, flushing, or rash. If any of these effects persist or worsen, inform your doctor.

Notify your doctor if you develop: breathing difficulties, swelling of the hands or feet, an irregular heartbeat, yellowing of the eyes or skin.

If you notice other effects not listed above, contact your doctor or pharmacist.

Precautions

Tell your doctor your medical history, especially if you have: heart disease, liver disease, allergies (especially drug allergies).

Limit intake of alcohol while taking this drug.

Drug Interactions

Tell your doctor of all prescription and nonprescription drugs you may use, especially if you have: cyclosporine, amiodarone, digoxin, rifampin, voriconazole.

Avoid any drugs that increase your heart-rate (the decongestants phenylephrine, pseudoephedrine and Ma Huang are examples). These drugs are commonly found in over-the-counter cough-and-cold products.

Do not start or stop any medicine without first consulting your doctor or pharmacist. Do not drink grapefruit juice while taking this medication unless instructed otherwise by your doctor.

Notes

Do not share this product with others.

Missed Dose

If you miss a dose, take it as soon as you remember. If it is near the time of the next dose, skip the missed dose and resume your usual dosing schedule. Do not double the dose to catch up.

Storage

Store at room temperature away from sunlight and moisture.

AMLODIPINE/BENAZEPRIL

Common Brand Name: Lotrel

Uses
This medication is used to treat high blood pressure (hypertension). This is a combination of a calcium channel-blocking drug (amlodipine) and an anglotension converting enzyme inhibitor (ACEI) (benazepril).

How to Use
Take this medication by mouth as prescribed, usually once a day.

Do not skip doses, increase your dose or stop taking this without your doctor's approval. It is important to continue taking medication for high blood pressure even if you do not feel ill. Most people with high blood pressure do not have any symptoms.

Side Effects
Headache, dizziness, lightheadedness, or fatigue may occur the first several days as your body adjusts to the medication. Cough, loss of appetite, change in taste, dry mouth, constipation increased sweating, or nasal congestion can also occur. If any of these effects continue or become bothersome, inform your doctor.

Notify your doctor if you develop: chest pain (angina), a rapid or pounding heartbeat, persistent sore throat or fever, difficulty swallowing, vision changes, muscle aches.

In the unlikely event you have an allergic reaction to this drug, seek immediate medical attention. Symptoms of an allergic reaction include: rash, itching, swelling, dizziness, trouble breathing.

If you notice other effects not listed above, contact your doctor or pharmacist.

Precautions
Tell your doctor if you have disease, heart disease, liver disease, diabetes, blood disorders, any allergies.

Limit intake of alcohol which enhances dizziness.

Because this medication may make you dizzy or lightheaded, use caution operating machinery or engaging in activities requiring alertness.

Rise slowly from a lying or seated position to minimize dizziness.

Drug Interactions

Tell your doctor of any over-the-counter or prescription medication you may take including: heart medications, potassium supplements, salt substitutes, medications for cough/ cold/allergies.

Do not start or stop any medicine without first consulting your doctor or pharmacist.

Notes

Lab tests may be done periodically while taking this medication to check its effectiveness and to prevent side effects.

Learn how to monitor your pulse and blood pressure.

Missed Dose

If you miss a dose, take it as soon as you remember. If it is near the time of the next dose, skip the missed dose and resume your usual dosing schedule. Do not double the dose to catch up.

Storage

Store this medication at room temperature between 59 and 86 degrees F (15 to 30 degrees C) away from heat and light.

Do not store in the bathroom. Keep this and all medications out of the reach of children.

AMOXICILLIN

Common Brand Names: Amoxil, Trimox

Uses
This medication is a penicillin-related antibiotic that is used to treat a wide variety of bacterial infections.

How to Use
Take this medication exactly as directed by your doctor. This drug may be taken with or without food.

Antibiotics work best when the amount of medicine in your body is kept at a constant level. Do this by taking the medication at evenly spaced intervals throughout the day and night.

Continue to take this medication until the full prescribed amount is finished even if symptoms disappear after a few days.

Stopping the medication too early may allow bacteria to continue to grow and may result in a relapse of the infection.

Side Effects
This medication may cause stomach upset, diarrhea, nausea or vomiting. If these effects persist or worsen, notify your doctor.

Inform your doctor if the following rare side effects occur: sore mouth, sore throat, fever, easy bruising or bleeding.

In the unlikely event you have an allergic reaction to this drug, seek immediate medical attention. Symptoms of an allergic reaction include: rash, itching, swelling, dizziness, trouble breathing.

If you notice other effects not listed above, contact your doctor or pharmacist.

Precautions
Before using this drug tell your doctor your medical history especially: kidney disease, stomach/intestinal problems, blood disorders, allergies to penicillin or cephalosporin antibiotics, any other allergies.

Use of this medication for prolonged or repeated periods may result in a secondary infection (e.g., oral, bladder or vaginal yeast infection).

Drug Interactions
Tell your doctor and pharmacist of all medications you may use both prescription and nonprescription, and especially: birth control pills, live vaccines, tetracycline.

This drug may interfere with the effectiveness of birth control pills. Discuss using other methods of birth control with your doctor.

Do not start or stop any medicine without first consulting your doctor or pharmacist.

Notes
This medication has been prescribed for your current condition only. Do not use it later for another infection or give it to someone else. A different medication may be necessary in those cases.

Missed Dose
If you miss a dose, take it as soon as you remember. If it is near the time of the next dose, skip the missed dose and resume your usual dosing schedule. Do not double the dose to catch up.

Storage
Keep at room temperature between 59 to 86 degrees F (15 to 30 degrees C) away from sunlight and moisture. Do not store in the bathroom.

AMOXICILLIN/CLAVULANATE

Common Brand Name: Augmentin

Uses
Amoxicillin/clavulanic acid is an antibiotic medicine used to treat a wide variety of bacterial infections.

How to Use
Take this medication as directed by your doctor, usually every 8 or 12 hours. This medication should be taken with food.

Antibiotics work best when the amount of medicine in your body is kept at a constant level. Therefore, take this drug at evenly spaced intervals.

Continue to take this medication until the full prescribed amount is finished even if symptoms disappear after a few days.

Stopping the medication too early may allow bacteria to continue to grow, which may decrease the effectiveness of the antibiotic in treating the infection.

Inform your doctor if your condition does not improve in a few days.

Side Effects
This medication may cause stomach upset, diarrhea, nausea, or vomiting during the first few days as your body adjusts to the medication. If these effects persist or worsen, contact your doctor promptly.

Tell your doctor immediately if any of these highly unlikely but very serious side effects occur: dark urine, stomach pain, yellowing eyes/skin.

An allergic reaction to this drug is unlikely, but seek immediate medical attention if it occurs. Symptoms of an allergic reaction include: rash, itching, swelling, dizziness, trouble breathing.

If you notice other effects not listed above, contact your doctor or pharmacist.

Precautions
Tell your doctor your medical history, especially if you have: blood disorders, kidney problems, liver disease, allergies or unusual reactions to penicillin or other antibiotics.

Use of this medication for prolonged or repeated periods may result in a secondary infection (e.g., oral or vaginal yeast infection). Contact your doctor if you notice white patches in your mouth, a change in vaginal discharge or other new symptoms.

Drug Interactions

Tell your doctor of all prescription and nonprescription medications you may take, especially if you have: probenecid, methotrexate, tetracyclines, live vaccines.

This antibiotic may cause false positive results in diabetic urine testing using Clinitest.

Do not start or stop any medicine without first consulting your doctor or pharmacist.

Notes

This medication has been prescribed for your current condition only. Do not use it later for another infection. Do not share this medication with others.

Missed Dose

If you miss a dose, take it as soon as you remember. If it is near the time of the next dose, skip the missed dose and resume your usual dosing schedule. Do not double the dose to catch up.

Storage

Store at room temperature away from moisture and sunlight. Do not store in the bathroom.

ANASTROZOLE

Common Brand Name: Arimidex

Uses
This medication is used in the treatment of post-menopausal breast cancer in women.

How to Use
Take this by mouth exactly as directed usually once a day.

This is a potent medication. Do not increase your dose or take this more often than directed.

Side Effects
Diarrhea, constipation, nausea, vomiting, loss of appetite, headache, hot flashes, dizziness, dry mouth, back pain, vaginal dryness and cough may occur. Bone pain sometimes worsens for a short time after this medicine is first started report this or any other changes to your doctor. Changes in diet such as eating several small meals or limited activity may help lessen nausea and vomiting.

Side effects that may be caused by blood clots including chest pains, shortness of breath, sudden severe headache, pain in legs or calves, slurred speech, sudden vision changes and severe weakness in arm or leg, should be reported immediately to your doctor.

Notify your doctor if you experience: breathing trouble, rash, vaginal bleeding, shortness of breath, chest pain, pain or swelling in the legs, swelling of the feet or ankles, weight gain, tingling of the hands or feet, depression.

If you notice other effects not listed above, contact your doctor or pharmacist.

Precautions
Before taking this, tell your doctor if you have other illnesses, liver disease, any allergies.

Drug Interactions
Tell your doctor of any nonprescription or prescription medication you may take.

Do not start or stop any medicine without first consulting your doctor or pharmacist.

Notes
Keep all doctor appointments and scheduled laboratory tests as your condition will be closely monitored.

Missed Dose
If you miss a dose, take it as soon as you remember. If it is near the time of the next dose, skip the missed dose and resume your usual dosing schedule. Do not double the dose to catch up.

Storage
Store at room temperature between 59 and 86 degrees F (15 to 30 degrees C) away from heat and moisture as directed.
Keep this and all medications out of the reach of children.

ASPIRIN

Common Brand Name: Aspirin

Uses
Aspirin is used to relieve mild-to-moderate pain, reduce fever, to reduce inflammation and swelling in conditions such as arthritis and is used in low doses as a "blood thinner" to prevent the formation of blood clots. It is effective in reducing the risk of stroke and offers a protective effect against heart attacks in men with chest pain.

How to Use
Take by mouth with food or after meals to prevent stomach upset.

Take this medication with 6 to 8 ounces (180-240ml) of water.

Do not lie down for at least 30 minutes after taking this drug.

Sustained release, long acting or enteric-coated preparations must be swallowed whole. Do not crush or chew them or the sustained activity may be destroyed and side effects increased.

Side Effects
Stomach upset is the most common side effect.

Others include heartburn, loss of appetite or dizziness. Notify your doctor if any of these symptoms persist or worsen.

Notify your doctor promptly if you develop: persistent ringing in the ears, difficulty hearing, dark urine, yellowing eyes, easy bruising, persistent stomach pain, black stools.

In the unlikely event you have an allergic reaction to this drug, seek immediate medical attention. Symptoms of an allergic reaction include: rash, itching, swelling, dizziness, breathing trouble.

If you notice other effects not listed above, contact your doctor or pharmacist.

Precautions
If you have any of the following health problems, consult your doctor before using aspirin: liver disease, kidney disease, bleeding disorders, ulcers, stomach/intestinal problems, nasal polyps, gout, asthma, allergies.

If you have congestive heart failure or are on a sodium-restricted diet, do not take effervescent aspirin tablets or powders because they are high in sodium.

If you have had oral surgery or your tonsils removed in the last seven days, do not use chewable aspirin tablets, effervescent aspirin or aspirin in crushed tablets or gargles.

This medicine may cause stomach bleeding. Daily use of alcohol, especially when combined with this medicine, may increase your risk for stomach bleeding. Check with your doctor or pharmacist for more information.

Aspirin that has a strong vinegar-like odor is old and should not be used.

Drug Interactions

Tell your doctor of all prescription and nonprescription drugs you may use, especially: "blood thinners" (anticoagulants or antiplatelet drugs such as warfarin, heparins, NSAIDs), acetazolamide, corticosteroids (e.g., prednisone), methotrexate, medication for gout, medication for diabetes.

If you have diabetes, regular high-dose use of aspirin may affect test results for urine sugar.

Aspirin is an ingredient in many over-the-counter products. To prevent an overdose of aspirin, read the labels carefully before taking other pain relievers or cold products to be sure they do not contain aspirin. Consult your pharmacist if you are uncertain your over-the-counter products contain aspirin.

Do not start or stop any medicine without first consulting your doctor or pharmacist.

Notes

There are many different dosage forms for aspirin products. Some have special coatings or contain buffers and some are long-acting. Ask your doctor or pharmacist for recommendations of the best product for you.

Missed Dose

If you miss a dose, take it as soon as you remember. If it is near the time of the next dose, skip the missed dose and resume your usual dosing schedule. Do not double the dose to catch up.

Storage

Store at room temperature between 59 and 86 degrees F (between 15 and 30 degrees C) away from moisture and sunlight. Do not store in the bathroom.

ATENOLOL

Common Brand Name: Tenormin

Uses
This medication is used for chest pain (angina), high blood pressure and irregular heartbeats, and to prevent additional heart attacks after an initial heart attack.

How to Use
Take this medication exactly as prescribed. Try to take it at the same time(s) each day.

Do not suddenly stop taking this medication without consulting your doctor. Some conditions may become worse when the drug is suddenly stopped.

Side Effects
You may experience dizziness, lightheadedness, drowsiness, and blurred vision as your body adjusts to the medication. Use caution engaging in activities requiring alertness.

Because beta-blockers reduce blood circulation to the extremities, your hands and feet may be more susceptible to the cold temperatures. Dress warm.

Inform your doctor if you develop: easy bruising or bleeding, difficulty breathing or wheezing swollen hands or feet, confusion, depression, fever and a sore throat.

In the unlikely event you have an allergic reaction to this drug, seek medical attention immediately. Symptoms of an allergic reaction include: rash, itching, swelling, dizziness, trouble breathing.

If you notice other effects not listed above, contact your doctor or pharmacist.

Precautions
Before taking this drug, tell your doctor if you have a history of: heart disease, kidney disease, liver disease, asthma, bronchitis, emphysema, any other lung disease, diabetes, overactive thyroid gland, any drug allergies.

Before having surgery, tell the doctor or dentist in charge that you are taking a beta-blocker.

In people with diabetes, atenolol can block symptoms of hypoglycemia (low blood sugar) such as changes in pulse (heart rate) sweating dizziness, and faintness.

Drug Interactions

Tell your doctor of all prescription and nonprescription drugs you may use, especially if you have: diuretics, cold preparations and nasal decongestants, other heart or high blood pressure medications, St John's wort.

Do not start or stop any medicine without first consulting your doctor or pharmacist.

Notes

Your doctor may want you to take your pulse (heart rate) each day while you take this medication. Learn how to monitor your pulse.

Missed Dose

If you miss a dose, take it as soon as you remember. If it is near the time of the next dose, skip the missed dose and resume your usual dosing schedule. Do not double the dose to catch up.

Storage

Store at room temperature between 59 and 86 degrees F (between 15 and 30 degrees C) away from moisture and sunlight. Do not store in the bathroom.

ATORVASTATIN

Common Brand name: Lipitor

Uses
Atorvastatin works by decreasing the amount of cholesterol that is made by the body. Atorvastatin is used, along with a cholesterol-lowering diet, to help lower cholesterol and fats (triglycerides) in the blood. Reducing cholesterol and triglycerides helps prevent strokes and heart attacks. Atorvastatin is one of several drugs that are referred to as "satins."

How to Use
Take this medication by mouth usually once daily with or without food; or as directed by your doctor. The dosage is based on your medical condition and response to therapy.

It may take up to several weeks before the full benefit of this drug takes effect.

It is important to continue taking this medication even if you feel well. Most people with high cholesterol or triglycerides do not feel sick.

Side Effects
Headache, nausea, diarrhea, constipation, gas, or stomach upset/pain may occur. If any of these effects persist or worsen, notify your doctor promptly.

Tell your doctor immediately if any of these unlikely but serious side effects occur: joint pain, muscle pain or weakness, fever, unusual tiredness, chest pain, swelling in the arms or legs, dizziness.

Tell your doctor immediately if any of these highly unlikely but very serious side effects occur: yellowing eyes and skin, dark urine, change in the amount of urine, vision problems, black stool, severe stomach pain.

An allergic reaction to this drug is unlikely, but seek immediate medical attention if it occurs. Symptoms of an allergic reaction include: rash, itching, swelling, severe dizziness, trouble breathing.

If you notice other effects not listed above, contact your doctor or pharmacist.

Precautions

This medication is not recommended for use if you have the following medical conditions: liver problems.

Tell your doctor your medical history, especially if you have: heart disease, eye problems (e.g., cataracts), thyroid problems, uncontrolled seizures, recent serious infection, recent major surgery, low blood pressure, alcohol use, any allergies (especially to other "statin" drugs).

Daily use of alcohol may increase your chance for serious side effects. Limit alcoholic beverages.

Drug Interactions

This drug is not recommended for use with mibefradil, azole antifungals (e.g., itraconazole, ketoconazole).

Ask your doctor or pharmacist for more details.

Tell your doctor of all prescription and nonprescription medication you may use, especially: cyclosporine, macrolide antibiotics (e.g., clarithromycin, erythromycin, troleandomycin), fibrates (e.g., gemfibrozil, clofibrate), niacin (nicotinic acid), antacids, digoxin, nefazodone, protease inhibitors (e.g., indinavir, ritonavir), rifampin.

Do not eat grapefruit or drink grapefruit juice while using this medication unless your doctor instructs you otherwise. Grapefruit juice may increase the level of this drug in your body.

Do not start or stop any medicine without first consulting your doctor or pharmacist.

Notes

Do not share this medication with others.

Laboratory and/or medical tests may be performed to monitor your cholesterol levels and to see if the medicine is causing unwanted side effects. For best results, this medication should be used along with exercise and a low-cholesterol/low-fat diet. Consult your doctor.

Missed Dose

If you miss a dose, take it as soon as you remember. If it is near the time of the next dose, skip the missed dose and resume your usual dosing schedule. Do not double the dose to catch up.

Storage

Store at room temperature between 56 and 86 degrees F (13 to 30 degrees C) away from light and moisture.

AZITHROMYCIN

Common Brand Name: Zithromax

Uses
Azithromycin is an antibiotic used to treat a wide variety of bacterial infections.

How to Use
This medication can be taken with or without food.

Avoid taking antacids with this since the absorption of this drug can be decreased. Wait at least 2 hours after taking this medication before taking an antacid.

Antibiotics work best when the amount of medicine in your body is kept at a constant level. Do this by taking the medication at the same time of the day on each day of treatment. Continue to take this medication until the full prescribed amount is finished even if symptoms disappear after a few days. Stopping the medication too early may allow bacteria to continue to grow and decreases the effectiveness of the medicine in treating the infection.

Side Effects
This medication may cause stomach upset, loose stools, loss of appetite, nausea, vomiting, or stomach cramps. If these symptoms persist or become severe, inform your doctor.

If you develop diarrhea while taking this medication, notify your doctor. Do not take any nonprescription medications to treat diarrhea without first consulting your doctor.

Notify your doctor if you develop: yellowing eyes or skin, dark urine, clay-colored stools.

In the unlikely event you have an allergic reaction to this drug, seek medical attention immediately. Symptoms of an allergic reaction include: rash, itching, swelling, dizziness, trouble breathing.

If you notice other effects not listed above, contact your doctor or pharmacist.

Precautions
Tell your doctor if you have allergies (especially drug allergies), liver problems, colitis and other stomach problems, kidney problems.

Use of this medication for prolonged or repeated periods may result in a secondary infection (e.g., oral, bladder or vaginal yeast infection).

Drug Interactions
Do not take aluminum- and magnesium-containing antacids simultaneously with azithromycin.

Tell your doctor of all over-the-counter and prescription medications you take, including: theophylline, warfarin, digoxin, cyclosporine, astemizole, terfenadine, triazolam, ergotamine, dihydroergotamine, certain drugs for high cholesterol (e.g., "statins").

Do not start or stop any medicine without first consulting your doctor or pharmacist.

Notes
This medication has been prescribed for your current condition only. Do not use it later for another infection or give it to someone else. A different medication may be necessary.

Missed Dose
If you miss a dose, take it as soon as you remember. If it is near the time of the next dose, skip the missed dose and resume your usual dosing schedule. Do not double the dose to catch up.

Storage
Store at room temperature away from sunlight and moisture.

BENAZEPRIL

Common Brand Name: Lotensin

Uses
This medication is an ACE inhibitor which prevents certain enzymes in the body from constricting blood vessels. This helps to lower blood pressure and makes the heart beat stronger. This medication is used to treat hypertension (high blood pressure), heart failure, and to prevent kidney problems in persons with diabetes.

How to Use
Take this medication exactly as prescribed. Try to take it at the same time each day so you remember to take it. Can be taken without regard to meals.

Do not stop taking this medication without consulting your doctor. Some conditions may become worse when the drug is suddenly stopped. Your dose may need to be gradually decreased.

It is important to continue taking this medication even if you feel well. Most people with high blood pressure do not feel sick.

Your doctor may schedule periodic visits to check your blood pressure and do laboratory work to see how effective the medication is.

Side Effects
Dizziness, headache, drowsiness, fatigue or cough may occur the first few days as your body adjusts to benazepril.

Notify your doctor if these effects continue or become bothersome.

To avoid dizziness or lightheadedness when rising from a seated or lying position, get up slowly.

Inform your doctor if you develop: chest pain, irregular heartbeat, tingling of the hands or feet, mouth sores, persistent sore throat, difficulty swallowing, dry cough, swelling of the face, lips, and tongue.

In the unlikely event you have an allergic reaction to this drug, seek immediate medical attention. Symptoms of an allergic reaction include: rash, itching, swelling, dizziness, trouble breathing.

If you notice other effects not listed above, contact your doctor or pharmacist.

Precautions

Tell your doctor your medical history, especially if you have: kidney or liver problems, certain rare autoimmune diseases such as lupus erythematosus or scleroderma, diabetes, heart or circulation problems, any allergies you have.

This medicine may make you more prone to sunburn. Wear protective clothing and a sunscreen containing a SPF of at least 15 if you become sun-sensitive.

Limit your intake of alcohol. Avoid overheating because it can increase dizziness and lightheadedness.

Inform your doctor/dentist you use this medication before undergoing medical/dental procedures.

Drug Interactions

Inform your doctor about all the medicine you use (both prescription and nonprescription), especially if you have: lithium, potassium supplements, potassium-sparing water pills, anti-inflammatory medicine (NSAID or ibuprofen-like drugs).

Do not start or stop any medicine without first consulting your doctor or pharmacist.

Notes

It is important to have your blood pressure checked regularly while taking this medication. Learn how to monitor your blood pressure. Discuss this with your doctor.

Missed Dose

If you miss a dose, take it as soon as you remember. If it is near the time of the next dose, skip the missed dose and resume your usual dosing schedule. Do not double the dose to catch up.

Storage

Store at room temperature away from sunlight and moisture.

BENZONATATE

Common Brand Name: Tessalon Perles

Uses
This medication dulls the cough reflex. It is used to relieve a cough due to colds or allergies. Its effects last for up to eight hours.

How to Use
This medication must be swallowed whole. Do not break or chew the capsules or allow them to dissolve in your mouth since the medication can numb the mouth and throat.

It is recommended to drink plenty of fluids (6-8 glasses a day) to help relieve cold symptoms.

Side Effects
Stomach upset, nausea, constipation, drowsiness, mild dizziness, nasal congestion or headache may occur the first several days as your body adjusts to the medication. If these effects continue or become bothersome, inform your doctor.

Notify your doctor if you develop: skin rash, numbness of the chest, tremors.

Because this medication may cause drowsiness or dizziness, use caution performing tasks requiring alertness.

If you notice other effects not listed above, contact your doctor or pharmacist.

Precautions
Tell your doctor if you have any allergies or illness.

Drug Interactions
Tell your doctor of any over-the-counter or prescription medication you may take.

Do not start or stop any medicine without first consulting your doctor or pharmacist.

Notes
Do not share this product with others.

Missed Dose

If you miss a dose, take it as soon as you remember. If it is near the time of the next dose, skip the missed dose and resume your usual dosing schedule. Do not double the dose to catch up.

Storage

Store at room temperature between 59 and 86 degrees F (between 15 and 30 degrees C) away from moisture and sunlight. Do not refrigerate.

BISOPROLOL/HCTZ

Common Brand Name: Ziac

Uses
This combination medication is used to treat hypertension (high blood pressure). Beta-blockers slow the heart rate.

Thiazide diuretics, also known as "water pills", reduce fluid accumulation in the body by increasing urination. Bisoprolol can be used for prevention of chest pain.

How to Use
Take this medication exactly as prescribed. Do not adjust the dose without consulting your doctor.

Take with food or milk if stomach upset occurs.

Because this drug increases urination, avoid taking a dose in the late evening before bedtime.

Do not suddenly stop taking this medication without consulting your doctor. Some conditions may become worse when the drug is suddenly stopped.

Side Effects
You may experience dizziness; lightheadedness; fugitive drowsiness; blurred vision; and low blood pressure and heart rate as your body adjusts to the medication. Use caution engaging in activities requiring alertness.

Because beta-blockers reduce blood circulation to the extremities, your hands and feet may be more susceptible to cold.

Thiazide diuretics can cause potassium loss from the body. It is advisable to eat foods or drink liquids high in potassium such as citrus juice, bananas, melons, raisins and dates. Use of salt substitutes also help prevent potassium loss. Sometimes potassium supplement medication may be prescribed by your doctor.

Inform your doctor if you develop: breathing difficulty, easy bruising or bleeding, swollen hands or feet, confusion or depression, excessive thirst, muscle cramps.

This medication may increase sensitivity to the sun. Avoid prolonged sun exposure. Wear protective clothing and use a sunscreen.

If you notice other effects not listed above, contact your doctor or pharmacist.

Precautions

You may want to check your pulse everyday while taking this drug. Discuss with your doctor what changes in your pulse rate mean.

Tell your doctor if you are allergic to sulfa drugs. You may also be allergic to this medication.

Drug Interactions

This drug is not recommended for use with dofetilide. Ask your doctor or pharmacist for more details.

Tell your doctor of all the prescription and nonprescription medicines you may use, especially if you have: other beta-blockers (e.g., propranolol), diuretics ("water pills"), St John's wort, warfarin, other medications for hypertension.

Do not start or stop any medicine without first consulting your doctor or pharmacist.

Notes

Do not share this product with others.

Missed Dose

If you miss a dose, take it as soon as you remember. If it is near the time of the next dose, skip the missed dose and resume your usual dosing schedule. Do not double the dose to catch up.

Storage

Store at room temperature away from sunlight and moisture.

BRIMONIDINE

Common Brand Name: Alphagan

IMPORTANT NOTE
The following information is intended to supplement, not substitute for, the expertise and judgment of your physician, pharmacist, or other healthcare professional. It should not be construed to indicate that use of the drug is safe, appropriate, or effective for you. Consult your healthcare professional before using this drug.

BRIMONIDINE OPHTHALMIC SOLUTION

Uses
This medication is used to treat glaucoma or (openangle) elevated fluid pressures in the eye.

How to Use
For best results this medication must be used routinely as directed. Continue using it for the full time prescribed.

To apply eye drops, wash hands first. To avoid contamination, do not touch the dropper tip or let it touch your eye or any other surface.

Tilt your head back, gaze upward and pull down the lower eyelid to make a pouch. Place dropper directly over eye and administer the prescribed number of drops. Look downward and gently close your eye for 1 to 2 minutes. Place one finger at the corner of the eye near the nose and apply gentle pressure. This will prevent the medication from draining away from the eye. Try not to blink and do not rub the eye.

Do not rinse the dropper. Replace cap after use.

If you are using another kind of eye drop, wait at least five minutes before applying other medications.

Side Effects
Red, itching eyes, blurred vision or eye discomfort, headache, foreign body sensation,

drowsiness or dry mouth may occur. If these continue or worsen, notify your doctor promptly.

Unlikely but report: dizziness, eyelid crusting, abnormal taste, palpitations, sensitivity to light, nasal dryness.

If you notice other effects not listed above, contact your doctor or pharmacist.

Precautions

Before using this drug, tell your doctor your medical history, especially if you have: allergies (especially drug allergies), liver or kidney disease, heart or blood vessel disease, depression, Raynaud's disease, low blood pressure (orthostasis).

Wait at least 15 minutes after using brimonidine drops before inserting soft contact lenses.

Limit alcohol use as this can contribute to the drowsiness effect that can occur with this drug. Use caution performing tasks that require alertness.

Drug Interactions

Tell your doctor of all nonprescription and prescription medication you may take, especially if you have: MAO inhibitors (e.g., phenelzine, tranylcypromine), sleep medications, sedatives, tranquilizers, anxiety medicine (e.g., diazepam), narcotic pain relievers (e.g., codeine, morphine), barbiturates (e.g., phenobarbital), psychiatric medications (e.g., amitriptyline, trazodone, chlorpromazine), certain antihistamines (e.g., diphenhydramine), muscle relaxants (e.g., cyclobenzaprine), beta-blockers (e.g., propranolol, metoprolol, timolol eye drops), high blood pressure medication, digoxin.

Do not start or stop any medicine without first consulting your doctor or pharmacist.

Notes

Do not share this medication with others.

Missed Dose

If you miss a dose, take it as soon as you remember. If it is near the time of the next dose, skip the missed dose and resume your usual dosing schedule. Do not double the dose to catch up.

Storage

Store at room temperature at or below 77 degrees F (25 degrees C) away from light and moisture. Do not freeze.

BRINZOLAMIDE

Common Brand Name: Azopt

Important Note
The following information is intended to supplement, not substitute for, the expertise and judgment of your physician, pharmacist or other healthcare professional. It should not be construed to indicate that use of the drug is safe, appropriate, or effective for you. Consult your healthcare professional before using this drug.

BRINZOLAMIDE OPHTHALMIC SUSPENSION

Uses
This medication is used to treat elevated eye (intraocular) pressure in glaucoma (open angle).

How to Use
This medication is generally used three times daily by placing one drop in the affected eye(s) as directed by your doctor. Shake the medication bottle well before use.

If you wear contact lenses, remove them before applying these eye drops. You may put them back in, 15 minutes after applying the drops.

To apply eye drops, wash hands first. To avoid contamination, do not touch the dropper tip or let it touch your eye or any other surface.

For best results, this medication must be used routinely as directed. Continue using it for the full time prescribed.

Tilt your head back, gaze upward and pull down the lower eyelid to make a pouch. Place dropper directly over eye and administer the prescribed number of drops. Look downward and gently close your eye for 1 to 2 minutes. Place one finger at the corner of the eye near the nose and apply gentle pressure. This will prevent the medication from draining away from the eye. Try not to blink and do not rub the eye.

Do not rinse the dropper. Replace cap after use.

If you are using another kind of eye drop, wait at least five minutes before applying other medications. Administer eye drops before eye ointments, to allow the eye drops to enter the eye.

Side Effects
Blurred vision, tearing; bitter, sour or unusual taste; dry eyes; headache; and dizziness may occur. If these persist or worsen, notify your doctor promptly.

If you notice any of the following serious side effects, stop using this medication and consult your doctor or pharmacist immediately: eye/eyelid problems (e.g., swelling, pain, redness, or discharge).

Tell your doctor immediately if you have any of these highly unlikely but very serious side effects include vision changes.

An allergic reaction to this drug is unlikely, but seek immediate medical attention if it occurs. Symptoms of an allergic reaction include: rash, itching, swelling, severe dizziness.

If you notice other effects not listed above, contact your doctor or pharmacist.

Precautions
Tell your doctor your medical history, including any allergies (especially to sulfas drugs), other eye conditions, kidney or liver disease.

This drug may make you dizzy or cause blurred vision; use caution engaging in activities requiring alertness such as driving or using machinery.

Drug Interactions
Tell your doctor of all prescription and nonprescription medication you may use, especially: dorzolamide and other glaucoma eye drops, oral carbonic anhydrase inhibitors (e.g., acetazolamide, dichlorphenamide, methazolamide), high-dose salicylates (e.g., aspirin for rheumatoid arthritis).

Notes
Do not share this medication with others.

Eye examinations and intraocular pressure will be monitored periodically to evaluate your progress.

Missed Dose
If you miss a dose, use it as soon as you remember.

If it is near the time of the next dose, skip the missed dose and resume your usual dosing schedule. Do not double the dose to catch up.

Storage
Store at room temperature between 39 and 86 degrees F (4 to 30 degrees C) away from light and moisture.

BUPROPION HCL

Common Brand Names: Wellbutrin, Zyban

Uses
This medication is used to treat depression and to prevent withdrawl with smoking cessations.

How to Use
This medication may be taken with food if stomach upset occurs. Take doses at regularly scheduled times each day.

Do not take more or less medication than prescribed and follow your doctor's instructions carefully. Taking more than the recommended dose of bupropion will increase your risk of having a seizure.

Do not stop taking this medication without notifying your doctor.

Since this drug may cause sleeplessness at first, it is best not to take this near bedtime.

It may take 4 weeks or more before the full effects of this medication are noticed.

Side Effects
This medication is generally well tolerated.

Dry mouth, headache, increased sweating, nausea/vomiting, constipation, anxiety, fatigue and blurred vision may occur. If these effects persist or worsen, notify your doctor.

Report promptly: unusual weight loss or gain, palpitations, agitation, trouble sleeping.

Unlikely but report promptly: tremor, dizziness, fainting, mood changes, slowed movements, difficulty urinating, decreased sex drive, drowsiness.

Very unlikely but report promptly: seizures, mental problems, fever, muscle aches, yellowing of the eyes or skin.

In the unlikely event you have an allergic reaction to this drug, seek medical attention immediately. Symptoms may include trouble breathing, rash, itching, swelling, or severe dizziness.

If you notice other effects not listed above, contact your doctor or pharmacist.

Precautions

Before taking bupropion HCL, tell your doctor if you have: history of seizures or head injury or brain tumor, heart disease, liver or kidney disease, eating disorder, diabetes, alcohol dependence, any allergies, the intent to quit smoking.

Because of the possibility this drug will make you dizzy and affect coordination, do not drive or operate machinery until you get used to the drug's effects.

Limit or avoid consumption of alcoholic beverages; alcohol can increase your risk of seizures. Chronic alcohol users who suddenly stop the intake of alcohol while taking bupropion HCL may increase the risk of having seizures.

Suddenly stopping certain tranquilizers (e.g., diazepam, chlordiazepoxide) is not recommended because doing so may increase the risk of having seizures.

Older adults may be more sensitive to the effects of this drug, especially the side effects.

Drug Interactions

Before taking bupropion tell your doctor of all nonprescription and prescription medications you may use especially: monoamine oxidase inhibitors (e.g., isocarboxazid, phenelzine, tranylcypromine, pargyline, selegiline, linezolid, furazolidone), levodopa, ritonavir, corticosteroids (e.g. prednisone), sedatives, adrenaline-like stimulants (e.g., ephedrine), products containing nicotine (e.g., patches or gum).

Also report use of drugs which might increase seizure risk (decrease seizure threshold) such as: phenothiazines (e.g., chlorpromazine), tricyclic antidepressants (e.g., amitriptyline), isoniazid (INH), theophylline.

Excess caffeine intake can increase the chance of seizures with this drug. Check all nonprescription/prescription drug labels for caffeine. Consult your doctor or pharmacist.

A certain product used to help quit smoking contains bupropion. Do not take that product while using this one.

Do not start or stop any medicine without first consulting your doctor or pharmacist.

Missed Dose

If you miss a dose, take it as soon as you remember. If it is near the time of the next dose, skip the missed dose and resume your usual dosing schedule. Do not double the dose to catch up.

Storage

Store at room temperature and keep away from moisture and sunlight. Do not store in the bathroom.

CALCITONIN SALMON

Common Brand Name: Miacalcin

Uses
Calcitonin, a hormone secreted by the thyroid gland, is important in calcium and bone metabolism. It is used to treat Paget's disease, to reduce high levels of calcium or to treat postmenopausal osteoporosis (bone loss).

How to Use
This medication is given as an injection just under the skin or into a muscle.

Use this medication exactly as prescribed. Do not stop using this medication or increase your dose without consulting your doctor.

Side Effects
Nausea, vomiting and flushing may occur the first several days as your body adjusts to the medication. These effects may be relieved somewhat by taking the injection just before bedtime.

Other side effects may include loss of appetite, salty taste, diarrhea, stomach upset, headache, dizziness, fever, eye pain, nasal congestion, itchy ear lobes, tender hands or feet, increased urination or redness or inflammation at the injection site. If any of these effects continue or become bothersome, inform your doctor.

Notify your doctor if you develop: chills, trouble breathing, hives or a skin rash.

In the unlikely event you have an allergic reaction to this drug, seek medical attention immediately. Symptoms of an allergic reaction include: rash, itching, swelling, dizziness, trouble breathing.

If you notice other effects not listed above, contact your doctor or pharmacist.

Precautions
Tell your doctor if you have allergies (especially drug allergies).

Drug Interactions
Tell your doctor of any over-the-counter or prescription medication you may take.

Do not start or stop any medicine without first consulting your doctor or pharmacist.

Notes
For treatment of postmenopausal osteoporosis, vitamin D and calcium supplements may be recommended. Talk to your doctor or nutritionist about this. Closely follow any dietary recommendations.

While using this, your doctor may schedule lab tests to monitor the effects of the medication.

This medication should be stored in the refrigerator before opening. Once opened, the product is only good for 30 days at room temperature.

Missed Dose
If you are using 2 doses daily and miss a dose, take the missed dose if you remember within 2 hours of when you should have injected the dose. If you do not remember within 2 hours, skip the missed dose and resume your usual dosing schedule.

If you are using 1 dose daily and miss a dose, take as soon as you remember, if you remember within the same day. If you remember the next day, skip the missed dose and resume your usual schedule.

If you use 1 dose every other day and miss a dose, take as soon as you remember if it is the same day. If not, inject the dose on the "off" day and skip the next day. Then continue with this schedule.

If you use 1 dose daily on 3 days a week and miss a dose: take the missed dose on the next day and move each subsequent injection back a day for that week. Resume your usual schedule the next week. Do not double the dose to catch up.

Storage
Refrigerate at 36 to 46 degrees F (2 to 8 degrees C). Do not freeze.

CAPTOPRIL

Common Brand Name: Capoten

Uses
Captopril belongs to a group of drugs called "ACE inhibitors." ACE inhibitors prevent certain substances in the body from constricting blood vessels. This helps to lower blood pressure and makes the heart beat stronger. This medication is used to treat hypertension (high blood pressure), heart failure, and kidney disease in certain diabetic patients.

How to Use
Captopril should be taken on an empty stomach, one hour before or two hours after a meal.

Take this medication exactly as prescribed. Try to take it at the same time each day.

Do not stop taking this medication without consulting your doctor. Some conditions may become worse when the drug is abruptly stopped. Your dose may need to be gradually decreased.

Consult your doctor before using salt substitutes or low salt milk.

It is important to continue taking this medication even if you feel well. Most people with high blood pressure do not feel sick.

Side Effects
Dizziness, headache, diarrhea, constipation, loss of appetite, nausea, loss of taste, flushing or fatigue may occur. If these effects persist or worsen, notify your doctor.

This medication can increase sensitivity to sunlight.

To avoid dizziness and lightheadedness when rising from a seated or lying position, get up slowly.

Inform your doctor if you develop: chest pain, tingling of the hands or feet, swelling of the tongue and lips, dry cough, persistent sore throat.

In the unlikely event you have an allergic reaction to this drug, seek immediate medical attention. Symptoms of an allergic reaction include: rash, itching, swelling, dizziness, trouble breathing.

If you notice other effects not listed above, contact your doctor or pharmacist.

Precautions

Tell your doctor your medical history, especially if you have: high blood levels of potassium, kidney problems, liver problems, salt-restricted diet, swelling (angioedema), heart problems, allergies (especially drug allergies).

This medicine may make you more prone to sunburn. Wear protective clothing and a sunscreen.

Limit your intake of alcohol and avoid overheating because this can aggravate dizziness and lightheadedness.

Drug Interactions

Inform your doctor about all the medicine you use (both prescription and nonprescription), especially if you have: lithium, potassium supplements, potassium-sparing water pills, anti-inflammatory medicine (NSAID like ibuprofen), other hypertension medications.

Avoid "stimulant" drugs that may increase your heart rate such as decongestants or caffeine. Decongestants can be found in cough-and-cold medicines.

Do not start or stop any medicine without first consulting your doctor or pharmacist.

Notes

It is important to have your blood pressure checked regularly while taking this medication. Learn how to monitor your blood pressure. Discuss this with your doctor.

Missed Dose

If you miss a dose, take it as soon as you remember. If it is near the time of the next dose, skip the missed dose and resume your usual dosing schedule. Do not double the dose to catch up.

Storage

Store at room temperature away from moisture and sunlight. Do not store in the bathroom.

CARBIDOPA/LEVODOPA

Common Brand Name: Sinemet

Uses
This combination medication is used to treat symptoms of Parkinson's disease.

How to Use
Take this drug as directed. Space the doses out over the waking day. It may take a few weeks before the full benefits of this medication are observed. If you are changing from plain levodopa to this drug, levodopa must be discontinued for 8 hours before taking this combination drug.

If stomach upset occurs, this drug may be taken with food or milk. Consult with your doctor.

Side Effects
May cause drowsiness, dizziness, headache, loss of appetite, stomach upset, nausea, vision changes, or trembling of the hands. These should subside as your body adjusts to the medication. If these symptoms persist or become bothersome, inform your doctor.

Notify your doctor if you develop: vomiting, difficulty swallowing, difficulty urinating, uncontrollable movements (especially twitching of the eyelid), chest pain, an irregular heartbeat, skin rash, mood or mental changes.

May cause dizziness especially when rising quickly from a seated or lying position. Change positions slowly and be careful on stairs.

If you notice other effects not listed above, contact your doctor or pharmacist.

Precautions
This medication can cause false results with urine glucose testing in diabetics. Blood glucose testing should be performed instead.

Tell your doctor if you have: glaucoma, history of skin cancer, breathing problems, heart disease, kidney disease, liver disease, endocrine disease, ulcers, depression, blood disorders.

Drug Interactions

Inform your doctor if you are taking medicine to treat depression or anxiety ("antidepressants" or Valium-like drugs), MAO inhibitors (e.g., furazolidone, linezolid, phenelzine, selegiline, tranylcypromine), phenytoin (Dilantin), iron vitamins, medication to treat high blood pressure (hypertension), other drugs to treat Parkinson's disease, any other prescription or non- prescription drugs.

Do not start or stop any medicine without first consulting your doctor or pharmacist.

Notes

Be sure your doctor knows your complete medical history and the medications you are taking.

Missed Dose

If you miss a dose, take as soon as remembered and take any remaining doses for that day at evenly spaced intervals.

If you miss a dose, take it as soon as you remember. If it is near the time of the next dose, skip the missed dose and resume your usual dosing schedule. Do not double the dose to catch up.

Storage

Store at room temperature away from sunlight and moisture. Do not store in the bathroom.

CARISOPRODOL

Common Brand Name: Soma

Uses

This medication relaxes muscles and relieves pain and discomfort associated with strains, sprains, spasms or other muscle injuries.

Muscle relaxers are for specific muscle injury and pain and should not be used for general body aches and pains.

How to Use

This medication may be taken with food or immediately after meals to prevent stomach upset.

Take this as directed. Do not increase your dose or take it more often than prescribed.

This medication provides temporary relief and must be used in addition to rest, physical therapy and other measures. Because this medication makes an injury temporarily feel better, do not attempt to lift or exercise too soon. Follow your doctor's instructions for recovery.

Side Effects

This medication may cause stomach upset, heartburn, headache, dizziness or drowsiness. If these symptoms persist or worsen, notify your doctor promptly.

Inform your doctor promptly if you develop: persistent stomach pain, rapid heart rate.

In the unlikely event you have an allergic reaction to this drug, seek immediate medical attention. Symptoms of an allergic reaction include: rash, itching, swelling, dizziness, trouble breathing.

If you notice other effects not listed above, contact your doctor or pharmacist.

Precautions

Tell your doctor your medical history, especially if you have: any liver or kidney disease, blood disorders, porphyria, asthma, any allergies.

When rising quickly from a sitting or lying position, dizziness or lightheadedness may occur. Change positions slowly.

Use caution engaging in activities requiring alertness (such as driving) if this drug makes you dizzy or drowsy.

Limit alcohol intake while taking this medication.

Drug Interactions

Tell your doctor of all over-the-counter and prescription medication you may take including: sedatives, tranquilizers, sleeping pills, narcotic pain relievers, medication for depression, certain antihistamines (e.g., diphenhydramine).

Many cough-and-cold products contain antihistamines which can cause drowsiness. Check labels carefully and consult your pharmacist if you have any questions. This drug may increase the drowsiness side effect of these medicines.

Do not start or stop any medicine without first consulting your doctor or pharmacist.

Missed Dose

If you miss a dose, take it as soon as you remember. If it is near the time of the next dose, skip the missed dose and resume your usual dosing schedule. Do not double the dose to catch up.

Storage

Store at room temperature between 59 and 86 degrees F (between 15 and 30 degrees C) away from moisture and sunlight. Do not store in the bathroom.

CEFPROZIL

Common Brand Name: Cefzil

Uses
This medication is a cephalosporin antibiotic used to treat a wide variety of bacterial infections such as sinusitis and respiratory tract infection.

How to Use
This medication is taken by mouth. To prevent stomach upset, it may be taken with food or milk.

The liquid form of this medication should shaken well before pouring each dose.

Antibiotics work best when the amount of medicine in your body is kept at a constant level. Do this by taking the medication at evenly spaced intervals throughout the day and night.

Continue to take this medication until the full prescribed amount is finished even if symptoms disappear after a few days.

Stopping the medication too early may allow bacteria to continue to grow resulting in a relapse of the infection. This drug requires an adjustment in dose for kidney problems.

Side Effects
This medication may cause stomach upset, diarrhea, loss of appetite, nausea or vomiting. Take with food or milk to minimize these effects. If these effects continue or become severe, inform your doctor promptly.

If any of the following effects occur, notify your doctor: headache, dizziness, fatigue, muscle aches, strange taste in the mouth.

Unlikely to occur but report promptly: fever, easy bleeding or bruising, change in the amount of urine, seizures.

An allergic reaction to this drug is unlikely, but seek immediate medical attention if it occurs. Symptoms of an allergic reaction include: difficulty breathing, skin rash, hives, itching.

If you notice other effects not listed above, contact your doctor or pharmacist.

Precautions

Tell your doctor your medical history, especially if you have: kidney problems, colitis or other stomach problems, allergies (especially to penicillins or cephalosporin antibiotics, other antibiotics, tartrazine, or any other medication).

Use of this medication for prolonged or repeated periods may result in a secondary infection (e.g., oral and bladder infection).

Drug Interactions

Tell your doctor of any over-the-counter or prescription medication you may take, including: probenecid, anticoagulants (blood thinners), other antibiotics.

Diabetics should be aware this medication may affect certain glucose test results. Talk to your doctor or pharmacist about the best way to monitor your glucose levels.

Do not start or stop any medicine without first consulting your doctor or pharmacist.

Notes

This medication has been prescribed for your current condition only. Do not use it later for another infection or give it to someone else. A different medication may be necessary.

Missed Dose

If you miss a dose, take it as soon as you remember. If it is near the time of the next dose, skip the missed dose and resume your usual dosing schedule. Do not double the dose to catch up.

Storage

Store tablets at room temperature between 59 and 86 degrees F (between 15 and 30 degrees C) away from moisture and sunlight. Do not store in the bathroom. Liquid suspensions should be stored in the refrigerator but not the freezer. Check the expiration date and discard any unused medication after that date. Reconstituted suspensions should be discarded in 2 weeks.

CEFUROXIME

Common Brand Names: Ceftin

Uses
This medication is a cephalosporin antibiotic and is used to treat a wide variety of bacterial infections.

How to Use
Take this medication with food as directed by your doctor.

Antibiotics work best when the amount of medicine in your body is kept at a constant level. Do this by taking the medication at evenly spaced intervals throughout the day and night.

Continue to take this medication until the full prescribed amount is finished even if symptoms disappear after a few days.

Stopping the medication too early may allow bacteria to continue to grow resulting in a relapse of the infection.

If the tablets cannot be swallowed, they can be crushed and mixed with food such as applesauce or pudding or drinks such as grape juice. The tablets have a strong bitter taste which may be hard to disguise. Notify your doctor if you are unable to take the medication because of the taste. It may be necessary to use a different medication.

Side Effects
This medication may cause stomach upset, diarrhea, loss of appetite, nausea or vomiting. Take with food or milk to minimize these effects. If they continue or become severe, inform your doctor promptly.

Inform your doctor promptly if any of these effects occur: headache, dizziness, fatigue, muscle aches, strange taste in the mouth, persistent fever, easy bruising or bleeding, persistent sore throat.

Though occurring rarely, seek immediate medical attention if you experience: seizures, jerky movements, severe drowsiness, dark urine, change in the amount of urine.

In the unlikely event you have an allergic reaction to this drug, seek immediate medical attention. Symptoms of an allergic reaction include: rash, itching, swelling, dizziness, trouble breathing.

If you notice other effects not listed above, contact your doctor or pharmacist.

Precautions
Tell your doctor your medical history, especially if you have: kidney problems, stomach/intestinal problems, any allergies.

Use of this medication for prolonged or repeated periods may result in a secondary infection (e.g., oral or bladder infection).

Drug Interactions
Tell your doctor of all medications you may use (both prescription and nonprescription), especially if you have: medication for gout (such as probenecid), live vaccines, other antibiotics.

Diabetics should be aware this medication may cause false positive urine glucose tests. Talk to your doctor or pharmacist about other ways to monitor your blood glucose.

Do not start or stop any medicine without first consulting your doctor or pharmacist.

Notes
This medication has been prescribed for your current condition only. Do not use it later for another infection or give it to someone else. A different medication may be necessary.

Missed Dose
If you miss a dose, take it as soon as you remember. If it is near the time of the next dose, skip the missed dose and resume your usual dosing schedule. Do not double the dose to catch up.

Storage
Store at room temperature away from sunlight and moisture.

CELECOXIB

Common Brand Name: Celebrex

Uses
This medication is a nonsteroidal anti-inflammatory drug (NSAID) which relieves pain and inflammation (swelling). It is used to treat pain, swelling and stiffness due to arthritis.

This drug works by blocking the enzyme in your body production of prostaglandins. Decreasing prostaglandins helps to reduce pain and swelling.

How to Use
Take by mouth, generally once or twice daily, as directed by your doctor. To decrease the chance of stomach upset, this drug is best taken with food. Dosage is based on your medical condition and response to therapy.

Take this medication with 6 to 8 ounces (180-240ml) of water.

Do not lie down for at least 30 minutes after taking this drug.

Side Effects
Stomach upset, diarrhea, gas or nausea may occur.

If these effects persist or worsen, notify your doctor promptly.

Very unlikely but report promptly: unusual fatigue, yellowing eyes or skin, severe headache, unexplained weight gain, change in amount of urine.

If you notice any of the following unlikely but very serious side effects, stop taking this drug and consult your doctor immediately: black stools, persistent stomach/ abdominal pain, vomit that looks like coffee grounds.

In the unlikely event you have an allergic reaction to this drug, seek immediate medical attention. Symptoms of an allergic reaction include rash, itching, swelling, dizziness or trouble breathing.

If you notice other effects not listed above, contact your doctor or pharmacist.

Precautions
Tell your doctor your medical history, including allergies or unusual reactions(especially allergies to drugs such as sulfas or NSAID like ibuprofen), kidney problems,

liver problems, heart disease, alcohol use, high blood pressure, swelling (edema), blood disorders (anemia), serious infections, stomach problems (bleeding or ulcers), asthma, growths in the nose (nasal polyps), dehydration, poorly controlled diabetes.

Caution is advised when this drug is used with older people, as they may be more sensitive to the side effects of this medication, especially stomach bleeding.

Drug Interactions
Tell your doctor of all prescription and nonprescription medications you use, especially if you have: fluconazole, lithium, "water pills" (diuretics, e.g., furosemide, hydrochlorothiazide), drugs for high blood pressure, ACE inhibitors (e.g., captopril, lisinopril), corticosteroids (e.g., prednisone), warfarin, NSAIDs (e.g., ibuprofen, naproxen).

Check all prescription and nonprescription medicine labels carefully since many contain pain relievers/fever reducers (NSAIDs such as ibuprofen, naproxen, or aspirin) which are similar to this drug. Aspirin, as prescribed by your doctor for reasons such as heart attack or stroke prevention (usually these dosages are 81-325 mg per day), should be continued. Take the aspirin dose before taking each dose of celecoxib. Consult your doctor or pharmacist for more details.

Do not start or stop any medicine without first consulting your doctor or pharmacist.

Notes
Do not share this medication with others.

Laboratory and/or medical tests may be performed to monitor your progress.

Missed Dose
If you miss a dose, take it as soon as you remember. If it is near the time of the next dose, skip the missed dose and resume your usual dosing schedule. Do not double the dose to catch up.

Storage
Store at room temperature between 59 and 86 degrees F (15-30 degrees C) away from light and moisture.

CEPHALEXIN

Common Brand Names: Keflex, Keftab

Uses
This medication is an antibiotic that is used to treat a variety of bacterial infections.

How to Use
Antibiotics work best when the amount of medicine in your body is kept at a constant level. Do this by taking the medication at evenly spaced intervals throughout the day and night.

This medication works best when taken on an empty stomach.

However, if stomach upset occurs, it may be taken with food.

Continue to take this medication until the full prescribed amount is finished even if symptoms disappear after a few days.

Stopping the medication too early may allow bacteria to continue to grow and decrease the effectiveness of the antibiotic in treating the infection.

Side Effects
This medication may cause stomach upset, diarrhea, loss of appetite, nausea, and vomiting. If these effects persist or worsen, inform your doctor promptly.

Unlikely to occur but report promptly: fever, easy bleeding or bruising, change in the amount of urine, seizures.

An allergic reaction to this drug is unlikely, but seek immediate medical attention if it occurs. Symptoms of an allergic reaction include: rash, itching, swelling, severe dizziness, trouble breathing.

If you notice other effects not listed above, contact your doctor or pharmacist.

Precautions
Before taking this medication, tell your doctor if you are allergic or have experienced any unusual reactions to any medications, especially: penicillins, cephalosporins.

Inform your doctor of any medical conditions, especially if you have: kidney disease.

Use of this medication for prolonged or repeated periods may result in a secondary infection (e.g., oral, bladder or vaginal yeast infection).

Drug Interactions
Tell your doctor of all prescription and nonprescription drugs you may use, especially if you have: medication for gout (e.g., probenecid).

Cephalosporins may cause false positive results in tests for sugar in the urine. Diabetics should use Clinistix rather than Clinitest tablets. Blood sugar testing is not affected.

Do not start or stop any medicine without first consulting your doctor or pharmacist.

Notes
This medication has been prescribed for your current condition only. Do not use it later for another infection or give it to someone else.

Missed Dose
If you miss a dose, take it as soon as you remember. If it is near the time of the next dose, skip the missed dose and resume your usual dosing schedule. Do not double the dose to catch up.

Storage
Store at room temperature away from moisture and sunlight. Do not store in the bathroom.

CETIRIZINE

Common Brand Name: Zyrtec

Uses
This medication is an antihistamine which provides relief of allergy symptoms such as watery eyes, runny nose, itching eyes, sneezing, itching and hives.

How to Use
Take this medication by mouth once a day as directed. May be taken with or without food.

Do not increase your dose or take this more often than directed.

Side Effects
Drowsiness, sleepiness, dry mouth, fatigue, dizziness, increased appetite, and nausea may occur. These effects should subside as your body adjusts to the medication. If they continue or become bothersome, inform your doctor.

Notify your doctor if you develop any of these serious effects while taking this medication: chest pain, rash, trouble breathing.

This medication may cause dizziness or drowsiness. Use caution engaging in activities requiring alertness, especially until you become used to this medicine. If you notice other effects not listed above, contact your doctor or pharmacist.

Precautions
Tell your doctor your medical history, especially if you have: liver or kidney disease, asthma, any blood disorders, any any allergies.

This medication can increase sensitivity to sunlight. Avoid prolonged sun exposure. Wear protective clothing and a sunscreen containing sun protection factor (SPF) of at least 15 when outdoors.

Drug Interactions
Tell your doctor of any over-the-counter and prescription medication you may take including: sedatives, tranquilizers, narcotic pain relievers, sleep medicine, drugs

for anxiety, barbiturates (e.g., phenobarbital), psychiatric medicines, other anti-histamines. This medicine may increase the drowsiness effects of these drugs.

Do not start or stop any medicine without first consulting your doctor or pharmacist.

Notes
This medication can affect results of allergy tests.

Remind your doctor you are taking this drug if you are scheduled for any tests.

Missed Dose
If you miss a dose, take it as soon as you remember. If it is near the time of the next dose, skip the missed dose and resume your usual dosing schedule. Do not double the dose to catch up.

Storage
Store between 59 and 86 degrees F (15 to 30 degrees C) away from heat and light. Do not store in the bathroom.

CIMETIDINE

Common Brand Name: Tagament

Uses
Cimetidine blocks secretion of acid from the stomach.

Prescription cimetidine is used to treat and prevent ulcers, to treat gastroesophageal reflux disorder (GERD), and to treat conditions associated with excessive acid secretion (e.g., Zollinger-Ellison Syndrome).

Nonprescription cimetidine is used to relieve heartburn and acid indigestion.

How to Use
This medication is taken by mouth. Take this as directed. Do not increase your dose, take this more often than prescribed or stop taking this without first consulting your doctor. If you are taking antacids in addition to this medication, stagger the doses so they are not taken at the same time. Try to space dosing of this medication and antacids by at least 2 hours.

Side Effects
Headache, fatigue, dizziness, loss of appetite, sleepiness, dry skin or dry mouth may occur as your body adjusts to the medication. Hair loss, increased sweating, anxiety, change in sex drive, breast enlargement in males and change in taste perceptions may also occur. If any of these effects continue or become bothersome, inform your doctor.

Notify your doctor if you develop: skin rash, hives, irregular heartbeat, diarrhea, mental confusion, depression, difficulty walking vision changes, trouble urinating, joint or muscle pain, ringing in the ears or breathing difficulty, yellowing eyes or skin, dark urine, black tarry stools, coffee ground-appearing vomit (may suggest internal bleeding).

If you notice other effects not listed above, contact your doctor or pharmacist.

Precautions
Tell your doctor if you have disease, allergies (especially drug allergies).

Do not change your dose without your doctor's approval.

Older adults may be more sensitive to the effects of this medication.

Drug Interactions

Tell your doctor of all medications you use (both prescription and nonprescription), especially if you have: antacids, alcohol, heart medication, blood thinners, anti-anxiety drugs, blood pressure medications, anti-seizure drugs, medications used for diabetes, antidepressants, narcotic pain medications (e.g., codeine), azole anti-fungals (e.g., ketoconazole), theophylline.

Cigarette smoking can affect this medication. Tell your doctor if you smoke and if you stop or start smoking while using this medication.

This medication is available in both prescription and over-the-counter formulations. Do not take both at the same time.

Do not start or stop any medicine without first consulting your doctor or pharmacist.

Notes

For best results, this medication is often used along with lifestyle changes such as stress-reduction programs, exercise and dietary changes. Talk to your health care professional about changes that you can benefit from. Laboratory tests may be done periodically while taking this medication to monitor results and prevent side effects.

Missed Dose

If you miss a dose, take it as soon as you remember. If it is near the time of the next dose, skip the missed dose and resume your usual dosing schedule. Do not double the dose to catch up.

Storage

Store at room temperature between 59 and 86 degrees F (15 to 30 degrees C) away from heat and light. Do not store in the bathroom.

CIPROFLOXACIN

Common Brand Name: Cipro

Uses
This medication is an antibiotic used to treat a wide variety of bacterial infections.

How to Use
Ciprofloxacin may be taken with or without food (also see next paragraph for more details). Take this medicine with a full glass of water.

If you take any of the following products, take them 6 hours before or 2 hours after taking this drug: zinc, iron, mineral supplements, sucralfate, didanosine, antacids that contain magnesium, calcium, or aluminum, and certain foods containing calcium (e.g., milk, yogurt, and calcium-enriched orange juice).

Drink plenty of fluids while using this medication unless your doctor tells you otherwise.

Antibiotics work best when the amount of medicine in your body is kept at a constant level. Do this by taking the medication at evenly spaced intervals throughout the day and night.

Continue to take this medication until the full prescribed amount is finished even if symptoms disappear after a few days.

Stopping the medication too early may allow bacteria to continue to grow resulting in a decrease in effectiveness in treating the infection.

Side Effects
This medication may cause stomach upset, loss of appetite, diarrhea, nausea, headache or dizziness during the first few days as your body adjusts to the medication. If these symptoms persist or become severe, inform your doctor.

Contact your doctor promptly if you experience the following: pain or tenderness (tendonitis) in arms or legs, seizures.

Notify your doctor if you develop: restlessness, vision changes, ringing in the ears, mental changes.

This medication may infrequently cause drowsiness.

In the unlikely event you have an allergic reaction to this drug, seek medical attention immediately. Symptoms of an allergic reaction include: rash, itching, swelling, fever, trouble breathing.

If you notice other effects not listed above, contact your doctor or pharmacist.

Precautions

Before taking this medication, tell your doctor your medical history especially if you have: epilepsy, kidney disease, tendon problems, nervous system disorders, liver disease, blood vessel problems, any drug allergies.

Use caution driving or performing tasks requiring alertness if this medication makes you dizzy or lightheaded. Limit alcohol intake.

This medication can increase sensitivity to sunlight. Avoid prolonged sun exposure. Wear protective clothing and a sunscreen containing a SPF of at least 15 when outdoors.

This drug may increase and/or prolong the effects of the caffeine in caffeine-containing products (coffee, colas, tea, etc.).

Drug Interactions

Tell your doctor of all the medications you may use (both prescription and nonprescription) especially if you have: other antibiotics, theophylline, warfarin, cyclosporine, live vaccines, probenecid, ropinirole, sucralfate, quinapril, didanosine, iron, zinc, mineral supplements, antacids that contain magnesium/aluminum/calcium.

This drug may increase and/or prolong the effects of caffeine.

Do not start or stop any medicine without first consulting your doctor or pharmacist.

Notes

This medication has been prescribed for your current condition only. Do not use it later for another infection or give it to someone else. A different medication may be needed in those cases.

Missed Dose

If you miss a dose, take it as soon as you remember. If it is near the time of the next dose, skip the missed dose and resume your usual dosing schedule. Do not double the dose to catch up.

Storage

Store at room temperature between 59 and 86 degrees F (between 15 and 30 degrees C) away from moisture and sunlight. Do not store in the bathroom.

CITALOPRAM

Common Brand Name: Celexa

Uses
Citalopram is used to treat depression.

This medication works by helping to restore the balance of certain natural chemicals in the brain.

How to Use
Take this medication by mouth usually once daily, with or without food; or as directed by your doctor.

The dosage is based on your medical condition and response to therapy.

It is important to continue taking this medication as prescribed even if you feel well. Also, do not stop taking this medication without consulting your doctor.

It may take up to several weeks before the full benefit of this drug takes effect.

Side Effects
Nausea, drowsiness, diarrhea, trouble sleeping, upset stomach, or dry mouth may occur. If any of these effects persist or worsen, notify your doctor promptly.

Tell your doctor immediately if any of these serious side effects occur: vomiting, loss of appetite, unusual or severe mental/mood changes, increased sweating/flushing, unusual fatigue, uncontrolled movements (tremor).

Tell your doctor immediately if any of these unlikely but serious side effects occur: blurred vision, stomach pain, fever, joint pain, muscle pain, unusually fast heartbeat, decreased interest in sex, changes in sexual ability, change in amount of urine.

Tell your doctor immediately if any of these highly unlikely but very serious side effects occur: weight changes, taste changes, unusual swelling of the hands/feet/face, seizures, painful and/or prolonged erection.

If you notice other effects not listed above, contact your doctor or pharmacist.

Precautions
Tell your doctor your medical history, especially if you have: liver problems, kidney

problems, seizures, heart problems, other mental/mood disorders thyroid problems, any allergies.

This drug may make you dizzy or drowsy; use caution engaging in activities requiring alertness such as driving or using machinery.

Drug Interactions

Certain medications taken with this product could result in serious, even fatal, drug interactions. Avoid taking monoamine oxidase inhibitors (e.g., furazolidone, isocarboxazid, linezolid, moclobemide, phenelzine, procarbazine, selegiline, tranylcypromine) within 2 weeks before or after treatment with this medication. Consult your doctor or pharmacist for additional information.

This drug is not recommended for use with: weight loss drugs (e.g., sibutramine, phentermine). Ask your doctor or pharmacist for more details.

Tell your doctor of all prescription and nonprescription medication you may use, especially: other SSRI antidepressants (e.g., fluoxetine, sertraline, fluvoxamine, paroxetine), nefazodone, trazodone, tramadol, venlafaxine, "triptan" migraine drugs (e.g., sumatriptan, zolmitriptan), tricyclic antidepressants (e.g., amitriptyline, nortriptyline), cimetidine, lithium, itraconazole, macrolide antibiotics (e.g., clarithromycin, erythromycin), any herbal/ natural products (e.g., melatonin, St John's wort, ayahuasca).

Tell your doctor if you take any drugs that cause drowsiness such as: medicine for sleep, sedatives, tranquilizers, anti- anxiety drugs (e.g., diazepam), narcotic pain relievers (e.g., codeine), psychiatric medicines (e.g., phenothiazines such as chlorpromazine), anti-seizure drugs (e.g., carbamazepine), muscle relaxants, certain antihistamines (e.g., diphenhydramine).

Do not start or stop any medicine without first consulting your doctor or pharmacist.

Missed Dose

If you miss a dose, take it as soon as you remember. If it is near the time of the next dose, skip the missed dose and resume your usual dosing schedule. Do not double the dose to catch up.

Storage

Store at room temperature between 59 and 86 degrees F (15 and 30 degrees C) away from light and moisture.

CLARITHROMYCIN

Common Brand Name: Biaxin

Uses

Clarithromycin is an antibiotic used to treat a wide variety of bacterial infections such as respiratory tract infections and skin infections. It is also used to treat peptic ulcers in combination with anti-ulcer medication.

How to Use

Regular release clarithromycin tablets may be taken with or without food. If stomach upset occurs, try taking it with food.

Extended release tablets (XL) must be taken with food and swallowed whole. Do not crush, break or chew them.

Antibiotics work best when the amount of medicine in your body is kept at a constant level. Do this by taking the medication at the same time(s) each day.

Continue to take this medication until the full prescribed amount is finished, even if symptoms disappear after a few days.

Stopping the medication too early may allow bacteria to continue to grow resulting in a relapse of the infection.

Side Effects

This medication may cause stomach upset, nausea, indigestion, loose stools, loss of appetite, vomiting, headache, abdominal pain, or a strange taste in the mouth the first few days as your body adjusts to it. If these symptoms continue or become severe, inform your doctor.

If you develop diarrhea while taking this medication, notify your doctor. Do not take any nonprescription medications to treat diarrhea without first consulting your doctor or pharmacist.

Unlikely but report promptly: dark urine, yellowing eyes/skin, mental/mood changes, an irregular heartbeat.

In the unlikely event you have an allergic reaction to this drug, seek medical attention immediately. Symptoms of an allergic reaction include: rash, itching, swelling, dizziness, trouble breathing.

Use of this medication for prolonged or repeated periods may result in a secondary infection (e.g., oral or bladder infection).

If you notice other effects not listed above, contact your doctor or pharmacist.

Precautions
Tell your doctor your medical history, especially if you have: other illnesses, allergies (especially drug allergies), liver disease, colitis, stomach problems, kidney problems, heart disease.

Drug Interactions
Tell your doctor of all drugs you may use, (prescription and nonprescription), especially of the following: barbiturates, benzodiazepines (e.g., midazolam, triazolam), carbamazepine, certain protease inhibitors (e.g., lopinavir, ritonavir), cyclosporine, digoxin, ergotamine (and related drugs), certain live vaccines, omeprazole, phenytoin, pimozide, theophylline, warfarin, certain drugs for high cholesterol (e.g., lovastatin).

Do not start or stop any medicine without first consulting your doctor or pharmacist.

Notes
This medication has been prescribed for your current condition only. Do not use it later for another infection or give it to someone else. A different medication may be necessary.

Missed Dose
If you miss a dose, take it as soon as you remember. If it is near the time of the next dose, skip the missed dose and resume your usual dosing schedule. Do not double the dose to catch up.

Storage
Store at room temperature between 68 and 77 degrees F (20 to 25 degrees C) away from moisture and sunlight. Do not store in the bathroom.

CLINDAMYCIN

Common Brand Name: Cleocin

Uses
An antibiotic used to treat a wide variety of bacterial infections.

How to Use
Clindamycin should be taken with food and a full glass (8 oz/240 ml) of water or other liquid unless your doctor directs you otherwise.

The oral solution of this product must be shaken well before using. Solution retains potency for 14 days at room temperature.

Antibiotics work best when the amount of medicine in your body is kept at a constant level. Do this by taking the medication at evenly spaced intervals throughout the day and night.

Continue to take this medication until the full prescribed amount is finished even if symptoms disappear after a few days.

Stopping the medication too early may allow bacteria to continue to grow resulting in a relapse of the infection.

Side Effects
This medication may cause stomach upset, diarrhea, nausea, vomiting, heartburn, cramps, bloating and weight loss which should disappear in a few days as your body adjusts to the medication. If these symptoms persist or become severe, inform your doctor.

If diarrhea becomes a problem, do not take any anti-diarrhea medications. Contact your doctor. Notify your doctor if the following effects occur: rash, hives, fever.

In the unlikely event you have an allergic reaction to this drug, seek medical attention immediately. Symptoms of an allergic reaction include: rash, itching, swelling, dizziness, trouble breathing.

If you notice other effects not listed above, contact your doctor or pharmacist.

Precautions
Before using this drug. tell your doctor your medical history especially if you have: liver or kidney disease, stomach or abdominal problems (colitis), any drug allergies.

Drug Interactions
Before you use this drug, tell your doctor about any other drugs you are taking including nonprescription drugs.

Do not start or stop any medicine without first consulting your doctor or pharmacist.

Notes
This medication has been prescribed for your current condition only. Do not use it later for another infection or give it to someone else. A different medication may be necessary in those cases.

Missed Dose
If you miss a dose, take it as soon as you remember. If it is near the time of the next dose, skip the missed dose and resume your usual dosing schedule. Do not double the dose to catch up.

Storage
Store at room temperature away from moisture and sunlight. Follow label warnings about whether or not to refrigerate liquid forms. Do not freeze. Do not store in bathroom.

CLONAZEPAM

Common Brand Name: Klonopin

Uses
This medication is used to treat seizure disorders or panic attacks.

How to Use
Take this medication exactly as prescribed. Try to take it at the same time each day so you get in the habit of taking it.

This medication may be taken with or without meals. However, if stomach upset occurs, take it with food.

Use this medication exactly as directed by your doctor. Do not increase your dose, use it more frequently or use it for a longer period of time than prescribed because this drug can be habit-forming. Also, if used for an extended period, do not suddenly stop using this drug without your doctor's approval.

Side Effects
Indigestion, change in appetite, nausea, seizures, drowsiness, dizziness, headache, tiredness or weakness may occur.

Mood changes, sleeplessness, excessive hair growth or loss of hair, blurred vision, dry mouth, sore gums, change in sex drive, muscle pain, and weight changes may also occur. If any of these effects persist or worsen, inform your doctor.

Notify your doctor if you develop: double vision, unusual eye movements, severe weakness, increased salivation, hallucinations, loss of coordination, a rapid or pounding heartbeat, difficulty speaking.

In the unlikely event you have an allergic reaction to this drug, seek immediate medical attention. Symptoms of an allergic reaction include: rash, itching, swelling, dizziness, trouble breathing.

If you notice other effects not listed above, contact your doctor or pharmacist.

Precautions
Tell your doctor your medical history, especially if you have: liver disease, kidney disease, glaucoma, lung disease, breathing disorders, any allergies you may have.

Because this medication may cause drowsiness, dizziness and/or blurred vision, use caution operating machinery such as driving.

Drug Interactions
Tell your doctor of all prescription and nonprescription medication you may use, especially if you have: cimetidine, disulfiram, narcotic pain relievers, sedatives, azole antifungals (e.g. ketoconazole, fluconazole, itraconazole) certain antidepressants (e.g., nefazodone and "SSRIs" such as fluoxetine), anti-seizure medications.

Limit alcohol intake while taking this medication because excessive drowsiness may occur.

Do not start or stop any medicine without first consulting your doctor or pharmacist.

Missed Dose
If you miss a dose, take it as soon as you remember. If it is near the time of the next dose, skip the missed dose and resume your usual dosing schedule. Do not double the dose to catch up.

Storage
Store at room temperature between 59 and 86 degrees F (15 to 30 degrees C) away from heat and light. Do not store in the bathroom.

CLONIDINE

Common Brand Name: Catapres

Uses
Clonidine relaxes and expands (dilates) blood vessels. It is used to treat high blood pressure (hypertension).

How to Use
Take this medication exactly as prescribed. Try to take it at the same time(s) each day.

Do not stop taking this medication without consulting your doctor. Some conditions may become worse when the drug is abruptly stopped. Your dose may need to be gradually decreased before it is stopped completely.

Tablets may be taken with food or milk to avoid stomach irritation.

It is important to continue taking this medication even if you feel well. Most people with high blood pressure do not feel sick.

Side Effects
Dizziness, drowsiness, headache, constipation, loss of appetite, fatigue, weakness, nasal congestion and dry eyes may occur the first several days as your body adjusts to the medication.

To avoid dizziness and lightheadedness when rising from a seated or lying position, get up slowly.

Inform your doctor if you develop: chest pain, difficulty breathing, difficulty urinating, skin rash, swelling of the hands or feet, yellowing of the eyes or skin.

If you notice other effects not listed above, contact your doctor or pharmacist.

Precautions
Tell your doctor if you have any medical conditions, especially: heart or circulatory problems, depression.

Before having surgery, including dental surgery, tell the doctor about your blood pressure medications.

Limit intake of alcohol.

Drug Interactions

Tell your doctor of all prescription and nonprescription drugs you may use, especially if you have: cough-and-cold products, beta-blockers (e.g., propranolol, timolol), drugs used for depression (e.g., amitriptyline, imipramine).

Do not start or stop any medicine without first consulting your doctor or pharmacist.

Notes

It is important to have your blood pressure checked regularly while taking this medication. Learn how to monitor your blood pressure. Discuss this with your doctor.

Do not allow anyone else to take this medication.

Missed Dose

If you miss a dose, take it as soon as you remember. If it is near the time of the next dose, skip the missed dose and resume your usual dosing schedule. Do not double the dose to catch up.

Storage

Store at room temperature between 59 and 86 degrees F (between 15 and 30 degrees C) away from moisture and sunlight. Do not store in the bathroom.

CLOPIDOGREL

Common Brand Name: Plavix

Uses
This medication is used to help prevent heart attacks, strokes and other problems caused by narrowed blood vessels ("hardening of the arteries").

How to Use
Take this medicine as directed, generally once daily by mouth, with or without food.

Side Effects
Stomach pain, diarrhea, headache or dizziness might occur. If these effects persist or worsen, notify your doctor promptly.

Unlikely but report promptly: black stools, "coffee-ground" appearing vomit, chest pain, swelling, unusual bleeding or bruising.

Very unlikely but report promptly: fever, persistent sore throat, mood changes, vision problems, fainting.

An allergic reaction to this drug is unlikely, but seek immediate medical attention if it occurs. Symptoms of an allergic reaction include: rash, itching, dizziness, trouble breathing.

If you notice other effects not listed above, contact your doctor or pharmacist.

Precautions
Before using this drug, tell your doctor your medical history, especially if you have: allergies (especially drug allergies), ulcers, abnormal bleeding or blood disorders, serious injury, recent surgery, liver disease.

Limit alcohol intake, as it may aggravate certain side effects of this medicine, especially stomach bleeding.

Use caution operating machinery or performing hazardous tasks as this medicine can cause dizziness.

Drug Interactions

Tell your doctor of all nonprescription and prescription medication you use, especially if you have: anticoagulants, warfarin, heparin, low molecular weight heparin, phenytoin, tamoxifen, tolbutamide, torsemide, fluvastatin. Do not take with aspirin or NSAIDs (e.g., ibuprofen, naproxen) unless instructed to do so by your doctor. Certain conditions are treated with clopidogrel in combination with aspirin. Consult your doctor or pharmacist for details.

Many nonprescription medicines contain aspirin or NSAIDs, so check your medicine labels carefully. Consult your pharmacist.

Do not start or stop any medicine without first consulting your doctor or pharmacist.

Notes

Do not share this medicine with others.

Inform all doctors and dentists involved in your care about your use of this drug.

Missed Dose

If you miss a dose, take it as soon as you remember. If it is near the time of the next dose, skip the missed dose and resume your usual dosing schedule. Do not double the dose to catch up.

Storage

Store at room temperature between 59 and 86 degrees F (15-30 degrees C) away from sunlight and moisture.

COLCHICINE

Common Brand Name: Colsalide

IMPORTANT NOTE
The following information is intended to supplement, not substitute for, the expertise and judgment of your physician, pharmacist or other healthcare professional. It should not be construed to indicate that use of the drug is safe, appropriate, or effective for you. Consult your healthcare professional before using this drug.

COLCHICINE (ORAL)

Uses
This medication is used to treat and prevent gout.

How to Use
To control a gout attack, start taking this medication at the first signs of an attack.

Take by mouth as directed. Colchicine is taken regularly to prevent gout attacks or only for episodes of acute gout attack.

Side Effects
Notify your doctor immediately if you experience the following symptoms (which may indicate that you need to stop taking the drug): nausea, stomach pain, vomiting, diarrhea.

Report to your doctor promptly: yellowing eyes or skin, sore throat, easy bruising or bleeding, muscle aches, numbness or tingling of legs and arms, fatigue, rash, itchy skin.

If you notice other effects not listed above, contact your doctor or pharmacist.

Precautions
Before using this drug, tell your doctor your medical history especially if you have: kidney or heart disease, stomach or intestinal problems, bleeding disorders, any drug allergies.

Alcohol can decrease the effectiveness of this drug. Also alcohol use can increase the chance of stomach problems with colchicine. Limit alcohol consumption while taking this.

If taking colchicine regularly to prevent and attack, take it regularly as directed by your doctor, eve if you start feeling well. If you take colchicine only to relieve an attack, follow the doctor's instructions.

Before having surgery, including dental surgery, tell your doctor you are taking colchicine.

If you are to take a urine test while using this medication, tell the doctor or laboratory personnel that you are taking colchicine because colchicine may affect the test results.

Drug Interactions
Before using this drug, tell your doctor of all prescription and nonprescription medicines you may use.

Do not start or stop any medicine without first consulting your doctor or pharmacist.

Notes
Colchicine relieves pain but only pain associated with gout. It should not be used for any other type of pain.

Do not allow anyone else to take this medication.

Missed Dose
If you miss a dose, take it as soon as you remember. If it is near the time of the next dose, skip the missed dose and resume your usual dosing schedule. Do not double the dose to catch up.

Storage
Store at room temperature between 59 and 86 degrees F (between 15 and 30 degrees C) away from moisture and sunlight. Do not store in the bathroom.

CONJUGATED ESTROGENS/ MEDROXYPROGESTERONE

Common Brand Names: Prempro, Premphase

Uses
This medication is a combination of hormones used as hormone replacement therapy (HRT) to treat symptoms of menopause and to prevent bone loss (osteoporosis) from occurring.

How to Use
Take this by mouth exactly as directed by your doctor. This may be taken with meals to prevent stomach upset.

Do not increase your dose, take this more often than directed or stop taking this without first consulting your doctor.

Side Effects
Headache, irritability, restlessness, mood changes, nausea, increase in uterine fibroids, weight changes, changes in sleeping patterns, fatigue, upset stomach, bloating, acne, change in sex drive or breast tenderness may occur. If these symptoms continue or become severe, inform your doctor immediately.

Notify your doctor immediately if any of the following occur: swelling ankles or feet, leg pain, chest pain, severe headache, vision problems, severe stomach/abdominal pain, depression, breathing problems, abnormal vaginal bleeding, lumps in the breast, one-sided weakness.

If you notice other effects not listed above, contact your doctor or pharmacist.

Precautions
Before taking this, tell your doctor if you have heart disease or circulation problems, asthma, migraine headaches, any previous cancers, blood disorders, liver disease, gallbladder disease, history of depression, diabetes, seizure disorders, undiagnosed abnormal vaginal bleeding, any allergies.

Two-drug combination hormone replacement therapy (estrogen and progestin menopause HRT) can infrequently cause breast cancer, heart disease (CHD/MI), stroke, or blood clots in the lung (PE) if used for a long period of time (greater than one year).

Therefore, the risks of use of HRT for a long period of time (more than one year) must be discussed with your doctor .

Use of two-drug HRT for short periods of time (less than one year) to relieve menopause symptoms may be considered. Discuss the risks and benefits with your doctor.

Cigarette smoking can increase the chance of blood-clots while taking this medication (especially in women past the age of 35).

Depending on strength, this drug may cause a patchy, darkening of the skin on the face (melasma). Higher strengths are more likely to cause melasma. Sunlight may intensify this darkening and you may need to avoid prolonged sun exposure and sunlamps.

Consult your doctor regarding use of sunscreens and protective clothing.

Drug Interactions
Tell your doctor of any nonprescription or prescription medication you may use, particularly: warfarin, steroids, antidepressants, thyroid, blood sugar medication.

This product can affect the results of certain lab tests. Make sure laboratory personnel and your doctors know you use this drug.

Do not start or stop any medicine without first consulting your doctor or pharmacist.

Notes
It is important to understand your therapy and to follow your doctor's instructions. Be sure to ask your doctor any questions you may have. Do not share this drug with others.

Missed Dose
If you miss a dose, take it as soon as you remember. If it is near the time of the next dose, skip the missed dose and resume your usual dosing schedule. Do not double the dose to catch up.

Storage
Store at room temperature between 59 and 77 degrees F (15 to 25 degrees C) as directed away from heat and light. Do not store in the bathroom.

Keep this and all medication away from children.

CONJUGATED ESTROGENS

Common Brand Name: Premarin

Uses
This medication is an estrogen hormone and is given to women who produce no or lower amounts of estrogen. It is used to reduce symptoms of menopause such as hot flashes, sweating chills, dizziness, and faintness. Estrogen vaginal cream is used to lessen uncomfortable changes in the vagina (e.g. dryness or soreness) and vulva that can develop with menopause.

How to Use
May be taken with food or immediately after a meal to prevent stomach upset.

Take this medication as prescribed. Follow the dosing schedule carefully. Be sure to ask your doctor or pharmacist if you have any questions.

Side Effects
Oral estrogens may cause dizziness, lightheadedness, headache, stomach upset, bloating, nausea, swelling in feet, or breast tenderness. These effects should disappear as your body adjusts to the medication.

Notify your doctor promptly if you experience: severe depression, calf pain, sudden severe headache, chest pain, shortness of breath, lumps in the breast, one-sided weakness, slurred speech, weakness or numbing in arm or leg, yellowing of the eyes or skin, changes in vaginal bleeding (spotting, breakthrough bleeding, prolonged or complete stoppage of bleeding), stomach pain, skin rash.

If you notice other effects not listed above, contact your doctor or pharmacist.

Precautions
Before you take this medication, tell your doctor your entire medical history, including: family medical history (especially breast lumps and cancer), high blood pressure, diabetes, asthma, epilepsy (seizures), migraine headaches, liver disease, heart disease, kidney disease, depression, uterine fibroid tumor, abnormal vaginal bleeding, blood clots or stroke, high cholesterol or triglycerides, gallbladder disease.

Before having surgery, tell the doctor that you take this drug.

Depending on strength, this drug may cause a patchy, darkening of the skin on the face (melasma). Higher strengths are more likely to cause melasma. Sunlight may intensify this darkening and you may need to avoid prolonged sun exposure and sunlamps.

Consult your doctor regarding use of sunscreens and protective clothing.

Cigarette smoking can increase the chance of blood-clots while taking this medication (especially in women past the age of 35).

Prolonged use of oral estrogens for many years increases the risk of developing breast cancer and endometrial cancer. It is important to have regular breast examinations and mammograms (x-ray pictures of the breasts) while taking oral estrogens.

Drug Interactions

Tell your doctor of all prescription and nonprescription drugs you may use, especially if you have: drugs used for seizures (e.g., phenytoin, phenobarbital, dilvalproex, valproic acid, carbamazepine).

Do not start or stop any medicine without first consulting your doctor or pharmacist.

Notes

Do not share this medication with others.

Missed Dose

If you miss a dose, take it as soon as you remember. If it is near the time of the next dose, skip the missed dose and resume your usual dosing schedule. Do not double the dose to catch up.

Storage

Store at room temperature between 59 and 86 degrees F (between 15 and 30 degrees C) away from moisture and sunlight. Do not store in the bathroom.

CYCLOBENZAPRINE

Common Brand Name: Flexeril

Uses
This medication relaxes muscles and relieves pain and discomfort associated with strains, sprains, spasms or other muscle injuries.

How to Use
May be taken with food if stomach upset occurs.

Take this medication as directed. Do not increase your dose or take it more often than prescribed.

Side Effects
May cause stomach upset, heartburn, constipation, headache, dizziness or drowsiness or dry mouth the first few days as your body adjusts to the medication. If these symptoms persist or become severe, notify your doctor.

Inform your doctor if you develop: muscle stiffness, skin rash, itching, rapid heart rate, swelling of the face, difficulty urinating.

When rising quickly from a sitting or lying position, dizziness or lightheadedness may occur. Change positions slowly and use caution on stairs.

Avoid activities requiring alertness if dizziness or drowsiness occurs.

If you notice other effects not listed above, contact your doctor or pharmacist.

Precautions
Before taking this drug, tell your doctor if you have: glaucoma, an overactive thyroid gland, heart disease, difficulty urinating, any allergies.

Drug Interactions
Tell your doctor of any over-the-counter or prescription medications you take, especially if you have: cimetidine, antidepressants, sedatives, tranquilizers, sleeping pills, narcotic pain medication (e.g., codeine), anti-allergy drugs, drugs used for asthma, cough-and-cold medicines.

Alcohol adds to the dizziness and drowsiness caused by cyclobenzaprine. Limit alcohol intake.

Do not start or stop any medicine without first consulting your doctor or pharmacist.

Notes

Do not use for longer than 3 weeks unless specifically instructed to do so.

This medication provides temporary relief and must be used in addition to rest, physical therapy and other measures.

Missed Dose

If you miss a dose, take it as soon as you remember. If it is near the time of the next dose, skip the missed dose and resume your usual dosing schedule. Do not double the dose to catch up.

Storage

Store at room temperature away from sunlight and moisture.

DIAZEPAM

Common Brand Names: Valium, Dizac

Uses
This medication is used to relieve nervousness and tension or improve sleep disturbances. It is also used to relieve symptoms of alcohol withdrawal such as tremors, or used to treat seizure disorders or as a skeletal muscle relaxant.

How to Use
Take with food or milk if stomach upset occurs. Take exactly as prescribed. Do not increase your dose or take more often than prescribed.

For insomnia, take 30 to 60 minutes prior to bedtime.

Do not stop taking this medication without your doctor's approval. Your dose may have to be gradually decreased if you have been taking it for some time.

Side Effects
This medication causes drowsiness and dizziness.

Avoid tasks requiring alertness.

Other side effects may include: stomach upset, blurred vision, headache, confusion, depression, impaired coordination, change in heart rate, trembling, weakness, memory loss, hangover effect (grogginess), dreaming or nightmares.

Notify your doctor if you develop: chest pain, change in heart rate, vision changes, yellowing of the eyes or skin.

In the unlikely event you have an allergic reaction to this drug, seek medical attention immediately. Symptoms of an allergic reaction include: rash, itching, swelling, dizziness, trouble breathing.

If you notice other effects not listed above, contact your doctor or pharmacist.

Precautions
Before using this drug, tell your doctor your medical history, especially if you have: liver or kidney disease, drug allergies.

Alcohol or other sedative-type drugs can lead to extreme drowsiness. Limit alcohol consumption while using this medication.

Older adults are usually more sensitive to the effects of this medication. Use cautiously.

Drug Interactions
Tell your doctor of all prescription and nonprescription drugs you may use, especially if you have: cimetidine, digoxin, disulfiram, levodopa, seizure medication, sleeping pills, narcotic pain medication (e.g., codeine), medication for depression, barbiturates, tranquilizers, sedatives, certain drowsiness-causing antihistamines (e.g., diphenhydramine), drugs used to treat allergies or colds, alcohol use.

Do not eat grapefruit or drink grapefruit juice unless your doctor instructs you otherwise.

Smoking can decrease the effectiveness of this drug.

Do not start or stop any medicine without first consulting your doctor or pharmacist.

Notes
Do not share this medication with others.

Missed Dose
If you miss a dose, take it as soon as you remember. If it is near the time of the next dose, skip the missed dose and resume your usual dosing schedule. Do not double the dose to catch up.

Storage
Store at room temperature between 59 and 86 degrees F (between 15 and 30 degrees C) away from moisture and sunlight. Do not store in the bathroom.

DICLOFENAC

Common Brand Names: Voltaren, Cataflam

Uses
This medication is a nonsteroidal anti-inflammatory drug that relieves pain and reduces inflammation (swelling). It is used to treat headaches, muscle aches, dental pain, and athletic injuries. It is commonly used to treat pain, swelling and stiffness associated with arthritis.

How to Use
Take this medication with food, milk, or antacids to prevent stomach upset.

Take this medication with 6 to 8 ounces (180-240ml) of water.

Side Effects
Stomach upset is the most common side effect.

Nausea, vomiting, bloating, gas, dizziness, drowsiness, blurred vision or loss of appetite may also occur. If any of these effects persist or worsen, notify your doctor.

Inform your doctor promptly if you develop: ringing in ears/ loss of hearing, vision changes.

If you notice any of the following unlikely but very serious side effects, stop taking this drug and consult your doctor or pharmacist immediately: black stools, persistent stomach/ abdominal pain, vomit that looks like coffee grounds.

An allergic reaction to this drug is unlikely, but seek immediate medical attention if it occurs. Symptoms of an allergic reaction include: rash, itching, swelling, severe dizziness, trouble breathing.

If you notice other effects not listed above, contact your doctor or pharmacist.

Precautions
Tell your doctor your medical history, especially if you have: liver or kidney disease, blood disorders, ulcers, heart disease, alcohol use, high blood pressure, eye disease, allergies (especially drug allergies).

Use caution when performing tasks requiring alertness. Limit alcohol intake as it may intensify the drowsiness effect of this medication.

This medicine may cause stomach bleeding. Daily use of alcohol, especially when combined with this medicine, may increase your risk for stomach bleeding. Check with your doctor or pharmacist for more information.

Do not take aspirin without consulting your doctor. Check the ingredients of any nonprescription medication you may be taking since many cough-and-cold formulas contain aspirin.

Infrequently, this medication may increase the skin's sensitivity to sunlight. If this happens to you, avoid prolonged sun exposure, wear protective clothing and use a sunscreen. Avoid sunlamps.

Caution is advised when this drug is used with older people.

Drug Interactions
Tell your doctor of all prescription and nonprescription drugs you may use, especially if you have: "blood thinners" such as warfarin, other arthritis medication, water pills, lithium.

Do not start or stop any medicine without first consulting your doctor or pharmacist.

Notes
In arthritis, it may take up to two weeks before the full effects of this medicine are noted. For best results, this medication must be taken regularly as directed by your doctor.

Missed Dose
If you miss a dose, take it as soon as you remember. If it is near the time of the next dose, skip the missed dose and resume your usual dosing schedule. Do not double the dose to catch up.

Storage
Store at room temperature away from moisture and sunlight. Do not store in the bathroom.

DIGOXIN

Common Brand Names: Digitek, Lanoxin

Uses
Digitalis medication works directly on the heart muscle to strengthen and regulate the heartbeat. It is used to treat certain heart conditions.

How to Use
Take this medication exactly as prescribed. Try to take it at the same time(s) each day.

May be taken with food or milk to avoid stomach irritation.

Do not stop taking this medication without consulting your doctor. Some conditions may become worse when the drug is suddenly stopped.

Side Effects
Diarrhea, loss of appetite, drowsiness, headache, dizziness, muscle weakness, and fatigue may occur as your body adjusts to the medication.

Inform your doctor if you develop: confusion, vomiting, visual disturbances (blurred vision or yellow/green halos around objects), rapid heart rate, slow pulse rate, skin rash, severe stomach upset, loss of appetite.

If you notice other effects not listed above, contact your doctor or pharmacist.

Precautions
Tell your doctor if you have a history of kidney disease, lung disease, thyroid problems, rheumatic fever.

Food high in fiber may decrease the absorption of digoxin. Be sure to take digoxin a few hours before or after eating something high in fiber (such as bran).

Difficulty breathing and swelling in your lower legs and ankles may be signs that your dose is too low. If normal activity causes shortness of breath or if you awaken frequently during the night due to shortness of breath, tell your doctor. Do not change your dose without consulting your doctor.

Before having surgery, including dental surgery, tell the doctor that you take digoxin.

Drug Interactions

Tell your doctor of all prescription and nonprescription medication you may use, especially: amphotericin, diuretics ("water pills"), corticosteroids (e.g., prednisone), amiodarone, neomycin, quinidine, cyclosporine, verapamil, quinine, thyroid medication, propafenone, sucralfate, erythromycin-like drugs, rifampin, bepridil, penicillamine, drugs used for cancer, tetracycline, dextrothyroxine, St John's wort.

Cholestyramine, colestipol or psyllium (Metamucil) should be taken at least 2 hours after digoxin to prevent interference. If you are taking aminosalicylic acid (PAS), antacids, kaolin-pectin, milk of magnesia or sulfasalazine, take it as far apart as possible from digoxin.

Do not start or stop any medicine without first consulting your doctor or pharmacist.

Notes

There are different brands of this medication available.

Not all are identical in action. Do not change brands without consulting your doctor or pharmacist.

Your doctor may want you to monitor your pulse rate every day while you take this medication. Discuss with your doctor what your pulse rate means.

To evaluate the effectiveness of this medication, your doctor may periodically take a blood sample to measure the amount of the drug in your body.

Do not allow anyone else to take your medication.

Missed Dose

If you miss a dose, take it as soon as you remember. If it is near the time of the next dose, skip the missed dose and resume your usual dosing schedule. Do not double the dose to catch up.

Storage

Store at room temperature between 59 and 86 degrees F (between 15 and 30 degrees C) away from moisture and sunlight. Do not store in the bathroom. Do not freeze liquid forms of this medication.

DILTIAZEM

Common Brand Names: Cartia XT, Cardizem, Tiazac

Uses
This drug is a calcium channel blocker. Calcium is involved in blood vessel contraction. By blocking calcium, diltiazem relaxes and widens blood vessels. Diltiazem is used to treat high blood pressure, chest pain (angina), or irregular heartbeat.

How to Use
The capsule(s) may be taken without regard to meals once daily in the morning. Swallow whole. Do not crush or chew the capsule. However, if you have difficulty swallowing, open the capsule, sprinkle the entire contents on a spoonful of applesauce, and take at once. Do not chew the mixture. Follow this with a cool glass of water.

Do not stop taking this drug without your doctor's permission.

Your dose may need to be gradually reduced.

Side Effects
This drug may cause dizziness and lightheadedness especially during the first few days. Avoid activities requiring alertness. When you sit or lie down for a while, get up slowly to allow your body to adjust and minimize dizziness. You may also experience bloating, heartburn, muscle cramps, headache, flushing, nasal congestion, sore throat, constipation or diarrhea. Inform your doctor if they become bothersome.

Notify your doctor if you develop: breathing difficulties, swelling of the hands or feet, an irregular heartbeat.

If you notice other effects not listed above, contact your doctor or pharmacist.

Precautions
Before taking this drug, tell your doctor if you have: heart problems, liver problems, lung diseases, allergies.

Limit intake of alcohol while taking this drug.

Drug Interactions

Tell your doctor of all prescription and nonprescription drugs you may use, especially if you have: cyclosporine, flecainide, beta-blockers (including eye drops), digoxin, lithium, disopyramide, high blood pressure medication, quinidine, rifampin, carbamazepine, cimetidine, St John's wort.

Avoid any drugs that increase your heart-rate (the decongestants phenylephrine and pseudoephedrine are examples). These drugs are commonly found in over-the-counter cough-and-cold products.

Do not start or stop any medicine without first consulting your doctor or pharmacist.

Notes

Do not share this product with others.

Missed Dose

If you miss a dose, take it as soon as you remember. If it is near the time of the next dose, skip the missed dose and resume your usual dosing schedule. Do not double the dose to catch up.

Storage

Store at room temperature away from sunlight and moisture.

DOXAZOSIN

Common Brand Name: Cardura

Uses
This medication relaxes and dilates (expands) blood vessels resulting in lowered blood pressure. It is used to treat hypertension (high blood pressure) and symptoms due to enlarged prostrate (benign prostatic hypertrophy).

How to Use
Take this medication exactly as prescribed. Try to take it at the same time each day. Take the first dose at bedtime to minimize the chances of getting dizzy or fainting.

It is important to continue taking this medication even if you feel well. Most people with high blood pressure do not feel sick.

Do not stop taking this medication without consulting your doctor. Some conditions may become worse when the drug is abruptly stopped. Your dose may need to be gradually decreased.

Side Effects
Dizziness, drowsiness, lightheadedness, headache, constipation, loss of appetite, dry mouth, tiredness, stuffy nose, blurred vision, dry eyes or trouble sleeping may occur the first several days as your body adjusts to the medication. If any of these effects continue or become bothersome, inform your doctor.

Notify your doctor if you experience: chest pain, depression, swelling of hands or feet, sexual problems.

Tell your doctor immediately if any of these highly unlikely but very serious side effects occur: persistent sore throat, fever, easy bleeding or bruising, nausea, stomach pain, yellowing eyes or skin, dark urine.

Males - though it is unlikely to occur, if you get a painful, prolonged erection, stop using this drug and seek immediate medical attention.

In the unlikely event you have an allergic reaction to this drug, seek immediate medical attention. Symptoms of an allergic reaction include: rash, itching, swelling, dizziness, trouble breathing.

If you notice other effects not listed above, contact your doctor or pharmacist.

Precautions
Tell your doctor your medical history, especially if you have: liver or kidney disease, allergies (especially to other similar drugs such as prazosin).

To avoid dizziness or fainting, get up slowly from a lying or seated position; especially when you first start using this drug or if your doctor changes your dosing.

Limit your intake of alcohol and avoid getting overheated because they may increase the dizziness and drowsiness effects of this drug. Use caution performing tasks requiring alertness such as driving or using machinery.

Drug Interactions
Inform your doctor about all the medicines you use (both prescription and nonprescription). Avoid any drugs that increase your heart rate or make you excited like decongestants because it may counteract your blood pressure medicine. Decongestants are commonly found in over-the-counter cough and cold products.

Do not start or stop any medicine without first consulting your doctor or pharmacist.

Notes
It is important to have your blood pressure checked regularly while taking this medication. Learn how to monitor your blood pressure. Discuss this with your doctor or pharmacist.

Your doctor may schedule lab tests periodically to see how the drug is working.

Missed Dose
If you miss a dose, take it as soon as you remember. If it is near the time of the next dose, skip the missed dose and resume your usual dosing schedule. Do not double the dose to catch up.

Storage
Store at room temperature away from sunlight and moisture.

DOXYCYCLINE

Common Brand Names: Vibramycin, Doryx

Uses
Doxycycline is an antibiotic used to treat a wide variety of bacterial infections.

How to Use
Take each dose with a full glass of water (4oz or 120 ml) or more. Do not lie down for 30 minutes after taking this drug to decrease irritation of your esophagus. Take with food or milk if stomach upset occurs unless your doctor directs you otherwise.

Avoid taking antacids containing magnesium, aluminum or calcium, sucralfate, iron preparations or vitamin (zinc) products within 2-3 hours of taking this medication. These products bind with the medicine preventing its absorption.

The liquid suspension form of this medicine must be shaken well before using.

Antibiotics work best when the amount of medicine in your body is kept at a constant level. Do this by taking the medicine at evenly spaced intervals throughout the day and night.

Continue to take this medication until the full prescribed amount is finished even if symptoms disappear after a few days.

Stopping the medication too early may allow bacteria to continue to grow resulting in a decrease in effectiveness in treating the infection.

Side Effects
This medication may cause stomach upset, diarrhea, nausea, headache or vomiting. If these symptoms persist or worsen, notify your doctor.

Very unlikely but report: stomach pain, yellowing of the eyes or skin, vision changes, mental changes.

Doxycycline increases sensitivity to sunlight.

In the unlikely event you have an allergic reaction to this drug, seek immediate medical attention. Symptoms of an allergic reaction include: rash, itching, swelling, dizziness, trouble breathing.

If you notice other effects not listed above, contact your doctor or pharmacist.

Precautions

Tell your doctor your medical history, especially if you have: liver problems, kidney problems, allergies (especially drug allergies), trouble swallowing, esophagus problems (e.g., hiatal hernia, gastrointestinal reflux disease).

Use of this medication for prolonged or repeated periods may result in a secondary yeast infection (of the mouth, bladder or vagina).

Doxycycline may make you more prone to sunburn. Wear protective clothing and avoid direct sunlight and use a sunscreen with a SPF of at least 15 while taking this medication.

Drug Interactions

Inform your doctor about all the medicines you may use (both prescription and nonprescription), especially if you have: other antibiotics, live vaccines, sucralfate, antacids, vitamins, warfarin, iron.

Do not start or stop any medicine without first consulting your doctor or pharmacist.

Notes

This medication has been prescribed for your current condition only. Do not use it later for another infection or give it to someone else. A different medication may be necessary.

Missed Dose

If you miss a dose, take it as soon as you remember. If it is near the time of the next dose, skip the missed dose and resume your usual dosing schedule. Do not double the dose to catch up.

Storage

Store at room temperature away from moisture and sunlight. Do not store in the bathroom.

ENALAPRIL

Common Brand Name: Vasotec

Uses
This medication prevents certain enzymes in the body from narrowing blood vessels. This helps to lower blood pressure and makes the heart beat stronger. This medication is used to treat high blood pressure, heart failure or to help diabetics prevent kidney problems.

How to Use
This medication may be taken without regard to meals. Take it exactly as prescribed and try to take it at the same time each day.

If you are given the liquid suspension form of this medicine, shake the bottle well before each use. Measure the liquid carefully and use as directed.

Do not stop taking this medication without consulting your doctor. Some conditions may become worse when the drug is abruptly stopped. Your dose may need to be gradually decreased before it is stopped completely.

Side Effects
Headache, diarrhea, constipation, nausea, fatigue or dry cough may occur the first several days as your body adjusts to the medication.

Unlikely, but report promptly if you develop: chest pain, tingling or swelling of the hands or feet, swelling of the face/ lips/tongue, yellowing of the skin or eyes, fever, dizziness, persistent sore throat.

In the unlikely event you have an allergic reaction to this drug, seek immediate medical attention. Symptoms of an allergic reaction include: rash, itching, swelling, severe dizziness, trouble breathing.

If you notice other effects not listed above, contact your doctor or pharmacist.

Precautions
Before taking this drug tell your doctor your medical history, especially history of: angioedema, high blood levels of potassium, kidney disease or kidney dialysis, salt restrictive diet, liver disease, heart problems, any drug allergies.

Consult your doctor before using salt substitutes or low salt milk.

To avoid dizziness and lightheadedness when rising from a seated or lying position, get up slowly.

Limit your intake of alcohol and use caution when exercising or during hot weather as these can aggravate dizziness and lightheadedness.

Drug Interactions

Inform your doctor about all the medicine you use (both prescription and nonprescription), especially if you take: lithium, potassium supplements, potassium-sparing water pills or other water pills (diuretics), high blood pressure drugs, NSAIDs (aspirin-like drugs).

Do not start or stop any medicine without first consulting your doctor or pharmacist.

Notes

It is important to have your blood pressure checked regularly while taking this medication. Learn how to monitor your blood pressure. Discuss this with your doctor.

Lab tests may be performed to monitor your progress.

Missed Dose

If you miss a dose, take it as soon as you remember. If it is near the time of the next dose, skip the missed dose and resume your usual dosing schedule. Do not double the dose to catch up.

Storage

Store tablets at room temperature away from sunlight and moisture. Do not store in the bathroom. Refrigerate the suspension between 36 to 46 degrees F (2 to 8 degrees C). The suspension should be discarded after 30 days.

ENTACAPONE

Common Brand Name: Comtan

Uses
This medication is used to treat Parkinson's Disease, in combination with levodopa-containing medicines. Entacapone must be used with your other Parkinson's Disease medicines in order to work.

How to Use
This medicine is taken by mouth, with or without food Entacapone generally is taken in conjunction with your levodopa/carbidopa medicine, or as directed.

Follow all instructions carefully; you may need to decrease the dosage of your levodopa/carbidopa, depending on the amount of levodopa you currently take. Your levodopa/carbidopa dosing schedule may change as well. Speak with your doctor regarding your medication regimen.

Do not suddenly stop using this drug: the dosage should be reduced gradually to minimize possible side effects. Consult your doctor or pharmacist for more information.

The manufacturer advises a maximum of 8 doses (1600mg) per day.

Side Effects
Diarrhea, drowsiness, upset stomach or dizziness may occur. If these effects persist or worsen, notify your doctor promptly.

Tell your doctor immediately if you have any of these unlikely but serious side effects: mental/mood changes, fainting, muscle coordination problems, muscle pain. This drug may cause a harmless discoloration (brownish-orange color) of your urine.

If you notice other effects not listed above, contact your doctor or pharmacist.

Precautions
Tell your doctor your medical history, including liver disease, any allergies, and other medications for Parkinson's disease.

To minimize dizziness and lightheadedness, get up slowly when rising from a seated or lying position.

This drug may make you dizzy or drowsy; use caution engaging in activities requiring alertness such as driving or using machinery. Limit alcoholic beverages.

Drug Interactions

Tell your doctor of all prescription and nonprescription medication you may use, especially if you have: most MAO inhibitors (e.g., furazolidone, linezolid, moclobemide, phenelzine, procarbazine), isoproterenol, adrenalin (epinephrine), norepinephrine, dopamine, dobutamine, alpha-methyldopa, apomorphine, isoetharine, bitolterol, probenecid, cholestyramine, certain antibiotics (e.g., erythromycin, ampicillin, rifamin, chloramphenicol).

According to the manufacturer, if you are prescribed the MAO inhibitor selegiline you may continue to take it while using entacapone.

Also, report use of any medicine that can make you drowsy, such as: sedatives, tranquilizers, anti-anxiety medicine, anti-seizure drugs, narcotic pain relievers (e.g., codeine), psychiatric medicines, certain drowsiness-causing antihistamines (e.g., diphenhydramine).

Do not start or stop any medicine without first consulting your doctor or pharmacist.

Notes

Do not share this medication with others.

Missed Dose

If you miss a dose, use it as soon as you remember.

If it is near the time of the next dose, skip the missed dose and resume your usual dosing schedule. Do not double the dose to catch up.

Storage

Store at room temperature—77 degrees F (25 degrees C)—away from light and moisture.

ESOMEPRAZOLE

Common Brand Name: Nexium

Uses
Esomeprazole is used to treat ulcers, esophagitis, and other conditions due to acid secretion (e.g., GERD). It works by blocking the production of acid in the stomach. When treating ulcers, this medication may be prescribed along with antibiotics.

How to Use
Take this medication by mouth usually once daily at least one hour before food; or take as directed by your doctor.

Do not crush or chew the capsules. Swallow the capsule(s) whole. If you have difficulty swallowing this medication whole, the capsule may be opened and the contents sprinkled into soft food (applesauce or yogurt) and taken as directed. Do not chew the food/medication mixture or make-up a supply in advance. Doing so may destroy the drug and/or increase side effects.

The dosage is based on your medical condition and response to therapy.

Side Effects
Headache, diarrhea, nausea, gas, stomach pain, constipation, or dry mouth may occur. If any of these effects persist or worsen, notify your doctor or pharmacist promptly.

Tell your doctor immediately if any of these serious side effects occur: throat pain, chest pain, severe stomach pain, coffee-ground vomit.

An allergic reaction to this drug is unlikely, but seek immediate medical attention if it occurs. Symptoms of an allergic reaction include: rash, itching, swelling, dizziness, trouble breathing.

If you notice other effects not listed above, contact your doctor or pharmacist.

Precautions
Tell your doctor your medical history, especially liver disease, any allergies you may have.

Drug Interactions

Tell your doctor or pharmacist of all prescription and nonprescription drugs you may use, especially: digoxin, diazepam, ketoconazole, itraconazole, iron supplements, vitamins with iron, cilostazol.

Do not start or stop any medicine without first consulting your doctor or pharmacist.

Notes

Do not share this medication with others.

Laboratory and/or medical tests may be performed to monitor your progress.

Missed Dose

If you miss a dose, take it as soon as you remember. If it is near the time of the next dose, skip the missed dose and resume your usual dosing schedule. Do not double the dose to catch up.

Storage

Store at room temperature between 59 and 86 degrees F (15 and 30 degrees C) away from light and moisture.

ESTRADIOL

Common Brand Name: Estrace

Uses
This medication is a hormone and is given to women whose bodies make little or not amounts of estrogen. It is used to reduce menopause symptoms (e.g., hot flashes), and to prevent brittle bones (osteoporosis).

How to Use
May be taken with food or immediately after a meal to prevent stomach upset.

Take this medication as prescribed. Follow the dosing schedule carefully. Be sure to ask your doctor if you have any questions.

Side Effects
May cause dizziness, lightheadedness, headache, stomach upset, bloating, or nausea. These effects should disappear as your body adjusts to the medication.

Notify your doctor promptly if you experience: severe depression, calf pain, sudden severe headache, chest pain, shortness of breath, lumps in the breast, one-sided weakness, slurred speech, weakness or tingling in the arm or leg, yellowing of the eyes or skin, changes in vaginal bleeding (spotting, breakthrough bleeding, prolonged or complete stoppage of bleeding), stomach pain, skin rash.

If you notice other effects not listed above, contact your doctor or pharmacist.

Precautions
Before you take this medication, tell your doctor your entire medical history, including: family medical history (especially breast lumps and cancer), high blood pressure, diabetes, asthma, epilepsy (seizures), migraine headaches, liver disease, heart disease, kidney disease, depression, uterine fibroid tumor, abnormal vaginal bleeding, blood clots or stroke, cholesterol or lipid problems, gallbladder disease.

Before having surgery, tell the doctor that you take this drug.

Depending on strength, this drug may cause a patchy, darkening of the skin on the face (melasma). Higher strengths are more likely to cause melasma. Sunlight may intensify this darkening and you may need to avoid prolonged sun exposure and sunlamps.

Consult your doctor regarding use of sunscreens and protective clothing.

Cigarette smoking can increase the chance of blood-clots while taking this medication (especially in women past the age of 35). Women who take estrogen should not smoke.

Long term use of estrogens is associated with an increase risk of cancer of the breast and endometrium. Women should have a regular physical exam and mammogram each year.

Drug Interactions
Tell your doctor of all prescription and nonprescription drugs you may use, especially if you have: hydantoins (e.g., phenytoin), barbiturates (e.g., phenobarbital), corticosteroids (e.g., prednisone).

This product can affect the results of certain lab tests. Make sure laboratory personnel and your doctors know you use this drug.

Do not start or stop any medicine without first consulting your doctor or pharmacist.

Missed Dose
If you miss a dose, take it as soon as you remember. If it is near the time of the next dose, skip the missed dose and resume your usual dosing schedule. Do not double the dose to catch up.

Storage
Store at room temperature between 59 and 86 degrees F (between 15 and 30 degrees C) away from moisture and sunlight. Do not store in the bathroom.

FELODIPINE

Common Brand Name: Plendil

Uses
This drug is a calcium channel blocker. Calcium is involved in blood vessel contraction. By blocking calcium, felodipine relaxes and widens the blood vessels. It is used to treat high blood pressure.

How to Use
Tablets should be swallowed whole. Do not crush or chew tablets.

This medication must be taken as directed to reduce blood pressure. It should be taken even if you do not feel sick. Most people with high blood pressure do not have any symptoms.

Try to take this medication at the same time each day.

Do not stop taking this medication suddenly without your doctor's permission. Some conditions can become worse if the medication is stopped too fast.

This drug is best taken without food (one hour before or two hours after a meal). If stomach upset occurs, it may be taken with a light meal.

Side Effects
This drug may cause dizziness, lightheadedness, and lower extremity swelling, especially during the first few days. Avoid activities requiring alertness. When you sit or lie down for a while, get up slowly to minimize dizziness and allow your body to adjust.

You may also experience headache, flushing, nausea, tingling hands and feet, cough, sleep disturbances and swollen gums. These effects should disappear as your body adjusts to the medication.

Inform your doctor if they become bothersome.

Notify your doctor if you develop: breathing difficulties, swelling of the face/hands/feet, an irregular heartbeat.

If you notice other effects not listed above, contact your doctor or pharmacist.

Precautions

Tell your doctor if you have disease, allergies (especially drug allergies).

Limit alcohol while taking this medication as it can enhance dizziness.

This medication may cause enlargement of the gums. This can be minimized by maintaining good oral hygiene with regular brushing, flossing and massaging of the gums.

Drug Interactions

Tell your doctor of any over-the-counter or prescription medication you may take, including: sedatives, tranquilizers, erythromycin antibiotics, cimetidine, ranitidine, phenytoin, beta-blockers, carbamazepine, digoxin, theophylline.

Avoid any drugs that increase your heart-rate (the decongestants phenylephrine and pseudoephedrine are examples). These drugs are commonly found in over-the-counter cough-and-cold products.

Do not eat grapefruit or drink grapefruit juice unless your doctor instructs you otherwise.

Do not start or stop any medicine without first consulting your doctor or pharmacist.

Notes

Do not share this product with others.

Missed Dose

If you miss a dose, take it as soon as you remember. If it is near the time of the next dose, skip the missed dose and resume your usual dosing schedule. Do not double the dose to catch up.

Storage

Store at room temperature between 59 and 86 degrees F (between 15 and 30 degrees C) away from moisture and sunlight. Do not store in the bathroom.

FENOFIBRATE

Common Brand Name: Tricor

Uses
This medication is used along with a non-drug program (including diet changes) to treat cholesterol, high trialycerides and lipid disorders.

How to Use
This drug is taken by mouth with food as directed.

Dosage is adjusted based on your condition and response. The maximum daily dose is 200 mg.

Separate doses of this drug and any bile acid resin drug (e.g., colestipol or cholestyramine) by at least 4 hours.

Full effects of this drug may take up to 3 months to occur.

Side Effects
Upset stomach, constipation, headache, dizziness or trouble sleeping may occur. If these effects persist or worsen, notify your doctor promptly.

Report promptly: muscle pain, tenderness, weakness, fever.

Very unlikely but report promptly: decreased sexual drive, yellowing eyes or skin, stomach pain.

In the unlikely event you have an allergic reaction to this drug, seek immediate medical attention. Symptoms of an allergic reaction include: rash, itching, swelling, dizziness, trouble breathing.

If you notice other effects not listed above, contact your doctor or pharmacist.

Precautions
Tell your doctor your medical history, including any allergies, diabetes, liver and/or kidney disease, gallbladder disease, low thyroid (hypothyroidism), muscle disorders.

Drug Interactions
Tell your doctor of all nonprescription and prescription medication you may use, especially: "blood thinners" (e.g., warfarin), "statin" drugs (e.g., lovastatin, simvast-

atin), cyclosporine, MAO Inhibitors (e.g., selegiline, furazolidone, tranylcypromine, phenelzine, moclobemide), certain diabetic medicine (sulfonylureas such as glipizide; and insulin), estrogens.

Do not start or stop any medicine without first consulting your doctor or pharmacist.

Notes

Do not share this medication with others.

Diet changes, weight loss (if overweight), exercise and drug therapy all are critical to reduce and control your cholesterol and lipids (fats in the blood). Consult your doctor about how to lower your heart disease risk factors.

Laboratory tests will be performed to monitor this drug for efficiency.

Missed Dose

If you miss a dose, take it as soon as you remember. If it is near the time of the next dose, skip the missed dose and resume your usual dosing schedule. Do not double the dose to catch up.

Storage

Store at room temperature away from light and moisture.

FEXOFENADINE

Common Brand Name: Allegra

Uses
This medication is an antihistamine used to relieve allergy symptoms such as watery, itchy, red eyes; sneezing, runny nose, itchy throat. Fexofenadine is also used for certain cases of itching skin (chronic idiopathic urticaria).

How to Use
Take this medication by mouth as directed, usually twice a day.

This may be taken with food or milk if stomach upset occurs.

Do not take antacids containing aluminum and magnesium (e.g., Mylanta or Maalox) within 2 hours of taking this medication.

Side Effects
Nausea, stomach upset, fatigue, headache, or earache may occur. If these effects continue or become severe, inform your doctor.

Tell your doctor immediately if any of these highly unlikely but very serious side effects occur: dizziness, fainting, irregular heartbeat.

Although drowsiness is uncommon at usual doses under normal circumstances, be aware that this medication may have such an effect before engaging in activities requiring alertness.

If you notice other effects not listed above, contact your doctor or pharmacist.

Precautions
Before taking this, tell your doctor if you have kidney disease, heart disease, any allergies.

Do not take this medication for several days before any allergy testing since test results can be affected.

Limit alcohol intake, as it may aggravate drug side effects.

Drug Interactions
Tell your doctor of any nonprescription or prescription medication you may use,

especially of drugs that may affect the heart rhythm (QTc prolongation) such as: cisapride, dofetilide, certain quinolone antibiotics (e.g., moxifloxacin), sotalol, amiodarone, phenothiazines (e.g., thioridazine), procainamide, quinidine, "water pills" (diuretics such as furosemide or hydrochlorothiazide).

Do not start or stop any medicine without first consulting your doctor or pharmacist.

Notes
Do not share this medication with others.

Missed Dose
If you miss a dose, take it as soon as you remember. If it is near the time of the next dose, skip the missed dose and resume your usual dosing schedule. Do not double the dose to catch up.

Storage
Store at room temperature between 68 and 77 degrees F (20 to 25 degrees C) away from light and moisture. Do not store in the bathroom.

FEXOFENADINE-PSEUDOEPHEDRINE

Common Brand Name: Allegra-D

Uses
This medication contains an antihistamine (fexofenadine) and decongestant (pseudoephedrine) used to relieve allergy symptoms such as itchy red eyes, stuffy nose and throat irritation.

How to Use
Take this medication by mouth on an empty stomach 1 hour before or two hours after meals as directed, usually twice daily. Taking this medicine with a high fat meal can decrease its effectiveness. Do not take antacids containing aluminum and magnesium within 2 hours of taking this medication. Swallow the medicine whole. Do not crush or chew the tablet, and do not take more than prescribed.

Important Note
Do not take this product within 14 days after stopping a monoamine oxidase inhibitor (see Drug Interactions).

Side Effects
Nausea, stomach upset, trouble sleeping, headache, or cold symptoms may occur. If these persist or worsen, notify your doctor promptly.

Unlikely but report promptly: dizziness, mental/mood changes, fast heartbeat, fever.

Tell your doctor immediately if any of these highly unlikely but very serious side effects occur: fainting, irregular heartbeat.

Although drowsiness is very uncommon at usual doses under normal circumstances, be aware that drowsiness may occur and may effect the ability to perfom tasks requiring alertness (e.g., driving).

If you notice other effects not listed above, contact your doctor or pharmacist.

Precautions
Tell your doctor your medical history, including allergies, kidney/urinary problems,

enlarged prostate, glaucoma (narrow angle), severe high blood pressure, heart disease, diabetes, thyroid problems (hyperthyroid).

Limit alcohol intake, as it may aggravate drug side effects, especially drowsiness. Older adults may be more sensitive to side effects.

Drug Interactions
Tell your doctor of all nonprescription and prescription medication you may use, especially: monoamine oxidase inhibitors (e.g., selegiline, furazolidone, phenelzine, tranylcypromine, moclobemide, procarbazine, linezolid), certain blood pressure drugs (e.g., methyldopa, mecamylamine, reserpine, prazosin), digoxin, all adrenaline-like drugs.

Report other drugs which affect the heart rhythm (QTc prolongation), such as: dofetilide, pimozide, quinidine, sotalol, procainamide, sparfloxacin, "water pills" (diuretics such as furosemide or hydrochlorothiazide).

Ask your doctor or pharmacist for more details.

Check the labels carefully on all nonprescription products, such as cough-and-cold medicines which contain antihistamines and decongestants. Consult your pharmacist before taking nonprescription cough and cold drugs with this medicine.

Do not take this medication for several days before any allergy testing since test results can be affected.

Do not start or stop any medicine without first consulting your doctor or pharmacist.

Notes
Do not share this medication with others.

Missed Dose
If you miss a dose, take it as soon as you remember. If it is near the time of the next dose, skip the missed dose and resume your usual dosing schedule. Do not double the dose to catch up.

Storage
Store at room temperature between 68 and 77 degrees F (20-25 degrees C) away from sunlight and moisture.

FLUCONAZOLE

Common Brand Name: Diflucan

Uses
This medication is an antifungal agent used to treat infections in certain areas of the body caused by yeast and yeast-like organisms.

How to Use
This medication works best when the amount of medicine in your body is kept at a constant level. Do this by taking the medication at evenly spaced intervals.

Take as directed since different conditions require different methods of use.

This drug is usually taken once daily. Another dosing method involves taking the drug for one week per month until treatment is completed.

Continue to take this medication until the full prescribed amount is finished even if symptoms disappear after a few days.

Stopping the medication too early may allow the yeast to continue to grow resulting in a decrease in effectiveness in treating the infection.

Side Effects
This medication may cause stomach upset, loss of appetite, altered taste, diarrhea, nausea, headache or dizziness during the first few days as your body adjusts to the medication.

If these symptoms persist or become severe, inform your doctor.

In the unlikely event you have an allergic reaction to this drug, seek immediate medical attention. Symptoms of an allergic reaction include: rash, itching, swelling, dizziness, trouble breathing.

If you notice other effects not listed above, contact your doctor or pharmacist.

Precautions
Tell your doctor your medical history, especially if you have: liver disease, kidney disease, any drug allergies.

Drug Interactions

Tell your doctor or pharmacist of all prescription and nonprescription drugs you may use, especially if you have: astemizole, cisapride, cimetidine, oral contraceptives, cyclosporine, oral antidiabetic drugs, phenytoin, rifampin, rifabutin, certain benzo-diazepines (e.g., alprazolam, triazolam), tacrolimus, terfenadine, theophylline, warfarin, zidovudine.

Do not start or stop any medicine without first consulting your doctor or pharmacist.

Notes

This medication has been prescribed for your current condition only. Do not use it later for another infection or give it to someone else. A different medicine may be needed.

Missed Dose

If you miss a dose, take it as soon as you remember. If it is near the time of the next dose, skip the missed dose and resume your usual dosing schedule. Do not double the dose to catch up.

Storage

Store at room temperature away from moisture and sunlight. Do not store in the bathroom.

FLUOXETINE

Common Brand Names: Prozac, Sarafem

Uses
Fluoxetine is used to treat depression, bulimia (an eating disorder), obsessive compulsive disorders (OCD).

This medication works by helping to restore the balance of certain natural chemicals in the brain.

How to Use
Take this medication by mouth usually once daily in the morning, with or without food; or as directed by your doctor.

The dosage is based on your medical condition and response to therapy. Some medical conditions may require a different dosing schedule (e.g., twice daily in the morning and at noon) as determined by your doctor. Take this medication exactly as prescribed.

It is important to continue taking this medication even if you feel well. Also, do not stop taking this medication without consulting your doctor.

It may take 4-6 weeks before the full benefit of this drug takes effect.

Side Effects
Nausea, headache, trouble sleeping, dry mouth, drowsiness, sweating, or upset stomach may occur. If any of these effects persist or worsen, notify your doctor promptly.

Tell your doctor immediately if any of these serious side effects occur: loss of appetite, unusual weight loss, unusual or severe mental/mood changes, uncontrolled movements (tremor), decreased interest in sex, flu-like symptoms (e.g., chills, fever, muscle aches, weakness).

Tell your doctor immediately if any of these unlikely but serious side effects occur: vision changes, trouble swallowing, swelling or white spots on the mouth and/or tongue, changes in sexual ability, painful and/or prolonged erection.

Tell your doctor immediately if any of these highly unlikely but very serious side effects occur: fainting, irregular/fast heartbeat.

An allergic reaction to this drug is unlikely, but seek immediate medical attention if it occurs. Symptoms of an allergic reaction include: rash, itching, swelling, dizziness, trouble breathing.

If you notice other effects not listed above, contact your doctor or pharmacist.

Precautions

Tell your doctor your medical history, especially if you have: liver problems, kidney disease, seizures, heart problems, diabetes, any allergies.

This drug may make you dizzy or drowsy; use caution engaging in activities requiring alertness such as driving or using machinery. Limit alcoholic beverages.

Liquid preparations of this product may contain sugar and/or small amounts of alcohol. Caution is advised if you have diabetes, alcohol dependence, or liver disease. Ask your doctor or pharmacist about the safe use of this product.

Caution is advised when using this product with older people because they may be more sensitive to the effects of the drug.

Drug Interactions

Certain medications taken with this product could result in serious, even fatal, drug interactions. Avoid taking MAO inhibitors (e.g., furazolidone, isocarboxazid, linezolid, moclobemide, phenelzine, procarbazine, selegiline, tranylcypromine) within 2 weeks, and avoid taking thioridazine within 5 weeks, before or after treatment with this medication.

Consult your doctor or pharmacist for additional information.

This drug is not recommended for use with: weight loss medicine (e.g., sibutramine, phentermine), thioridazine.

Ask your doctor or pharmacist for more details.

Tell your doctor of all prescription and nonprescription medication you may use, especially: other SSRI antidepressants (e.g., citalopram, sertraline), nefazodone, trazodone, venlafaxine, "triptan" migraine drugs (e.g., sumatriptan, zolmitriptan), tramadol, tricyclic antidepressants (e.g., amitriptyline, nortriptyline), flecainide, propafenone, haloperidol, clozapine, lithium, tryptophan, "blood thinners" (e.g., warfarin), anti-seizure drugs (e.g., carbamazepine, phenytoin/hydantoins), herbal/natural products (e.g., St John's wort, ayahuasca).

Tell your doctor if you take any drugs that cause drowsiness such as: medicine for sleep, tranquilizers, anti-anxiety drugs (e.g., alprazolam), narcotic pain relievers (e.g., codeine), muscle relaxants, psychiatric medicine (e.g., phenothiazines such as chlorpromazine), certain antihistamines (e.g., diphenhydramine).

Check the labels on all your medicines (e.g., cough-and-cold products) because they may contain drowsiness-causing ingredients. Ask your pharmacist about the safe use of these products.

Report other drugs which affect the heart rhythm such as: dofetilide, pimozide, sotalol, quinidine, procainamide, sparfloxacin, "water pills" (diuretics such as furosemide or hydrochlorothiazide).

Ask your doctor or pharmacist for more details.

Fluoxetine may affect the amount of glucose (sugar) in your blood. If you take any anti-diabetes medication (e.g., glipizide, glyburide, metformin), your dosage of these drugs may need to be adjusted when fluoxetine is started or discontinued. Consult your doctor.

Do not start or stop any medicine without first consulting your doctor or pharmacist.

Notes
Do not share this medication with others.

Laboratory and/or medical tests may be performed to monitor your progress and any adverse effects.

Missed Dose
If you miss a dose, take it as soon as you remember. If it is near the time of the next dose, skip the missed dose and resume your usual dosing schedule. Do not double the dose to catch up.

Storage
Store at room temperature between 59 and 86 degrees F (15 and 30 degrees C) away from light and moisture.

FLUTICASONE

Common Brand Names: Flonase, Flovent

Uses
This is a nasal corticosteroid that works directly on nasal tissue to reduce swelling and inflammation. The medication is used to treat itching, runny nose, postnasal drip, nasal congestion and sneezing in people with a history of runny nose and allergy.

How to Use
To get the most benefit from this medication, make sure you understand how to use the nasal spray properly. Ask your doctor or pharmacist to show you how to use the pump and nasal adapter.

Shake gently before each use. Before using the medication for the first time, the unit must be "primed" with 3 to 4 pumps of the spray.

Use this medication exactly as prescribed. Do not use more than two sprays in each nostril daily. It may take a few days before the benefits of the medication are noticed. If no improvement occurs after several days, notify your doctor.

Side Effects
The more common side effects are nose bleeding, blood in nasal mucus, or nasal burning or irritation. Less common or rare occurrences are headache, sneezing, runny nose, nasal dryness, congestion, or stomach upset. If these effects continue or become bothersome, inform your doctor.

Long-term use of nasal steroids may cause fungal infections of the nose or throat. Inform your doctor if you develop an infection. The medication may be discontinued while the infection is treated.

Very unlikely to occur but report: vision problems, headache, increased thirst or urination, unusual weakness, weight loss, nausea, dizziness.

In the very unlikely event you have an allergic reaction to this drug, seek immediate medical attention. Symptoms of an allergic reaction include: rash, itching, swelling, dizziness, trouble breathing.

If you notice other effects not listed above, contact your doctor or pharmacist.

Precautions

Tell your doctor your medical history, especially if you have: any allergies, eye problems (glaucoma, cateracts), infections, recent nasal surgery, nasal sores.

If you are prescribed doses higher than those usually recommended, avoid exposure to chickenpox or measles. If you do become exposed, notify your doctor promptly.

Though very unlikely, it is possible this medication will be absorbed into your bloodstream. This may cause undesirable side effects that may require additional treatment. This is especially true for those who have used this for an extended period if they also have serious medical problems such as serious infections, injuries or surgeries. This precaution applies for up to one year after stopping use of this drug. Consult your doctor or pharmacist for more details.

Drug Interactions

Tell your doctor of all other prescription or nonprescription medicines you use, especially if you have: other nasal products (such as cold products), other corticosteroids (e.g., prednisone), antibiotics.

Do not start or stop any medicine without first consulting your doctor or pharmacist.

Notes

Do not share this medication with others.

Watering or itching eyes often associated with allergies are not significantly relieved by this medication.

Inform all your doctors you use (or have used) this medication.

Missed Dose

If you miss a dose, take it as soon as you remember. If it is near the time of the next dose, skip the missed dose and resume your usual dosing schedule. Do not double the dose to catch up.

Storage

Store at room temperature and keep away from moisture and sunlight.

FOLIC ACID

Common Brand Name: Folic Acid

Uses
Folic acid is used to treat or prevent certain anemias caused by poor diet, pregnancy or other conditions.

How to Use
Take this medication as directed.

Follow dietary recommendations made by your doctor or nutritionist.

Side Effects
Folic acid usually has very few side effects

If you experience any unusual effects from taking this medicine, notify your doctor.

In the unlikely event you have an allergic reaction to this drug, seek immediate medical attention. Symptoms of an allergic reaction include: rash, itching, swelling, dizziness, trouble breathing.

If you notice other effects not listed above, contact your doctor or pharmacist.

Precautions
Tell your doctor your medical history, especially anemia (e.g., pernicious anemia), any drug or food allergies.

Drug Interactions
Tell your doctor of all prescription and nonprescription medications you may use, especially: phenytoin, primidone vitamin preparations.

Do not start or stop any medicine without first consulting your doctor or pharmacist.

Notes
Folic acid is found naturally in leafy green or yellow vegetables. Eat more of these foods to increase the amount of folic acid in your diet.

Do not allow anyone else to take this medication.

Missed Dose
If you miss a dose, take it as soon as you remember. If it is near the time of the next dose, skip the missed dose and resume your usual dosing schedule. Do not double the dose to catch up.

Storage
Store at room temperature between 59 and 86 degrees F (between 15 and 30 degrees C) away from moisture and sunlight. Do not store in the bathroom.

FOSINOPRIL

Common Brand Name: Monopril

Uses

ACE inhibitors prevent certain substances in the body from constricting blood vessels. This helps to lower blood pressure and makes the heart beat stronger. Thiazides are diuretics (water pills) that help to reduce blood pressure. This medication is used to treat hypertension (high blood pressure).

How to Use

This medication may be taken without regard to meals.

Take this medication exactly as prescribed. Try to take it at the same time each day.

Do not stop taking this medication without consulting your doctor. Some conditions may become worse when the drug is abruptly stopped. Your dose may need to be gradually decreased.

It is important to continue taking this medication even if you feel well. Most people with high blood pressure do not feel sick.

Side Effects

Dizziness, headache, diarrhea, constipation, loss of appetite, nausea, loss of taste, flushing, fatigue, cough or increased urination may occur. If these effects persist or worsen, notify your doctor.

This medication can increase sensitivity to sunlight.

To avoid dizziness and lightheadedness when rising from a seated or lying position, get up slowly.

Inform your doctor if you develop: chest pain, tingling of the hands or feet, persistent sore throat.

In the unlikely event you have an allergic reaction to this drug, seek immediate medical attention. Symptoms of an allergic reaction include: rash, itching, swelling, dizziness, trouble breathing.

If you notice other effects not listed above, contact your doctor or pharmacist.

Precautions

Tell your doctor your medical history, especially if you have: scheduled medical or dental procedures, heart problems, allergies (especially sulfa drugs).

This medicine may make you more prone to sunburn. Wear protective clothing and a sunscreen.

Limit your intake of alcohol and avoid overheating because this can aggravate dizziness and lightheadedness.

Avoid "stimulant" drugs that may increase your heart rate such as decongestants or caffeine. Decongestants are commonly found in over-the-counter cough-and-cold medicine.

Drug Interactions

This drug is not recommended for use with dofetilide. Ask your doctor or pharmacist for more details.

Inform your doctor about all the medicine you use (both prescription and non-prescription), especially if you have: lithium, potassium supplements, potassium-sparing water pills, anti- inflammatory medicine (NSAIDs such as ibuprofen), digoxin.

If you take antacids, colestipol or cholestyramine, take this medicine 1 hour before or 4 hours after the cholesterol lowering medicine because of decreased absorption.

Do not start or stop any medicine without first consulting your doctor or pharmacist.

Notes

It is important to have your blood pressure checked regularly while taking this medication. Learn how to monitor your blood pressure. Discuss this with your doctor.

Missed Dose

If you miss a dose, take it as soon as you remember. If it is near the time of the next dose, skip the missed dose and resume your usual dosing schedule. Do not double the dose to catch up.

Storage

Store at room temperature away from sunlight and moisture.

FUROSEMIDE

Common Brand Name: Lasix

Uses
Furosemide is a diuretic. Diuretics are referred to as "water pills" because they decrease the amount of water retained in the body by increasing urination. Diuretics are used to treat edema (fluid retention and swelling, especially of the hands and feet caused by heart failure and other diseases) and hypertension (high blood pressure).

How to Use
May take with food or milk if stomach upset occurs.

If this medication is taken in the late afternoon or evening, you may need to get up during the night to urinate. If you are able to take this medicine once a day it may be best to take it in the morning.

Side Effects
This drug may cause dizziness and lightheadedness especially during the first few days as your body adjusts to it.

Rise slowly from a seated or lying position. It may also increase sensitivity to sunlight.

Blurred vision, loss of appetite, itching, stomach upset, headache and weakness may also occur during initial therapy as your body adjusts to the medication.

Inform your doctor if you develop muscle cramps, pain, nausea or vomiting while taking this medication. It may be a sign of low blood potassium. This medication can cause a loss of potassium from the body.

Contact your doctor if you experience: dry mouth, thirst, unusual bleeding or bruising, rash, yellow eyes or skin, severe nausea or vomiting, ringing in ears.

This medication increases urination. Expect this effect.

In the unlikely event you have an allergic reaction to this drug, seek medical attention immediately. Symptoms of an allergic reaction include: rash, itching, swelling, dizziness, trouble breathing.

If you notice other effects not listed above, contact your doctor or pharmacist.

Precautions

Before using this drug, tell your doctor your medical history especially if you have: kidney problems, unusual decrease in urine output, liver disease, diabetes, drug allergies.

This drug may reduce the potassium levels in your blood. Ask your doctor about adding potassium to your diet. A potassium supplement may be prescribed by your doctor.

Furosemide may make you more sensitive to sunlight. Use a sunscreen that has a skin protection factor (SPF) of at least 15 and wear protective clothing, including a hat. Contact your doctor if you develop a sever reaction from the sun while taking this medication.

Alcohol may intensify side effects. Limit your alcohol intake.

Use caution when exercising heavily, especially during hot weather. Contact your doctor if you become sick with severe vomiting or diarrhea.

Drug Interactions

Tell your doctor of all prescription and nonprescription drugs you may use, especially if you have: warfarin, lithium, aminoglycosides (e.g., neomycin, kanamycin, gentamicin), large doses of salicylates (aspirin and aspirin-like drugs), sucralfate, ginseng, ethacrynic acid or other diuretics ("water pills"), digoxin, diabetic medications, NSAIDS (e.g., ibuprofen, naproxen), cisplatin, blood pressure medication, probenecid, cyclosporine.

Do not start or stop any medicine without first consulting your doctor or pharmacist.

Notes

Do not share this medication with others.

Missed Dose

If you miss a dose, take it as soon as you remember. If it is near the time of the next dose, skip the missed dose and resume your usual dosing schedule. Do not double the dose to catch up.

Storage

Store at room temperature away from moisture and sunlight. Do not store in the bathroom.

GABAPENTIN

Common Brand Name: Neurontin

Uses
This medication is taken with other medications to help control seizure disorders and is also used to treat certain chronic pain problems.

How to Use
Take this medication by mouth exactly as prescribed.

During the first few days your doctor may gradually increase your dose to allow your body to adjust to the medication. To minimize side effects, take the very first dose at bedtime. For best effects, take this medication at evenly spaced times throughout the day and night. This will ensure a constant level of drug in your body. Do not take this more often or increase your dose without consulting your doctor. Do not stop taking this medicine suddenly. Your doctor may want you to gradually lower the amount taken before stopping it completely.

Side Effects
This drug is usually well tolerated. Drowsiness, dizziness, unsteadiness, fatigue or nausea may occur. If these effects persist or worsen, notify your doctor.

Unlikely to occur but report promptly: mental or mood changes, tingling or numbness of the hands or feet, swelling of ankles, vision problems, fever, unusual bleeding.

Very unlikely to occur but report promptly: fainting, difficulty moving, stiffness, uncontrolled movements, stomach or abdominal pain, leg pain, chest pain, trouble breathing.

If you notice other effects not listed above, contact your doctor or pharmacist.

Precautions
Tell your doctor your medical history, especially if you have: kidney disease, drug allergies.

Use caution operating machinery or engaging in activities that require alertness. Limit alcohol intake as it may increase the dizziness/drowsiness effect of this drug.

Drug Interactions

Tell your doctor of any over-the-counter or prescription medication you use, especially if you have: other medication for seizures, antacids.

Because antacids may interfere with the absorption of this medication, it is best to take gabapentin at least 2 hours after taking an antacid. Do not take them at the same time.

Do not start or stop any medicine without first contacting your doctor or pharmacist.

Notes

Laboratory tests may be done periodically while taking this medication to monitor the effects. See your doctor regularly.

Missed Dose

If you miss a dose, take it as soon as you remember. If it is near the time of the next dose, skip the missed dose and resume your usual dosing schedule. Do not double the dose to catch up.

Storage

Store this medication at room temperature between 59 and 86 degrees F (between 15 and 30 degrees C) away from heat and light Do not store in the bathroom. Keep this and all medications out of the reach of children.

The oral solution form of this drug must be refrigerated between 36-46 degrees F (2-8 degrees C).

GALANTAMINE

Common Brand Name: Reminyl

Uses
This medication is used to treat the memory and behavioral symptoms of Alzheimer's disease.

How to Use
Take this medication by mouth, usually twice daily with food (at the morning and evening meals), or as directed.

Drink plenty of fluids with this medication unless instructed otherwise. Your dose will be adjusted over time (titrated) until the right amount of medicine is determined.

Use this medication exactly as prescribed to minimize the occurrence of side effects. Do not stop taking it or increase the dose unless instructed to do so by your doctor.

If you are using the liquid form of this drug, read the manufacturer's instruction sheet that comes with the bottle.

Follow the directions exactly.

If you have not taken the drug for several days, contact your doctor to re-establish your dosing schedule. To minimize gastrointestinal side effects, you will be restarted at the lowest dose. The dosage will then gradually be increased.

It may take at least four weeks of continued use before full benefit of this drug takes effect.

The recommended maximum total daily dose is 24 mg.

Side Effects
Nausea, vomiting, diarrhea, dizziness, decreased appetite or weight loss may occur. If any of these effects persist or worsen, notify your doctor or pharmacist promptly.

Tell your doctor immediately if any of these unlikely but serious side effects occur: fainting, new-onset or worsening heartburn, unusually slow heartbeat, chest pain, stomach pain, loss of bladder control or difficulty urinating.

If you notice other effects not listed above, contact your doctor or pharmacist.

132

Precautions

Tell your doctor your medical history, especially if you have: heart problems (e.g., bradycardia, AV block, arrhythmia), stomach/intestinal problems (peptic ulcer disease, GERD), difficulty urinating, convulsions, lung disease (severe asthma, obstructive pulmonary disease), liver or kidney disease, recent tobacco use, recent/frequent alcohol use, any allergies (including allergy to daffodil plants) and other medications for the treatment of alzheimer's disease.

This drug may make you dizzy; use caution when performing activities that require alertness such as driving or using machinery. Limit alcoholic beverages because it may cause dizziness and make your stomach more likely to bleed.

Caution is advised when using this drug with older people, as they may be more sensitive to drug side effects.

Drug Interactions

Tell your doctor of all prescription and nonprescription medication you may use, especially: anticholinergic drugs (e.g., benztropine, scopolamine oxybutynin tolterodine), cholinergic drugs (e.g., bethanechol), other cholinesterase inhibitors (e.g., donepezil), succinylcholine-type muscle blocking drugs.

Also report use of heart drugs (those which decrease heart rate or block AV impulse conduction) such as: digoxin, beta-blockers (e.g., metoprolol, propranolol), calcium channel blockers (e.g., diltiazem, verapamil).

Do not start or stop any medicine without first consulting your doctor or pharmacist.

Notes

Do not share this medication with others.

Missed Dose

If you miss a dose, take it as soon as you remember. If it is near the time of the next dose, skip the missed dose and restart your usual dosing schedule. Do not double your dose to catch up.

Storage

Store at room temperature between 59 and 86 degrees F (15 to 30 degrees C) and away from light and moisture. Do not store in bathroom.

GATIFLOXACIN

Common Brand Name: Tequin

Uses
This medication is a quinolone antibiotic used to treat certain types of infections (e.g., respiratory tract infections, sinus infections, and urinary tract infections).

How to Use
Take this medication by mouth, generally once daily, as directed by your doctor. Drink plenty of fluids while using this drug, unless instructed otherwise. The length of treatment depends on your condition and response to therapy.

Take this medication exactly as prescribed. Do not exceed the recommended dose of this medication.

Antibiotics work best when the amount of medicine in your body is kept at a constant level. This is done by taking the medication at evenly spaced intervals (e.g., every 24 hours).

Continue to take this medication until the full-prescribed amount is finished, even if symptoms disappear after a few days.

Stopping the medicine too early may allow bacteria to continue to grow, resulting in a relapse of the infection.

Avoid taking didanosine, sucralfate, aluminum/magnesium- containing antacids, iron or zinc preparations, or vitamin/mineral products within 4 hours of taking this medicine.

These products may bind with this medicine and interfere with its absorption. Consult your pharmacist for more information.

Side Effects
Nausea, stomach pain, diarrhea, mild dizziness or headache may occur. If any of these effects persist or worsen, notify your doctor promptly.

Tell your doctor immediately if you have any of these unlikely but serious side effects: white patches in the mouth, unusual vaginal itching or discharge.

Tell your doctor immediately if you have any of these very unlikely but serious side effects: chest pain, seizures, mental/mood changes, muscle/tendon pain or swelling.

Tell your doctor immediately if any of these highly unlikely but very serious side effects occur: fainting, fast/slow/irregular heartbeat.

Allergic reactions to this drug are unlikely, but seek immediate medical attention if they occur. Symptoms of an allergic reaction include: rash, itching, swelling, dizziness, trouble breathing.

If you notice other effects not listed above, contact your doctor or pharmacist.

Precautions

Tell your doctor your medical history, including allergies (especially to quinolone antibiotics such as ciprofloxacin), kidney disease, diabetes, seizures, tendon problems (e.g., tendonitis, bursitis), heart problems (e.g., QTc interval prolongation, bradycardia, arrhythmia, myocardial infarction), brain disorders (e.g., cerebral atherosclerosis, tumors or increased intracranial pressure), low blood potassium (hypokalemia).

This drug may make you dizzy. Use caution engaging in activities requiring alertness such as driving or using machinery. Limit alcohol intake because it can intensify the dizziness effect of this medication.

Use of this medication for prolonged or repeated periods may result in a secondary infection (e.g., oral or bladder infection).

Patients with diabetes may experience changes in blood sugar due to infection or use of this medication. Monitor your blood glucose levels frequently while using this medication and notify your doctor promptly if you experience symptoms of high or low blood sugar. Symptoms of high blood sugar include increased thirst and urination. Symptoms of low blood sugar include dizziness, sweating, hunger and fast pulse.

Though gatifloxacin has not been shown to make skin sensitive to the sun, other drugs very similar to this one have. Therefore, avoid excessive sunlight and sun lamps. Consult your doctor or pharmacist for more information.

Drug Interactions

Tell your doctor of all prescription and nonprescription medication you may use, especially if you have: drugs for diabetes (e.g., glyburide, insulin), NSAIDs (e.g., ibuprofen, naproxen), drugs that decrease potassium levels such as certain "water pills" (e.g., furosemide, hydrochlorothiazide), didanosine, sucralfate, digoxin, probenecid, warfarin, magnesium/aluminum- containing antacids, iron preparations, zinc supplements, vitamin/mineral supplements, erythromycin.

Report other drugs which affect the heart rhythm (QTc prolongation), such as: amiodarone, dofetilide, pimozide, sotalol, quinidine, procainamide.

Ask your doctor or pharmacist for more details.

Do not start or stop any medicine without first consulting your doctor or pharmacist.

Notes

Do not share this medication with others. Do not use this medication for another infection, unless directed to do so by your doctor.

Laboratory and/or medical tests may be performed to monitor your progress.

Dose may need to be adjusted dependent upon kidney function.

Missed Dose

If you miss a dose, take it as soon as you remember. If it is near the time of the next dose, skip the missed dose and resume your usual dosing schedule. Do not double the dose to catch up.

Storage

Store at room temperature between 59 and 86 degrees F (15 to 30 degrees C) away from light and moisture.

GEMFIBROZIL

Common Brand Name: Lopid

Uses
This medication is used to lower high cholesterol and/or triglyceride levels in the blood. High levels of cholesterol or triglycerides may block the blood vessels, increasing the risk of heart disease. For best results, this medication must be used along with an exercise program and a low-cholesterol, low-fat diet.

How to Use
Take this medication as prescribed. It is usually taken 30 minutes before your morning or evening meals.

It may take a few weeks to months before the full effects of this medication are noticed.

Side Effects
Stomach upset, heartburn, gas, diarrhea, nausea, abdominal pain, vomiting, skin rash, or unusual tiredness may occur during the first few days as your body adjusts to the medication. If these effects persist or become bothersome, inform your doctor.

Notify your doctor if you experience: muscle pain, weakness, fever, chills, severe stomach pain with nausea and vomiting.

If you notice other effects not listed above, contact your doctor or pharmacist.

Precautions
Tell your doctor if you have bladder problems, kidney problems, liver problems, allergies (especially drug allergies).

If this medication makes you dizzy or lightheaded, avoid driving or engaging in activities requiring alertness.

If you take insulin or oral diabetes medication, your dose may need to be changed because gemfibrozil may, in some instances, increase the amount of sugar in your blood. Ask your doctor if you need to change your dose.

Drug Interactions

Before you take gemfibrozil, tell your doctor of any over-the-counter or prescription drugs you are taking, especially if you have: anticoagulants ("blood thinners"), lovastatin, or other cholesterol lowering drugs.

Do not start or stop any medicine without first consulting your doctor or pharmacist.

Notes

Your doctor may periodically perform lab tests during treatment to evaluate the effectiveness of the medication and to prevent the side effects of increased liver function tests. Know what your cholesterol level is and understand what it means. Your doctor, pharmacist or nutritionist can provide you with valuable information.

Do not allow anyone else to take this medication.

Missed Dose

If you miss a dose, take it as soon as you remember. If it is near the time of the next dose, skip the missed dose and resume your usual dosing schedule. Do not double the dose to catch up.

Storage

Store at controlled room temperature 68-77 degrees F (20-25 degrees C), away from light and moisture.

GLIMEPIRIDE

Common Brand Name: Amaryl

Uses
Glimepiride is used along with diet to treat diabetes. It can be used with insulin, metformin, or thiazolidinediones ("glitazones") in certain cases.

How to Use
Take this by mouth exactly as prescribed, usually once a day with breakfast or the first main meal of the day.

Your dose may be adjusted initially every 1-2 weeks to determine the most effective dose for you. Follow dosing instructions closely and keep all doctors appointments.

It is important that you regularly test your urine or blood for sugar as discussed with your doctor.

Side Effects
Stomach pain, gas, bloating or diarrhea are most common but should subside as your body adjusts to the medication.

Also, skin rash/itching, dizziness and nausea may occur. Sun sensitivity/rash occurs rarely. If any of these effects continue or become severe, inform your doctor.

Notify your doctor if you develop: symptoms of high blood sugar (e.g., thirst increase, reduced hunger, frequent urination), symptoms of low blood sugar (e.g., increased heart rate, nervousness, sweating, hunger, numbness/tingling of the hands or feet).

Promptly report any of these serious side effects: persistent sore throat or fever, unusual bruises/bleeding, headache, shortness of breath, yellowing skin or eyes (jaundice).

If you notice other effects not listed above, contact your doctor or pharmacist.

Precautions
Before taking this drug, tell your doctor if you have been hospitalized for diabetes

or have any of the following medical problems: kidney disease, liver disease, heart disease, any allergies.

During times of stress such as fever, infection, injury or surgery, it may be more difficult to control your blood sugar.

Consult your doctor or pharmacist as additional medication may be required.

Drug Interactions

Tell your doctor of any nonprescription or prescription medication you may take particularly: "water pills" (diuretics), thyroid hormone, steroids, estrogen hormone, sulfa drugs, azole-type antifungals (e.g., itraconazole, ketoconazole), quinolone antibiotics (e.g., ciprofloxacin, levofloxacin), phenytoin, isoniazid, aspirin or aspirin-like drugs (e.g., NSAIDs), "blood thinners" (e.g., warfarin), asparaginase, MAO inhibitors (e.g., phenelzine, tranylcypromine), phenothiazines (e.g., chlorpromazine, thioridazine), H2-blockers (e.g., famotidine, ranitidine), pentamidine, octreotide, cyclosporine, beta-blockers (e.g., metoprolol, propranolol).

Do not start or stop any medicine without first consulting your doctor or pharmacist.

Notes

This medication is not a substitute for proper diet and exercise. It is recommended to attend a diabetes education program to understand diabetes and all aspects of its treatment including diet, exercise, personal hygiene, medications and getting regular eye-and-foot exams.

Lab tests will be done periodically while taking this to monitor its effects and prevent side effects. You may be asked to monitor your own blood sugar.

Controlling high blood sugar helps prevent heart disease, strokes, kidney disease and circulation problems.

Missed Dose

If you miss a dose, take it as soon as you remember. If it is near the time of the next dose, skip the missed dose and resume your usual dosing schedule. Do not double the dose to catch up.

Storage

Store this at room temperature between 59 and 86 degrees F (15 and 30 degrees C) away from heat and light. Do not store in the bathroom. Keep this and all medications out of the reach of children.

GLIPIZIDE

Common Brand Name: Glucotrol

Uses
This medication is used in the treatment of non-insulin dependent diabetes. It must be used in conjunction with proper diet and exercise to help decrease blood sugar levels.

How to Use
This medication should be taken 30 minutes before a meal.

Take this medication at the same time(s) each day in order to maintain a constant blood level. Monitor blood glucose levels daily while taking this medication.

Side Effects
Headache, stomach upset, loss of appetite, diarrhea, nausea or vomiting may occur as your body adjusts to the medication.

This medication can cause low blood sugar (hypoglycemia). The symptoms include chills, cold sweat, shaking, rapid heart rate, weakness, headache, fainting. If you experience these symptoms, eat a quick source of sugar such as table sugar, orange juice, a piece of candy,honey or non-diet soda. Tell your doctor about the reaction. To help prevent hypoglycemia, eat meals on a regular schedule and do not skip meals.

Symptoms of high blood sugar (hyperglycemia) include confusion, drowsiness, flushing, rapid breathing or fruity breath, increased urination, increased thirst, increased hunger, odor. If any of these symptoms occur, contact your doctor.

This medication can increase sensitivity to sunlight.

Inform your doctor if you develop: itchy skin, dark urine, fever, sore throat, swelling of the hands or feet, unusual bleeding or bruising.

If you notice other effects not listed above, contact your doctor or pharmacist.

Precautions
Tell your doctor your medical history, especially if you have: high blood pressure, liver problems, kidney problems, allergies (especially drug allergies).

Avoid alcohol while taking this medication. It can cause facial flushing, nausea, vomiting, dizziness or stomach pain.

This medication may make you more prone to sunburn. Wear protective clothing and a sunscreen.

Drug Interactions

Inform your doctor about all the medicines you use (both prescription and nonprescription) especially if you have: blood thinners (e.g., warfarin), MAO inhibitors (e.g., furazolidone, linezolid, phenelzine, selegiline, tranylcypromine), beta-blockers (e.g., metoprolol, propranolol, including certain glaucoma eye medicines), aspirin-like drugs, probenecid.

Do not start or stop any medicine without first consulting your doctor or pharmacist.

Notes

It is recommended to attend a diabetes education program to understand diabetes and all aspects of its treatment including diet, exercise, personal hygiene, medications and getting regular eye exams.

Controlling high blood sugar helps prevent heart disease, strokes, kidney disease and circulation problems.

Missed Dose

If you miss a dose, take it as soon as you remember. If it is near the time of the next dose, skip the missed dose and resume your usual dosing schedule. Do not double the dose to catch up.

Storage

Store at room temperature away from sunlight and moisture.

GLYBURIDE

Common Brand Names: Dia Beta, Micronase, Glynase PresTab

Uses
This medication is used in the treatment of diabetes.

How to Use
May be taken with food or milk if stomach upset occurs.

Take this medication at the same time(s) each day in order to maintain a constant blood level. Monitor blood glucose levels regularly while taking this medication.

This medication must be used along with a proper diet and an exercise program.

Side Effects
Headache, stomach upset, loss of appetite, nausea, diarrhea or vomiting may occur as your body adjusts to the medication.

Inform your doctor if you develop: itchy skin, dark urine, fever, sore throat, swelling of the hands or feet, unusual bleeding or bruising.

This medication can cause low blood sugar (hypoglycemia). The symptoms include chills, cold sweat, shaking, rapid heart rate, weakness, headache, fainting. If you experience these symptoms, eat a quick source of sugar such as table sugar, orange juice, honey, non-diet soda. Tell your doctor about the reaction. To help prevent hypoglycemia, eat meals on a regular schedule and do not skip meals.

Symptoms of high blood sugar (hyperglycemia) include confusion, drowsiness, flushing, rapid breathing, or fruity breath odor. If these symptoms occur, contact your doctor.

This medication can increase sensitivity to sunlight.

In the unlikely event you have an allergic reaction to this drug, seek immediate medical attention. Symptoms of an allergic reaction include rash, itching, swelling, dizziness or trouble breathing.

If you notice other effects not listed above, contact your doctor or pharmacist.

Precautions
Tell your doctor your medical history, especially if you have: high blood pressure, liver or kidney disease, any allergies.

Avoid alcohol while taking this medication. It can cause facial flushing, nausea, vomiting, dizziness or stomach pain.

This medication may make you prone to sunburn. Wear protective clothing and a sunscreen containing SPF of at least 15.

Drug Interactions
Inform your doctor about all the medicines you use (both prescription and nonprescription) especially if you are using: warfarin, monoamine oxidase inhibitors (e.g., furazolidone, linezolid, phenelzine, selegiline, tranylcypromine), beta-blockers (e.g., metoprolol, propranolol, timolol), certain "water pills" (diuretics such as hydrochlorothiazide), corticosteroids (e.g., prednisone), glaucoma eye medicines, aspirin-like drugs, probenecid.

Do not start or stop any medicine without first consulting your doctor or pharmacist.

Notes
It is important you wear or carry medical identification indicating you are a diabetic.

It is recommended you attend a diabetes education program to understand diabetes and all aspects of its treatment including diet, exercise, personal hygiene, medications and getting regular eye exams.

Controlling high blood sugar helps prevent heart disease, strokes, kidney disease and circulation problems.

Missed Dose
If you miss a dose, take it as soon as you remember. If it is near the time of the next dose, skip the missed dose and resume your usual dosing schedule. Do not double the dose to catch up.

Storage
Store at room temperature away from moisture and sunlight. Do not store in the bathroom.

GLYBURIDE/METFORMIN

Common Brand Name: Glucovance

Uses
This combination medication is used, along with diet and exercise programs, to control high blood sugar in diabetic patients (type 2 diabetes). One ingredient works by helping the body make more natural insulin and the other ingredient works by making the body use the natural insulin more effectively.

Controlling blood sugar helps diabetics prevent heart disease, strokes, kidney disease, blindness, and circulation problems.

How to Use
Take this medication by mouth, usually twice daily with meals or as directed by your doctor. Try to take this medication at the same time(s) each day. To avoid negative side effects take this medication with food or milk.

Do not skip meals, drink too much alcohol, or exercise without having recently eaten. These activities can cause your blood sugar to get too low and cause serious side effects.

Side Effects
Nausea, metallic taste, diarrhea, or stomach pain, may occur as your body adjusts to the effects of the medication. If these effects persist or worsen, notify your doctor.

In some cases, this medication may cause low blood sugar (hypoglycemia). Symptoms of low blood sugar are: lightheadedness, dizziness, shakiness, sweating, chills, hunger.

If the symptoms listed above occur, use your prescribed glucose liquid or tablets, or drink a glass of orange juice or non-diet soda in order to raise your blood sugar level quickly.

Tell your doctor immediately if you have any of these serious side effects: severe nausea, vomiting, diarrhea, stomach pain.

Stop taking this medication and tell your doctor immediately if you have any of these unlikely but serious side effects: rapid breathing, unusual drowsiness, muscle aches, unusually fast or slow heartbeat.

If you notice other effects not listed above, contact your doctor or pharmacist.

Precautions

Tell your doctor your medical history, including any allergies, kidney disease, liver disease, heart conditions, serious infections, stroke, dehydration, metabolic conditions (e.g., acidosis), certain hormonal conditions (adrenal/pituitary insufficiency), recent or planned surgeries.

Limit alcohol consumption while using this medication.

Caution is advised when using this drug with older people because they may be more sensitive to the effects of the drug.

Drug Interactions

Tell your doctor of all prescription and nonprescription medication you may use, especially if you have: "blood thinners" (e.g., warfarin), MAO inhibitors (e.g., furazolidone, linezolid, phenelzine, selegiline, tranylcypromine), beta-blockers (e.g., metoprolol, propranolol), aspirin-like drugs (salicylates or NSAIDs such as ibuprofen, naproxen), probenecid, sulfa drugs, quinolone antibiotics (e.g., ciprofloxacin), "water pills" (e.g., thiazide diuretics), corticosteroids (e.g., prednisone), thyroid drugs, estrogens, phenytoin, isoniazid, niacin, decongestants or diet pills, certain psychiatric medication (phenothiazines), calcium channel blockers (e.g., verapamil, diltiazem), cimetidine, drugs removed by the kidney (using cationic renal secretion) including ranitidine and digoxin.

If you are scheduled to have any diagnostic procedures using iodine contrast material (x-ray), tell your doctor that you are taking this product. This medication generally is stopped before your procedure, and withheld for 2 days after the procedure.

Consult your doctor for more details.

Do not start or stop any medicine without first consulting your doctor or pharmacist.

Notes

This medication is not a substitute for proper diet and exercise. It is recommended to attend a diabetes education program to understand diabetes and all aspects of its treatment, including diet, exercise, personal hygiene, medications and the importance of having regular eye and foot exams.

Do not share this medication with others.

Laboratory and/or medical tests (e.g., kidney function and blood counts) will be performed in order to monitor your progress and response to this medication.

Missed Dose
If you miss a dose, take it as soon as you remember. If it is near the time of the next dose, skip the missed dose and resume your usual dosing schedule. Do not double the dose to catch up.

Storage
Store at room temperature between 36 and 86 degrees F (2 to 30 degrees C) away from light and moisture.

HUMAN INSULIN 70/30

Common Brand Name: Humulin 70/30

Uses
Insulin is used to treat diabetes mellitus.

How to Use
Insulin must be injected. Learn the proper way to inject insulin. Check the dose carefully.

Clean the injection site with rubbing alcohol. Change the injection site daily to prevent skin bulges or pockets. Do not inject cold insulin. The insulin container you are currently using can be kept at room temperature for up to one month.

Insulin is frequently injected 30 minutes before a meal. Some inject at bedtime. Ask your pharmacist or nurse for details of injecting insulin as it varies depending on your insulin treatment plan.

Monitor your urine or blood sugar as prescribed. Keep track of your results. This is very important in order to determine the correct insulin dose.

Follow all of your doctor's directions carefully.

Side Effects
Insulin may cause minor and usually temporary side effects such as rash, irritation or redness at the injection site.

To help prevent hypoglycemia, eat meals on a regular schedule.

Too much insulin can cause low blood sugar (hypoglycemia). The symptoms include cold sweat, shaking, rapid heart rate, weakness, headache and fainting which, if untreated, may lead to slurred speech and other behaviors that resemble drunkenness. If you experience these symptoms, eat a quick source of sugar such as glucose (glutose, etc.) table sugar, orange juice, honey or non-diet soda. Tell your doctor about the reaction.

Too little insulin can cause symptoms of high blood sugar (hyperglycemia) which include confusion, drowsiness, rapid breathing, fruity breath odor, increased urination, increased hunger, or unusual thirst. If these symptoms occur, contact your doctor. Your insulin dose needs adjustment.

In the unlikely event you have an allergic reaction to this drug, seek medical attention immediately. Symptoms of an allergic reaction include: rash, itching, swelling, dizziness, trouble breathing.

If you notice other effects not listed above, contact your doctor or pharmacist.

Precautions
Tell your doctor if you have had allergic reactions, especially to beef, pork or human insulin and of your medical history especially if you have: thyroid problems, kidney or liver disease, any current infection.

Dosage adjustments may be required when you become ill, are under stress, or when quitting smoking. Consult your doctor if you catch a cold or the flu, become nauseated or if your blood glucose levels are high.

Fat deposits can occur if injection site is not rotated.

Check your sugar readings before and after exercise. You may need a snack beforehand.

Drug Interactions
Before you use insulin, tell your doctor of all prescription and nonprescription drugs you are taking especially: beta-blockers (acebutolol, atenolol, betaxolol, esmolol, metoprolol, carteolol, nadolol, penbutolol, pindolol, propranolol, timolol, bisoprolol), fenfluramine, MAO inhibitors (e.g., furazolidone, linezolid, phenelzine, selegiline, tranylcypromine), salicylates (aspirin-like compounds), dexfenfluramine, steroids (e.g., prednisone, hydrocortisone), sulfa antibiotics, water pills, ACE inhibitors, octreotide, isoniazid, niacin, estrogens, cold and allergy drugs, drugs that contain alcohol or sugar.

Other medications can affect the action of insulin and can alter the results of urine tests for sugar or ketones.

Do not start or stop any medicine without first consulting your doctor or pharmacist.

Notes
It is recommended you attend some type of diabetes education program to understand diabetes and the importance of meals, exercise, personal hygiene, use of other medications and getting regular eye and medical exams.

Controlling high blood sugar helps prevent heart disease, eye problems, strokes, kidney disease and circulation problems.

Do not allow anyone else to use this medication.

Missed Dose

Call your doctor if you should miss a dose. Your doctor will give you complete instructions as to what to do. Be aware of symptoms of high/low blood sugar.

Storage

Insulin may be stored under refrigeration up to the expiration date noted on the package and must be discarded after that date. Consult your pharmacist for the storage requirements of your particular form/type of insulin, including room temperature storage options. Do not expose insulin to heat or sunlight. Do not freeze.

HUMAN INSULIN NPH

Common Brand Name: Humulin N

Uses
Insulin is used to treat diabetes mellitus.

How to Use
Insulin must be injected. Learn the proper way to inject insulin. Check the dose carefully.

Clean the injection site with rubbing alcohol. Change the injection site daily to prevent skin bulges or pockets. Do not inject cold insulin. The insulin container you are currently using can be kept at room temperature. The length of time you can store it at room temp. depends on the product. Consult your pharmacist.

Insulin is frequently injected 30 minutes before a meal. Some inject at bedtime. Ask your pharmacist or nurse for details of injecting insulin as it varies depending on your insulin treatment plan.

Monitor your urine or blood sugar as prescribed. Keep track of your results. This is very important in order to determine the correct insulin dose.

Follow all of your doctor's directions carefully.

Side Effects
Insulin may cause minor and usually temporary side effects such as rash, irritation or redness at the injection site.

To help prevent hypoglycemia, eat meals on a regular schedule.

Too much insulin can cause low blood sugar (hypoglycemia). The symptoms include cold sweat, shaking, rapid heart rate, weakness, headache and fainting which, if untreated, may lead to slurred speech and other behaviors that resemble drunkenness. If you experience these symptoms, eat a quick source of sugar such as glucose (glutose, etc.) table sugar, orange juice, honey or non-diet soda. Tell your doctor about the reaction.

Too little insulin can cause symptoms of high blood sugar (hyperglycemia) which include confusion, drowsiness, rapid breathing, fruity breath odor, increased urination or unusual thirst. If these symptoms occur, contact your doctor. Your insulin dose needs adjustment.

In the unlikely event you have an allergic reaction to this drug, seek medical attention immediately. Symptoms of an allergic reaction include: rash, itching, swelling, dizziness, trouble breathing.

If you notice other effects not listed above, contact your doctor or pharmacist.

Precautions

Tell your doctor if you have had allergic reactions, especially to beef, pork or human insulin and of your medical history especially if you have: thyroid problems, kidney or liver disease, any current infection.

Dosage adjustments may be required when you become ill, are under stress, or when quitting smoking. Consult your doctor if you catch a cold or the flu, become nauseated or if your blood glucose levels are high. Your insulin dose may need to be adjusted.

Fat deposits on the skin can occur if injection site is not rotated.

Check your sugar readings before and after exercise. You may need a snack beforehand.

Drug Interactions

Before you use insulin, tell your doctor of all prescription and nonprescription drugs you are taking especially: beta-blockers (acebutolol, atenolol, betaxolol, esmolol, metoprolol, carteolol, nadolol, penbutolol, pindolol, propranolol, timolol, bisoprolol), fenfluramine, monoamine oxidase inhibitors (e.g., furazolidone, linezolid, phenelzine, selegiline, tranylcypromine), salicylates (aspirin-like compounds), dexfenfluramine, steroids (e.g., prednisone, hydrocortisone), sulfa antibiotics, water pills, ACE inhibitors, octreotide, isoniazid, niacin, estrogens, cold and allergy drugs, drugs that contain alcohol or sugar.

Other medications can affect the action of insulin and can alter the results of urine tests for sugar or ketones.

Do not start or stop any medicine without first consulting your doctor or pharmacist.

Notes

It is recommended you attend some type of diabetes education program to understand diabetes and the importance of meals, exercise, personal hygiene, use of other medications and getting regular eye and medical exams.

Controlling high blood sugar helps prevent heart disease, strokes, kidney disease and circulation problems.

Missed Dose

Call your doctor if you should miss a dose. Your doctor will give you complete instructions as to what to do. Be aware of symptoms of high/low blood sugar.

Storage

Insulin may be stored under refrigeration up to the expiration date noted on the package and must be discarded after that date. Consult your pharmacist for the storage requirements of your particular form/type of insulin, including room temperature storage options. Do not expose insulin to heat or sunlight. Do not freeze.

HYDROCHLOROTHIAZIDE

Common Brand Names: HydroDIURIL, Esidrix, Microzide

Uses
This medication is a "water pill" (diuretic) that decreases the amount of water in the body by increasing urination. It is used to decrease body fluid and swelling of the hands or feet (edema), and for high blood pressure.

How to Use
Because this drug increases urination, it is best taken early in the day.

This drug may be taken by mouth with food or milk to reduce stomach upset.

Side Effects
This drug may cause dizziness and lightheadedness especially during the first few days as your body adjusts to it.

Rise slowly from a seated or lying position to minimize the dizziness or light-headedness.

Blurred vision, loss of appetite, itching, stomach upset, headache and weakness may also occur during initial therapy as your body adjusts to the medication. If these effects persist or worsen, notify your doctor promptly.

Inform your doctor promptly if you develop: muscle cramps, weakness, pain, nausea, vomiting.

In the unlikely event you have an allergic reaction to this drug, seek immediate medical attention. Symptoms of an allergic reaction include: rash, itching, swelling, dizziness, trouble breathing.

If you notice other effects not listed above, contact your doctor or pharmacist.

Precautions
Tell your doctor your medical history, especially about: gout, diabetes, liver problems, urinary problems, kidney problems, any allergies (especially to sulfa medications).

Thiazide diuretics may increase sensitivity to sunlight. Avoid prolonged sun exposure. If you become sun sensitive, use a sunblock containing sun protection factor (SPF) of at least 15 and wear protective clothing when outdoors.

Drug Interactions
This drug is not recommended for use with dofetilide. Ask your doctor or pharmacist for more details.

Inform your doctor about all the medicines you may use (both prescription and nonprescription), especially if you take: lithium, digoxin, oral drugs used for diabetes, aspirin, NSAIDs (e.g., ibuprofen, naproxen), hydrochlorothiazide.

If you take colestipol or cholestyramine for high cholesterol, take them 1 hour before or 4 hours after because these drugs can decrease the amount that is absorbed into your body Do not start or stop any medicine without first consulting your doctor or pharmacist.

Notes
Do not share this medication with others.

This drug may reduce the potassium levels in your blood. Ask your doctor about increasing your dietary potassium. Sometimes a potassium supplement medication will be prescribed by your doctor.

Missed Dose
If you miss a dose, take it as soon as you remember. If it is near the time of the next dose, skip the missed dose and resume your usual dosing schedule. Do not double the dose to catch up.

Storage
Store at room temperature away from moisture and sunlight. Do not store in the bathroom.

HYDROCODONE/IBUPROFEN

Common Brand Name: Vicoprofen

Uses
This medication is used for short-term relief of pain. It is not recommended for such chronic conditions as arthritis.

How to Use
This medication is taken by mouth, usually one tablet every 4 to 6 hours as necessary for pain. Dosage should not exceed 5 tablets per day. Treatment is for 10 days or less unless otherwise directed. Follow all instructions exactly to receive good pain relief. Contact your doctor or pharmacist if your pain is not relieved.

Take this medication with 6 to 8 ounces (180-240ml) of water.

After a period of time, this medicine may not work as well. If this occurs, consult your doctor or pharmacist.

Prolonged or excessive use of this product may cause dependency (or addiction). Do not increase your dosage or use more often than directed.

Side Effects
Mild headache, dizziness, drowsiness, nausea or constipation might occur. If these persist or worsen, notify your doctor promptly.

Unlikely but report promptly: unusual bleeding or bruising.

Very unlikely but report promptly: stiff neck, yellowing eyes or skin, unusual change in amount of urine, fast heartbeat, fever, severe headache, ringing in the ears, eye problems, mental/mood changes.

If you notice any of the following unlikely but very serious side effects, stop taking this drug and consult your doctor or pharmacist immediately: black stools, persistent stomach/ abdominal pain, vomit that looks like coffee grounds.

In the unlikely event you have an allergic reaction to this drug, seek medical attention immediately. Symptoms of an allergic reaction include: rash, itching, swelling, severe dizziness, trouble breathing/slow, very shallow breathing.

If you notice other effects not listed above, contact your doctor or pharmacist.

Precautions

Tell your doctor your medical history, especially if you have: allergies (especially drug allergies), asthma, recent head injury, brain disorders (e.g., cancer), stomach/intestinal ulcers, high blood pressure, blood disorders, alcoholism, current smoking, kidney problems, lung diseases, heart problems, liver disease, diabetes, thyroid problems (hypothyroid), enlarged prostate (males), urinary problems.

Use caution when performing tasks requiring alertness or when using machinery. Limit alcohol intake.

This medicine may cause stomach bleeding. Daily use of alcohol, especially when combined with this medicine, may increase your risk for stomach bleeding. Check with your doctor or pharmacist for more information.

Caution is advised when this product is used with older people.

Drug Interactions

Tell your doctor of all nonprescription and prescription medication you may use, especially if you have: blood pressure medicine (including ACE inhibitors such as lisinopril or enalapril), anticholinergics/antihistamines such as diphenhydramine or propantheline, antidepressants, MAO inhibitors (e.g., linezolid, selegiline, furazolidone, tranylcypromine, phenelzine), tricyclics (e.g., amitriptyline), aspirin or other NSAIDs such as naproxen, "blood-thinners" such as warfarin or heparin, "water pills" (diuretics), lithium, methotrexate, other narcotic pain relievers such as codeine, corticosteroids (e.g., prednisone), cimetidine.

Also report the use of drugs that cause drowsiness such as: anti-seizure drugs, anti-anxiety drugs, muscle relaxants, psychiatric drugs, sedatives, sleeping pills.

Certain cough-and-cold and pain reliever medicines contain narcotics (e.g., codeine) or aspirin-like pain relievers (NSAIDs) which are very similar to the drugs in this product.

Do not start or stop any medicine without first consulting your doctor or pharmacist.

Notes

Do not share this medication with others.

To help minimize constipation from this product, drink plenty of fluid, use a high fiber diet and exercise if possible.

Laboratory tests will be done to monitor for side effects.

Missed Dose

If you miss a dose, take it as soon as you remember. If it is near the time of the next dose, skip the missed dose and resume your usual dosing schedule. Do not double the dose to catch up.

Storage
Store at room temperature between 68 and 77 degrees F (20-25 degrees C) away from light and moisture.

HYDROCODONE WITH APAP

Common Brand Names: Vicodin, Lorcet, Lortab

Uses
This medication is used to relieve moderate-to-severe pain.

How to Use
Take this medication by mouth, exactly as prescribed. To prevent upset stomach, take with food or milk.

Pain medications work best in preventing pain before it occurs. Once the pain becomes intense, the medication is not as effective in relieving it.

Use this medication exactly as directed by your doctor. Do not increase your dose, take it more frequently, or use it for a longer period of time than prescribed because this drug can be habit-forming. Also, if used for an extended period of time, do not suddenly stop using this drug without your doctor's approval.

When used for extended periods, this drug may not work as well and may require different dosing. Talk with your doctor if this medication stops working well.

Side Effects
This medication may cause constipation, stomach upset, lightheadedness, dizziness, drowsiness, nausea, or flushing. If any of these effects persist or worsen, contact your doctor or pharmacist promptly.

Tell your doctor immediately if you have any of these unlikely but serious side effects: loss of coordination, confusion, irregular heartbeat, slow/irregular breathing, anxiety, tremors.

An allergic reaction to this drug is unlikely, but seek immediate medical attention if it occurs. Symptoms of an allergic reaction include: rash, itching, swelling, severe dizziness, trouble breathing.

If you notice other effects not listed above, contact your doctor or pharmacist.

Precautions
Tell your doctor your medical history, especially if you have: liver or kidney conditions, history of alcohol use, heart problems, abdominal/stomach problems,

breathing problems, seizure disorders, drug dependency, severe diarrhea, drug allergies.

Avoid alcoholic beverages, because they may increase certain side effects of this drug. Use caution when performing tasks requiring alertness such as driving or using heavy machinery.

This product contains acetaminophen, which may cause liver damage. Daily use of alcohol, especially when combined with acetaminophen, may increase your risk for liver damage. Check with your doctor or pharmacist for more information.

Caution is advised when prescribing or using this drug with older people or the very young since they may be more sensitive to the effects of this medication.

Drug Interactions

Tell your doctor of all prescription and nonprescription drugs you use, including: MAO inhibitors (e.g., furazolidone, linezolid, phenelzine, selegiline, tranylcypromine), psychiatric drugs, tranquilizers, sleep medications, rifampin, other narcotic pain relievers, barbiturates, anti-seizure drugs, drowsiness-causing antihistamines (e.g., diphenhydramine), isoniazid, zidovudine, sulfinpyrazone, cimetidine.

Before taking pain relievers, cough-and-cold medicines or allergy products, read their labels to be sure that they do not also contain acetaminophen. An overdose of acetaminophen can be harmful. If you are uncertain your medicines contain acetaminophen, ask your pharmacist.

Do not start or stop any medicine without first consulting your doctor or pharmacist.

Notes

To prevent constipation, increase your intake of fiber, drink plenty of water and exercise.

This medication has been prescribed for your current condition only. Do not use it later for another condition unless told to do so by your doctor. A different medication may be necessary in those cases. Do not share this medication with others.

Missed Dose

If you miss a dose, take it as soon as you remember. If it is near the time of the next dose, skip the missed dose and resume your usual dosing schedule. Do not double the dose to catch up.

Storage

Store at room temperature away from light and moisture.

HYDROXYZINE

Common Brand Names: Atarax, Vistaril

Uses
This medication is used for motion sickness, anxiety, alcohol withdrawal symptoms, rash, hives, watery eyes, runny nose, itching, and sneezing due to allergies or the common cold. It is also used as a sleep aid (for insomnia).

How to Use
May be taken with food or milk if stomach upset occurs.
Shake suspensions well before taking.

Side Effects
May cause drowsiness, dizziness, headache, constipation, loss of appetite (less likely with cyproheptadine), stomach upset, vision changes, irritability, dry mouth and nose. These effects should subside as your body adjusts to the medication. If they persist or become bothersome, inform your doctor.
Notify your doctor if you develop: breathing difficulties, pounding or irregular heartbeat, ringing in the ears, difficulty urinating, confusion.
If you notice other effects not listed above, contact your doctor or pharmacist.

Precautions
Tell your doctor your medical history, especially if you have: glaucoma (narrow angle), stomach ulcers, difficulty urinating (e.g., enlarged prostate), heart disease, high blood pressure, seizures, lung problems, overactive thyroid.
Change from a seated or lying position slowly to avoid dizziness. Use caution in performing activities requiring alertness. Limit alcohol intake to avoid excessive drowsiness.
Caution is advised when using this drug with older people because they may be more sensitive to the effects of the drug.

Drug Interactions
Tell your doctor of all the medications you may use (both prescription and nonpre-

scription), especially if you have: sleeping pills, sedatives, tranquilizers, muscle relaxants, medication for depression, seizure medications, narcotic pain relievers, other medications for colds/hay fever/allergies.

Because this medication may affect allergy testing, you may have to stop using this medication for several days before the tests are performed. Consult your doctor about this.

Do not start or stop any medicine without first consulting your doctor or pharmacist.

Notes
Do not share this product with others.

Missed Dose
If you miss a dose, take it as soon as you remember. If it is near the time of the next dose, skip the missed dose and resume your usual dosing schedule. Do not double the dose to catch up.

Storage
Store at room temperature between 59 and 86 degrees F (between 15 and 30 degrees C) away from moisture and sunlight. Do not store in the bathroom. Do not freeze liquid forms of this medication.

IBUPROFEN

Common Brand Names: Motrin, Advil

Uses
This medication is used to treat pain and reduce inflammation. It is used to treat headaches, muscle aches, dental pain, arthritis, or athletic injuries. Some NSAIDs are also used to reduce fever.

How to Use
Take this medication by mouth with a full glass of water (8oz. or 240ml) as directed by your doctor. The dosage is based on your medical condition and response to therapy.

If stomach upset occurs while taking this medication, take it with food, milk, or an antacid. Do not lie down for at least 30 minutes after taking this drug.

In certain conditions (e.g., arthritis), it may take up to two weeks, taken regularly, before the full benefit of this drug takes effect.

If you use this for migraine headache, and the pain is not relieved or it worsens after the first dose, seek immediate medical attention.

Side Effects
Upset stomach, nausea, vomiting, heartburn, headache, diarrhea, constipation, drowsiness, and unusual fatigue may occur. If any of these effects persist or worsen, notify your doctor.

Tell your doctor immediately if any of these serious side effects occur: stomach pain, swelling of the feet or ankles, ringing in the ears (tinnitus).

Tell your doctor immediately if any of these unlikely but serious side effects occur: vision changes, joint pain, muscle pain or weakness, easy bruising or bleeding, persistent sore throat and fever.

Tell your doctor immediately if any of these highly unlikely but very serious side effects occur: changes in amount or color of urine, yellowing of the eyes or skin.

If you notice any of the following unlikely but serious side effects, stop taking this medication and consult your doctor immediately: black stools, persistent stomach/ abdominal pain, vomit that looks like coffee grounds.

An allergic reaction to this drug is unlikely, but seek immediate medical attention if it occurs. Symptoms of an allergic reaction include: rash, itching, swelling, dizziness, trouble breathing.

If you notice other effects not listed above, contact your doctor or pharmacist.

Precautions

Tell your doctor your medical history, especially if you have: kidney problems, liver problems, stomach problems (e.g., ulcers), heart disease (e.g., arrhythmias, heart failure), high blood pressure (hypertension), diabetes, blood problems (e.g., anemia, bleeding disorders, porphyria), asthma, eye problems, severe or long-lasting headaches, any allergies.

This drug may make you dizzy or drowsy. Use caution engaging in activities requiring alertness such as driving or using machinery.

This medication may make you more sensitive to the sun. Avoid prolonged sun exposure, use a sunblock containing skin protection factor (SPF) of at least 15, and wear protective clothing when outdoors.

This medicine may cause stomach bleeding. Daily use of alcohol and this medicine may increase your risk for stomach bleeding. If you consume 3 or more alcoholic beverages per day, check with your doctor before using this medication.

Older adults may be more sensitive to the effects of the drug, especially side effects such as stomach bleeding and kidney problems.

Drug Interactions

Tell your doctor of all prescription and nonprescription medication you may use, especially: warfarin, other medications for arthritis (e.g., aspirin, methotrexate), "water pills" (diuretics), lithium, anti-ulcer medication (e.g., cimetidine), high blood pressure medication such as ACE inhibitors (e.g., captopril, lisinopril), and beta-blockers (e.g., metoprolol, propranolol), probenecid, phenytoin, cyclosporine, sulfa drugs, medicine for diabetes (e.g., glipizide, glyburide), alendronate, other NSAIDs.

Check the labels on all your medicines because they may contain aspirin or other aspirin-like NSAIDs (e.g., ibuprofen, naproxen). Ask your pharmacist about the safe use of those products.

Do not start or stop any medicine without first consulting your doctor or pharmacist.

Notes

Do not share this medication with others.

Laboratory and/or medical tests may be performed to monitor your progress.

Missed Dose

If you miss a dose, take it as soon as you remember. If it is near the time of the next dose, skip the missed dose and resume your usual dosing schedule. Do not double the dose to catch up.

Storage

Store at room temperature between 36 and 86 degrees F (2 to 30 degrees C) away from light and moisture.

INDOMETHACIN

Common Brand Name: Indocin

Uses
Indomethacin treats the pain, swelling and stiffness associated with arthritis, gout, bursitis or tendonitis.

How to Use
Take with food or immediately after meals to prevent stomach upset.

Take this medication with 6 to 8 ounces (180-240ml) of water.

Sustained release or long acting preparations must be swallowed whole. Do not crush or chew them or the sustained activity may be destroyed and side effects increased.

Side Effects
Stomach upset is the most common side effect. If this persists or becomes severe, notify your doctor.

Headache, heartburn, loss of appetite, lightheadedness, dizziness, bloating, constipation, diarrhea, nervousness, or drowsiness may occur as your body adjusts to the medication.

Notify your doctor promptly if you develop any of these serious side effects while taking this medication: vision changes, ringing in ears/loss of hearing.

If you notice any of the following unlikely but very serious side effects, stop taking this drug and consult your doctor or pharmacist immediately: black stools, persistent stomach/ abdominal pain, vomit that looks like coffee grounds.

An allergic reaction to this drug is unlikely, but seek immediate medical attention if it occurs. Symptoms of an allergic reaction include: rash, itching, swelling, severe dizziness, trouble breathing.

If you notice other effects not listed above, contact your doctor or pharmacist.

Precautions
Tell your doctor your medical history, especially if you have: liver or kidney disease, blood disorders, ulcers, heart disease, alcohol use, high blood pressure, eye disease,

mental disturbances, brain diseases (such as Parkinson's disease), any allergies (especially drug allergies).

Use caution when performing tasks requiring alertness. Limit alcohol intake as it may intensify the drowsiness effect of this medication.

This medicine may cause stomach bleeding. Daily use of alcohol, especially when combined with this medicine, may increase your risk for stomach bleeding. Check with your doctor or pharmacist for more information.

Do not take aspirin without consulting your doctor. Check the ingredients of any nonprescription medication you may be taking since many cough-and-cold formulas contain aspirin.

Infrequently, this medication may increase the skin's sensitivity to sunlight. If this happens to you, avoid prolonged sun exposure, wear protective clothing and use a sunscreen. Avoid sunlamps.

Caution is advised when this drug is used with older people.

Drug Interactions
Tell your doctor of all prescription and nonprescription drugs you may use, especially if you have: "blood thinners" (e.g., warfarin), other arthritis medication, "water pills" (diuretics), lithium, antihypertensive medications.

Do not start or stop any medicine without first consulting your doctor or pharmacist.

Notes
In arthritis, it may take up to four weeks before the full effects of this medicine are noted. For best results, this must be taken regularly, as directed by your doctor.

Missed Dose
If you miss a dose, take it as soon as you remember. If it is near the time of the next dose, skip the missed dose and resume your usual dosing schedule. Do not double the dose to catch up.

Storage
Store at room temperature away from sunlight and moisture.

INSULIN GLARGINE

Common Brand Name: Lantus

Uses
Insulin glargine is used to treat diabetes mellitus. Like other insulin products, it works by helping sugar (glucose) get into cells but has a more long-acting (over 24 hours) effect.

How to Use
Learn all preparation and usage instructions, including how to inject this medication properly, and how to manage your blood sugar (e.g., blood glucose monitoring, high or low blood sugar symptoms, treatment for high or low blood sugar).

If any of this information is unclear, consult your doctor or pharmacist.

Before injecting each dose, clean the injection site with rubbing alcohol. It is important to change the location of the injection site daily to avoid problem areas under the skin (lipodystrophy). The Abdomen has the best absorption.

Inject this medication under the skin (SC) usually once daily at bedtime; or use as directed by your doctor.

The dosage is based on your medical condition and response to therapy. Measure each dose very carefully; even small changes in the amount of insulin may have a large effect on your blood sugar levels.

If you experience any of the symptoms of low blood sugar (listed below in side section section), take a quick source of sugar such as glucose tablets, table sugar, orange juice, honey, or non-diet soda. Promptly contact your doctor.

Insulin glargine is not recommended to be given into a vein (IV). Severe low blood sugar may result.

Do not mix this type of insulin with other insulin products or with other intravenous (IV) solutions.

Before using, inspect this product visually for particles or discoloration. If either is present, do not use the liquid.

Learn how to store and discard needles and medical supplies safely. Consult your pharmacist.

Side Effects

Injection site reactions (e.g., pain, redness, irritation) may occur. If any of these effects persist or worsen, notify your doctor.

Tell your doctor immediately if any of these serious side effects of low blood sugar (hypoglycemia) occur: fainting, cold sweats, shaking/tremor, unusually fast heartbeat, headache, slurred speech, seizures.

Tell your doctor immediately if any of these serious side effects of high blood sugar (hyperglycemia) occurs: unusual drowsiness, confusion, rapid breathing, fruity breath odor, increased urination, unusual thirst increased hunger.

An allergic reaction to this drug is unlikely, but seek immediate medical attention if it occurs. Symptoms of an allergic reaction include: rash, itching, swelling, dizziness, trouble breathing.

If you notice other effects not listed above, contact your doctor or pharmacist.

Precautions

Tell your doctor your medical history, especially if you have: kidney problems, liver problems, nerve disease (e.g., diabetic neuropathy), thyroid problems, any allergies (especially to other insulin products).

Fever, serious infection or injury, emotional stress, or major surgery may increase your blood sugar level temporarily which may make this medication less effective. Consult your doctor for details and a treatment plan.

Caution is advised when using this drug with older people because they may be more sensitive to its effect on blood sugar.

Drug Interactions

Tell your doctor of all prescription and nonprescription medication you may use, especially: other insulin products (e.g., Regular, NPH), oral diabetes medicine (e.g., glyburide, pioglitazone), ACE inhibitors (e.g., enalapril, lisinopril), beta-blockers (e.g., metoprolol, propranolol), disopyramide, fibrates (e.g., clofibrate, gemfibrozil), fluoxetine, MAO inhibitors (e.g., furazolidone, isocarboxazid, linezolid, moclobemide, phenelzine, procarbazine, selegiline, tranylcypromine), propoxyphene, salicylates (e.g., aspirin), octreotide, sulfa antibiotics (e.g., sulfamethoxazole), corticosteroids (e.g., prednisone), danazol, diuretics, sympathomimetic drugs (e.g., albuterol, epinephrine), isoniazid, certain psychiatric medicine (e.g., phenothiazines such as chlorpromazine), somatropin, thyroid medicine, estrogens and progestins (including birth control pills), clonidine, lithium, pentamidine, guanethidine, reserpine.

Drinking alcohol may affect your blood sugar level. Limit alcoholic beverages.

Do not start or stop any medicine without first consulting your doctor or pharmacist.

Notes

Do not share this medication with others.

Laboratory and/or medical tests will be performed to monitor your progress.

It is recommended that you attend a diabetes education program to understand diabetes and all the important aspects of its treatment including meals, exercise, personal hygiene, medications, and getting regular eye and medical exams.

It is very important to eat regularly scheduled, balanced meals while using this medication. If you have any questions or concerns about your diet, consult your doctor. Also, following a doctor-approved exercise plan will help control your diabetes.

Missed Dose

If you miss a dose, take it as soon as you remember. If it is near the time of the next dose, skip the missed dose and resume your usual dosing schedule. Do not double the dose to catch up.

Storage

The unopened vial/cartridge of medication is best stored in the refrigerator between 36 and 46 degrees F (2 and 8 degrees C). Do not freeze. The unopened vial/cartridge may also be stored at room temperature below 86 degrees F (30 degrees C), but must be discarded after 28 days.

After you have opened the medication, you may store it in the refrigerator or at room temperature, but it must be discarded after 28 days.

Protect insulin from direct sunlight, heat, and moisture.

IPRATROPIUM/ ALBUTEROL

Common Brand Name: Combivent

Uses
This medication is used to treat chronic obstructive pulmonary disease disease (bronchitis or emphysema).

How to Use
Make sure you understand how to use the inhaler properly. Shake the canister well before use. After exhaling, place your lips around the inhaler mouthpiece. Depress the spray and inhale deeply. Hold your breath as long as it is comfortable in order to allow the medicine to be absorbed in the lungs. When more than one inhalation is prescribed, wait at least one minute between puffs.

Use this medication as directed. Do not increase your dose or use this more frequently than directed. Excessive use may lead to a loss of effectiveness while increasing the chance for side effects. Do not stop using this medication without first consulting your doctor.

If you find yourself using this more than usual, or your symptoms do not improve or worsen after using this, contact your doctor immediately.

Side Effects
Headache, nausea, coughing, dry mouth or sinus congestion may occur. If these continue or are bothersome, notify your doctor.

Uncommon effects include: palpitations or irregular heartbeat, chest pain, change in sputum color (infection).

Very unlikely but report: dizziness, nervousness, hair loss, fever, coordination problems.

In the unlikely event you have an allergic reaction to this drug, seek medical attention immediately. Symptoms of an allergic reaction include: rash, itching, swelling, dizziness, trouble breathing.

If you notice other effects not listed above, contact your doctor or pharmacist.

Precautions

Before using this drug, tell your doctor your medical history, especially if you have: heart/liver/kidney diseases, high blood pressure, narrow-angle glaucoma, prostate enlargement or bladder problems, seizures, thyroid problems, diabetes, allergies (including soy products or peanuts).

Drug Interactions

Tell your doctor of all over-the-counter or prescription medication you may use, including: all asthma drugs, blood pressure or chest pain medications, beta-blockers (e.g., propranolol), levodopa, digoxin, certain antidepressants (e.g., amitriptyline, doxepin), MAO inhibitors (e.g., furazolidone, phenelzine, selegiline, tranylcypromine), ritodrine, other "adrenalin" drugs, thyroid drugs, caffeine, antihistamines (often found in cough/cold preparations), antispasmodics (e.g., atropine, clidinium, propantheline), drugs used to treat Parkinson's disease, diuretics (e.g., hydrochlorothiazide).

Do not start or stop any medicine without first consulting your doctor or pharmacist.

Notes

Do not share this inhaler with anyone else.

Missed Dose

If you miss a dose, take it as soon as you remember. If it is near the time of the next dose, skip the missed dose and resume your usual dosing schedule. Do not double the dose to catch up.

Storage

Store at room temperature between 59 and 86 degrees F (15-30 degrees C) away from sunlight and moisture. Exposure to temperatures above 120 degrees F may cause bursting.

IPRATROPIUM BROMIDE

Common Brand Name: Atrovent

Uses
This medication is inhaled into the lungs where it opens breathing passages. It is used to treat breathing disorders such as chronic onbstructive pulmonary disease (COPD), chronic bronchitis or emphysema.

How to Use
This medication is inhaled into the lungs using special breathing (nebulizer) equipment usually 3 to 4 times a day (6 to 8 hours apart). A health care professional will demonstrate the proper way to measure the medication and use the equipment. Make sure you understand how to operate the machine and ask any questions you may have. Be sure to read and understand the patient instructions that come with the medication. Use this medication as directed. Do not increase your dose or take this more frequently than directed. Excessive use may lead to a loss of effectiveness while increasing the chance for side effects.

Do not stop using this medication without first consulting your doctor.

Side Effects
This medication may cause dizziness, headache, nausea, dry mouth, cough, hoarseness, or blurred vision. These effects should disappear as your body adjusts to the medication.

If they persist or become bothersome, inform your doctor.

Notify your doctor if you experience any of these serious effects while taking this medication: rash, itching, irregular heartbeat, chest pains, rapid heartbeat.

If this drug comes in contact with the eye, temporary blurring of your vision may occur.

If you notice other effects not listed above, contact your doctor or pharmacist.

Precautions
Before using this medication, tell your doctor your medical history, especially if

you have: glaucoma, prostate trouble, any allergies (especially to atropine/other belladonna derivatives).

Drug Interactions
Tell your doctor of all nonprescription or prescription medication you may take particularly: antispasmodics (e.g., atropine, clidinium, propantheline), antihistamines (often found in cough/cold preparations), medication for Parkinson's disease.

Do not start or stop any medicine without first consulting your doctor or pharmacist.

Notes
It may be preferable to use the nebulizer with a mouthpiece rather than a face mask to reduce the chance of the solution coming into contact with the eyes and causing blurred vision. To get maximal effect from the inhaler, proper use is necessary.

Missed Dose
If you miss a dose, take it as soon as you remember. If it is near the time of the next dose, skip the missed dose and resume your usual dosing schedule. Do not double the dose to catch up.

Storage
This medication should be stored at room temperature away from light. Avoid freezing.

IRBESARTAN

Common Brand Name: Avapro

Uses
This drug is used to treat high blood pressure (hypertension). It works by preventing the narrowing of blood vessels. High blood pressure reduction helps prevent strokes, heart attacks, and kidney problems.

How to Use
Take this medication by mouth as prescribed, and learn proper usage. Consult your pharmacist.

Be sure to follow the dosing instructions closely. Do not increase your dose, skip any doses or stop taking this without first consulting your doctor.

Before using potassium supplements or salt substitutes, consult your doctor or pharmacist.

It is important to continue taking this medication even if you do not feel sick. Most people with high blood pressure do not have any symptoms.

Side Effects
Infrequent side effects such as dizziness, diarrhea, stomach upset, stuffed nose or dry mouth may occur the first several days as your body adjusts to the medication. If any of these effects persist or worsen, contact your doctor.

Unlikely to occur but report promptly: abdominal pain, persistent sore throat, muscle weakness, unusual fatigue, joint or muscle aches, fever, major change in the amount of urine eliminated.

In the unlikely event you have an allergic reaction to this drug, seek immediate medical attention. Symptoms of an allergic reaction include: rash, itching, swelling, dizziness, breathing trouble.

If you notice other effects not listed above, contact your doctor or pharmacist.

Precautions
Tell your doctor your medical history, including kidney or liver disease, congestive heart failure, diabetes, allergies (especially drug allergies).

To avoid dizziness and lightheadedness when rising from a seated or lying position, get up slowly. Also limit your intake of alcoholic beverages which will aggravate these effects.

Use caution performing tasks requiring alertness if this medication causes you to feel dizzy.

Caution is advised when this drug is used with older people. They may be more sensitive to the effects of this drug.

Drug Interactions
Tell your doctor of all over-the-counter or prescription medication you may take including: other drugs for blood pressure (e.g., diuretics-"water pills"), aspirin or aspirin-related pain or fever drugs, drugs that can cause kidney problems (e.g., amphotericin, gentamicin).

Do not take any over-the-counter medication for allergies or cough or colds without consulting your doctor or pharmacist. Many of the products contain ingredients which may interact with the effects of this medication.

Do not start or stop any medicine without first consulting your doctor or pharmacist.

Notes
Laboratory tests will be done periodically to monitor for possible side effects.

Learn how to monitor your pulse and blood pressure. Talk to your health care professional about this.

Missed Dose
If you miss a dose, take it as soon as you remember. If it is near the time of the next dose, skip the missed dose and resume your usual dosing schedule. Do not double the dose to catch up.

Storage
Store at room temperature between 59 and 86 degrees F (15 to 30 degrees C) away from heat and light. Do not store in the bathroom.

ISOSORBIDE MONONITRATE S. A.

Common Brand Name: Imdur, ISMO

Uses
This medication relaxes blood vessels allowing more blood to flow through. This improves blood flow to the heart. Oral isosorbide mononitrate s.a. is used to prevent angina (chest pain). This medication is NOT for treating an attack of chest pain that is already happening.

How to Use
This medication is best taken on an empty stomach with a full glass of water.

Take exactly as prescribed. To be effective in preventing chest pain, you must continue taking this drug even if you feel well.

Sustained-release or long acting tablets and capsules must be swallowed whole. Crushing or chewing them destroys the long action and may increase side effects.

Do not stop taking this drug suddenly without consulting your doctor. Some conditions may become worse when the drug is suddenly stopped. Your dose may need to be gradually decreased.

Notify your doctor if the medication does not appear to be as effective. Do not increase your dose or take it more often than prescribed without consulting your doctor.

Side Effects
Headache, dizziness, flushing, rapid heartbeat or restlessness may occur as your body adjusts to the medication. If they persist or become bothersome, inform your doctor.

To prevent dizziness and lightheadedness when rising from a seated or lying position, get up slowly.

Notify your doctor if you experience: blurred vision, dry mouth, skin rash, nausea.

Headache is often a sign the medication is working. Treat headaches with an aspirin or non-aspirin pain reliever as recommended by your doctor. If the headaches continue or become severe, notify your doctor.

In the unlikely event you have an allergic reaction to this drug, seek medical attention immediately. Symptoms of an allergic reaction include: rash, itching, swelling, dizziness, trouble breathing.

If you notice other effects not listed above, contact your doctor or pharmacist.

Precautions
Before using this medication tell your doctor your medical history especially if you have: heart problems, head injury or surgery, glaucoma, thyroid conditions, anemia, alcohol usage, drug allergies.

Use caution engaging in activities that require alertness or in operating machinery if this medication makes you dizzy or drowsy.

Alcoholic beverages may increase the risk of fainting or of experiencing dizziness.

Drug Interactions
Tell your doctor of all medications you may use including prescription and nonprescription drugs, especially if you have: drugs for high blood pressure, certain migraine drugs (ergot alkaloids), sildenafil, high doses of aspirin.

Do not start or stop any medicine without first consulting your doctor or pharmacist.

Notes
Some persons may develop a tolerance to the effects of this medication over time. Notify your doctor if the medication appears to be losing its effectiveness or if the chest pain continues while taking this drug.

Missed Dose
If you miss a dose, take it as soon as you remember. If it is near the time of the next dose, skip the missed dose and resume your usual dosing schedule. Do not double the dose to catch up.

Storage
Store this medication away from heat or flame. Always keep this medication in its original container. Keep container closed tightly to avoid moisture.

LANSOPRAZOLE

Common Brand Name: Prevacid

Uses
Lansoprazole is used to treat various acid-related stomach and/or throat (esophagus) problems (e.g., GERD, ulcers, erosive esophagitis, or Zollinger-Ellison Syndrome).

It may also be used to treat ulcers associated with long-term use of certain pain/anti-inflammatory drugs (NSAIDs).

Lansoprazole works by blocking the production of acid in the stomach.

When using this medication to treat stomach ulcers caused by Helicobacter pylori, it may be prescribed along with certain antibiotics (e.g., amoxicillin, clarithromycin).

How to Use
Take this medication by mouth, usually once daily, before a meal; or as directed by your doctor.

The dosage and length of treatment is based on your medical condition and response to therapy.

Do not crush or chew the capsules. Swallow the capsule(s) whole. If you have difficulty swallowing this medication whole, the capsule may be opened and the contents sprinkled into soft food (e.g., applesauce, cottage cheese, yogurt), or emptied into a small amount (2 oz or 60 ml) of juice and taken as directed.

Rinse the container with an additional small amount of juice and drink the contents to make sure the entire dose was taken. Do not chew the food/medication mixture or make up a supply in advance.

Doing so may destroy the drug and/or increase side effects.

If you take sucralfate in addition to this medication, take your dose of lansoprazole at least 30 minutes before your sucralfate.

Side Effects
Headache, diarrhea, gas, or constipation, may occur. If any of these effects persist or worsen, notify your doctor.

Tell your doctor immediately if any of these serious side effects occur: stomach/abdominal pain, rash, back pain, unusual tiredness, dizziness, vomiting.

Tell your doctor immediately if any of these unlikely but serious side effects occur: chest pain, dark urine, yellowing eyes or skin.

Tell your doctor immediately if any of these highly unlikely but very serious side effects occur: persistent fever or sore throat, easy bruising or bleeding.

An allergic reaction to this drug is unlikely, but seek immediate medical attention if it occurs. Symptoms of an allergic reaction include: rash, itching, swelling, trouble breathing.

If you notice other effects not listed above, contact your doctor or pharmacist.

Precautions
Tell your doctor your medical history, especially if you have: liver problems, any allergies.

Drug Interactions
Tell your doctor of all prescription and nonprescription medication you may use, especially: theophylline, digoxin, azole antifungals (e.g., ketoconazole, itraconazole), ampicillin, iron supplements, sucralfate.

Do not start or stop any medicine without first consulting your doctor or pharmacist.

Notes
Do not share this medication with others.

Laboratory and/or medical tests may be performed to monitor your progress.

Missed Dose
If you miss a dose, take it as soon as you remember. If it is near the time of the next dose, skip the missed dose and resume your usual dosing schedule. Do not double the dose to catch up.

Storage
Store at room temperature between 59 and 86 degrees F (15 to 30 degrees C) away from light and moisture.

LATANOPROST

Common Brand Name: Xalatan

Uses
This medication is used along with other medicines to treat glaucoma and other problems related to high pressure within the eye.

How to Use
One drop is placed in the affected eye(s) once daily in the evening.

Avoid touching the dropper tip to your eye. This will help protect the bottle from becoming contaminated with bacteria. Pull the lower lid out forming a pouch and place one drop in the eye.

Apply pressure to the inside corner of the eye for 1 to 2 minutes. This will keep the medicine in the eye area longer. If more than one eye medication is being used, wait 5 minutes before using the next eye drop.

The preservative in this product may be absorbed by contact lenses. Contact lenses should be removed before using this drug.

Lenses may be reinserted 15 minutes after use of latanoprost.

Side Effects
Blurred vision, burning and stinging, a sensation of a foreign body in the eye, dry eye, lid crusting or discomfort can occur. Report these problems if they persist.

Notify your doctor if any of the following occur: eye pain, red eye, itching/swelling/increased brown coloration of the eye, darkening of the eyelid or eyelash.

Very unlikely but report: rapid vision changes, flu symptoms, chest pain, rash, headaches.

Precautions
Tell your doctor your medical history, especially if you have: kidney or liver diseases, any allergies, high blood pressure, swollen or itching eyes, contact lens use.

This medication can cause a darkening of the eye (iris) when given for several years. If only one eye is being treated, only one eye might darken. The consequences of this are unknown. Consult your eye doctor.

If you develop an eye infection, trauma or have eye surgery, check with your doctor about the continued use of the same dropper bottle. A new dropper bottle may be needed.

Drug Interactions
Tell your doctor of all nonprescription or prescription medication you may use, especially of eye drops containing thimerosal preservative (consult your pharmacist). If such drops are used, wait 5 minutes after using latanoprost.

Do not start or stop any medicine without first consulting your doctor or pharmacist.

Missed Dose
If you miss a dose, take it as soon as you remember. If it is near the time of the next dose, skip the missed dose and resume your usual dosing schedule. Do not double the dose to catch up.

Storage
Store unopened bottles in the refrigerator between 36 to 46 degrees F (2 to 8 degrees C). Once opened, the bottle may be stored at room temperature no higher than 77 degrees F (25 degrees C) for six weeks. Keep away from light and moisture. Do not store in the bathroom.

LETROZOLE

Common Brand Name: FEMARA

Uses
This medication is used to treat advanced breast cancer in women after menopause (change of life).

How to Use
Take by mouth once daily with or without food or as directed. Do not stop taking this medication unless instructed to do so by your doctor or pharmacist. Continue to take your other medications unless instructed otherwise.

Side Effects
This drug is generally well tolerated. Fatigue, nausea, constipation, diarrhea, headache, drowsiness or dizziness may occur. If these persist or worsen, notify your doctor promptly. Bone pain sometimes worsens for a short time after this medicine is first started; report this and any other changes to your doctor.

Unlikely but report promptly: chest pain, stomach pain, trouble breathing, hot flushes, rash, itching.

Very unlikely but report promptly: swelling/redness/weakness/ pain in legs or arms, vision problems, unusual vaginal bleeding.

If you notice other effects not listed above, contact your doctor or pharmacist.

Side effects that may be caused by blood clots including chest pains, shortness of breath, sudden severe headache, pain in legs or calves, slurred speech sudden vision changes and severe weakness in arm or leg, should be reported immediately to your doctor.

Precautions
Tell your doctor your medical history, especially if you have: liver problems, allergies (especially drug allergies).

Limit alcohol intake as it may increase the side effects of this drug.

Caution performing tasks requiring mental alertness (e.g., driving), since it is possible this drug may cause drowsiness.

Drug Interactions

Tell your doctor of all nonprescription and prescription medication you may use, especially of drugs that cause drowsiness such as: sedatives, tranquilizers, psychiatric medications, certain cough-and-cold products containing antihistamines (e.g., diphenhydramine), anti-seizure drugs, muscle relaxants, narcotic pain relievers (e.g., codeine).

Do not start or stop any medicine without first consulting your doctor or pharmacist.

Notes

Do not share this medication with others.

Missed Dose

If you miss a dose, use it as soon as you remember.

If it is near the time of the next dose, skip the missed dose and resume If you miss a dose, take it as soon as you remember. If it is near the time of the next dose, skip the missed dose and resume your usual dosing schedule. Do not double the dose to catch up.

Storage

Store at room temperature between 59 and 86 degrees F (15-30 degrees C) away from light and moisture.

LEVOFLOXACIN

Common Brand Name: LEVAQUIN

Uses
This medication is an antibiotic used to treat a wide variety of bacterial infections including urinary tract infections, skin infections or respiratory tract infections.

How to Use
Take by mouth, usually once daily or as directed.

May take with or without food. Drink plenty of water.

If you take any of the following items, take them 2 hours before or 2 hours after taking this drug: zinc, iron, sucralfate, or antacids that contain magnesium or aluminum.

Antibiotics work best when the amount of medicine in your body is kept at a constant level. Do this by taking the medication at the same time of day or night.

Continue to take this medication until the full prescribed amount is finished even if symptoms disappear after a few days.

Stopping the medication too early may allow bacteria to continue to grow resulting in a decrease in effectiveness in treating the infection.

Side Effects
This medication may cause loss of appetite, trouble sleeping, diarrhea, nausea, headache or dizziness during the first few days as your body adjusts to the medication. If these symptoms persist or become severe, inform your doctor.

Very unlikely but report promptly: muscle pain, tenderness in the arms or legs, vaginal discomfort, abdominal pain, vision changes, seizures, confusion, drowsiness, mental/mood changes, irregular heartbeat, restlessness.

Notify your doctor immediately if an allergic reaction to this medication occurs. Symptoms of an allergic reaction include: difficulty breathing, skin rash, hives or itching.

If you notice other effects not listed above, contact your doctor or pharmacist.

Precautions

Before taking this medication, tell your doctor your medical history especially if you have: epilepsy, kidney disease, tendon problems, nervous system disorders, liver disease, blood vessel disease, drug allergies.

Use caution driving or performing tasks requiring alertness if this medication makes you dizzy, lightheaded or drowsy. Limit alcohol intake.

Because this medication may make you more sensitive to the sun, avoid prolonged sun exposure. Wear protective clothing and use a sunscreen containing an SPF of at least 15 when outdoors.

Drug Interactions

Before taking this drug, tell your doctor of all over-the-counter or prescription drugs you may take especially if you have: theophylline, other antibiotics, anticoagulants (blood thinners), NSAID (e.g., ibuprofen, aspirin), antacids, sucralfate, iron, zinc, diabetes medication, live vaccines, quinapril.

Do not start or stop any medicine without first consulting your doctor or pharmacist.

Notes

This medication has been prescribed for your current condition only. Do not use it later for another infection or share it with someone else. A different medication may be needed in those cases.

Missed Dose

If you miss a dose, take it as soon as you remember. If it is near the time of the next dose, skip the missed dose and resume your usual dosing schedule. Do not double the dose to catch up.

Storage

Store at room temperature between 59 and 86 degrees F (between 15 and 30 degrees C) away from moisture and sunlight. Do not store in the bathroom. Keep container tightly closed.

LEVOTHYROXINE

Common Brand Names: SYNTHROID, Levoxyl, Levothroid

Uses
Thyroid replacement therapy is prescribed when not enough thyroid hormone is secreted from the thyroid gland.

How to Use
Take this medication on an empty stomach.

It is usually taken as a single daily dose before breakfast.

Do not stop taking this medication unless consulting with your doctor. Replacement therapy is usually taken for life.

Side Effects
Symptoms of low thyroid levels include fatigue, muscle aches, constipation, dry skin, weight gain, slow heart rate, sensitivity to cold, or dry brittle hair that tends to fall out easily. These symptoms should disappear as your body adjusts to the medication. If they persist or become bothersome, inform your doctor.

Symptoms of high thyroid levels include headache, chest pain, increased pulse rate, rapid or irregular heartbeat, shortness of breath, trembling, sweating, diarrhea, weight loss. If you experience any of these effects, contact your doctor. Your dose may need to be adjusted.

If you notice other effects not listed above, contact your doctor or pharmacist.

Precautions
Before using this drug, tell your doctor your medical history, especially if you have: heart problems, diabetes, adrenal gland problems, pituitary gland problems, any allergies (including drug allergies).

Thyroid replacement drugs should not be used for weight control.

Drug Interactions
Some medicines can increase or decrease the effects of thyroid replacement hormone in your body. Inform your doctor about all the medicines you use (both prescription

and nonprescription), especially about: warfarin, drugs that may increase heart rate or blood pressure such as decongestants or caffeine (decongestants may be found in nonprescription cough-and-cold medicines), estrogen products, digoxin, diabetes medicines.

Certain medicines may decrease absorption of this drug into your bloodstream. Therefore, take this medicine 4 hours apart from: calcium or iron supplements, aluminum or calcium antacids, cholestyramine or colestipol, sucralfate or sodium polystyrene sulfonate.

Do not start or stop any medicine without first consulting your doctor or pharmacist.

Notes

There are different brands of thyroid hormones available.

Do not change brands without first consulting your doctor or pharmacist.

Lab tests should be done periodically to monitor the effectiveness of this medication.

Missed Dose

If you miss a dose, take it as soon as you remember. If it is near the time of the next dose, skip the missed dose and resume your usual dosing schedule. Do not double the dose to catch up.

Storage

Store at room temperature away from sunlight and moisture. Do not store in the bathroom.

LISINOPRIL

Common Brand Names: Zestril, Prinivil

Uses
This medication prevents certain substances in the body from narrowing blood vessels. This helps to lower blood pressure and increases the supply of blood and oxygen to the heart. This medication is used to treat high blood pressure, heart failure or to help diabetics prevent kidney problems.

How to Use
This medication may be taken without regard to meals. Take it exactly as prescribed and try to take it at the same time each day.

Do not stop taking this medication without consulting your doctor. Some conditions may become worse when the drug is abruptly stopped. Your dose may need to be gradually decreased before it is completely stopped.

Side Effects
Headache, diarrhea, constipation, nausea, fatigue or dry cough may occur the first several days as your body adjusts to the medication.

Unlikely, but report promptly if you develop: chest pain, tingling or swelling of the hands or feet, swelling of the face/ lips/tongue, yellowing of the skin or eyes, fever, dizziness, persistent sore throat.

In the unlikely event you have an allergic reaction to this drug, seek immediate medical attention. Symptoms of an allergic reaction include: rash, itching, swelling, dizziness, trouble breathing.

If you notice other effects not listed above, contact your doctor or pharmacist.

Precautions
Before taking this drug tell your doctor your medical history, especially history of: angioedema (swelling of the lips, tongue, or face), high blood levels of potassium, kidney disease or kidney dialysis, salt restrictive diet, liver disease, heart problems, any drug allergies.

Consult your doctor before using salt substitutes or low salt milk.

To avoid dizziness and lightheadedness when rising from a seated or lying position, get up slowly.

Limit your intake of alcohol and use caution when exercising or during hot weather as these can aggravate dizziness and lightheadedness.

Drug Interactions

Inform your doctor about all the medicine you use (both prescription and nonprescription), especially if you take: lithium, potassium supplements, potassium-sparing water pills or other water pills (diuretics), high blood pressure drugs, NSAIDs (aspirin-like drugs).

Avoid "stimulant" drugs that may increase your heart rate such as decongestants or caffeine. Decongestants are commonly found in over-the-counter cough-and-cold medicines.

Do not start or stop any medicine without first consulting your doctor or pharmacist.

Notes

It is important to have your blood pressure checked regularly while taking this medication. Learn how to monitor your blood pressure. Discuss this with your doctor.

Lab tests may be performed to monitor your progress and to make certain there are no unwanted side effects.

Missed Dose

If you miss a dose, take it as soon as you remember. If it is near the time of the next dose, skip the missed dose and resume your usual dosing schedule. Do not double the dose to catch up.

Storage

Store at room temperature away from sunlight and moisture. Do not store in the bathroom.

LISINOPRIL/HCTZ

Common Brand Name: ZESTORETIC

Uses
ACE inhibitors prevent certain substances in the body from constricting blood vessels. This helps to lower blood pressure and makes the heart beat stronger. Thiazides are diuretics (water pills) that help to reduce blood pressure. This medication is used to treat hypertension (high blood pressure).

How to Use
This medication may be taken without regard to meals.

Take this medication exactly as prescribed. Try to take it at the same time each day.

Do not stop taking this medication without consulting your doctor. Some conditions may become worse when the drug is abruptly stopped. Your dose may need to be gradually decreased.

It is important to continue taking this medication even if you feel well. Most people with high blood pressure do not feel sick.

Side Effects
Dizziness, headache, diarrhea, constipation, loss of appetite, nausea, loss of taste, flushing, fatigue, cough or increased urination may occur. If these effects persist or worsen, notify your doctor.

This medication can increase sensitivity to sunlight.

To avoid dizziness and lightheadedness when rising from a seated or lying position, get up slowly.

Inform your doctor if you develop: chest pain; tingling of the hands or feet; swelling in your lips, tongue, and face.

In the unlikely event you have an allergic reaction to this drug, seek immediate medical attention. Symptoms of an allergic reaction include: rash, itching, swelling, dizziness, trouble breathing.

If you notice other effects not listed above, contact your doctor or pharmacist.

Precautions

Tell your doctor your medical history, especially if you have: scheduled medical or dental procedures, heart problems, allergies (especially sulfa drugs).

This medicine may make you more prone to sunburn. Wear protective clothing and a sunscreen.

Limit your intake of alcohol and avoid overheating because this can aggravate dizziness and lightheadedness.

Avoid "stimulant" drugs that may increase your heart rate such as decongestants or caffeine. Decongestants are commonly found in over-the-counter cough-and-cold medicine.

Drug Interactions

This drug is not recommended for use with dofetilide. Ask your doctor or pharmacist for more details.

Inform your doctor about all the medicine you use (both prescription and non-prescription), especially if you have: lithium, potassium supplements, potassium-sparing water pills, anti-inflammatory medicine (NSAIDs such as ibuprofen), digoxin.

If you take colestipol or cholestyramine, take this medicine 1 hour before or 4 hours after the cholesterol lowering medicine because of decreased absorption.

Do not start or stop any medicine without first consulting your doctor or pharmacist.

Notes

It is important to have your blood pressure checked regularly while taking this medication. Learn how to monitor your blood pressure. Discuss this with your doctor.

Missed Dose

If you miss a dose, take it as soon as you remember. If it is near the time of the next dose, skip the missed dose and resume your usual dosing schedule. Do not double the dose to catch up.

Storage

Store at room temperature away from sunlight and moisture.

LORATADINE

Common Brand Name: Claritin

Uses
Loratadine is an antihistamine that provides relief of symptoms of seasonal and allergic rhinitis such as watery eyes, runny nose, itching eyes, and sneezing. It is also used for hives.

How to Use
Take this medication by mouth once a day or as directed.

Do not increase your dose or take this more often than directed.

Do not take this medication for several days before allergy testing since test results can be affected.

Side Effects
This medication may cause headache, thirst, blurred vision, dry mouth and dry nose. These effects should decrease as your body adjusts to the medication. If they continue or become bothersome, inform your doctor.

Notify your doctor if you develop: rapid or pounding heartbeat, dizziness, unusual weakness.

Loratadine does not usually cause drowsiness when used at recommended doses and under normal circumstances. However, be sure of the drug's effects before engaging in activities that require alertness.

An allergic reaction to this drug is unlikely, but seek immediate medical attention if it occurs. Symptoms of an allergic reaction include: rash, itching, swelling, severe dizziness, trouble breathing.

May discolor urine (this is harmless).

If you notice other effects not listed above, contact your doctor or pharmacist.

Precautions
Tell your doctor if you have any of the following conditions: heart disease, kidney disease, liver disease, high blood pressure, breathing problems, any allergies.

Limit alcohol intake, as it may worsen drowsiness with this medication.

Drug Interactions

Tell your doctor of any over-the-counter or prescription medication you may take.

Do not start or stop any medicine without first consulting your doctor or pharmacist.

Notes

Do not share this medication with others.

Missed Dose

If you miss a dose, take it as soon as you remember. If it is near the time of the next dose, skip the missed dose and resume your usual dosing schedule. Do not double the dose to catch up.

Storage

Store at room temperature between 59 and 86 degrees F (15 to 30 degrees C) away from heat and light. Do not store in the bathroom.

LORATADINE WITH PSEUDOEPHEDRINE

Common Brand Names: CLARITIN-D 12 HOUR, CLARITIN-D 24 HOUR

Uses
Loratadine is an antihistamine that provides relief from symptoms of seasonal and allergic rhinitis (e.g., hay fever) such as watery eyes, runny nose, itching eyes and sneezing.

Pseudoephedrine is a decongestant that relieves congestion, promotes sinus draining and improves breathing.

How to Use
Swallow the tablet whole with a full glass of water.

Do not chew or crush the tablet, as doing so will destroy the long action and may increase the side effects.

Do not increase the dose or take this more frequently than prescribed.

Side Effects
May cause difficulty in sleeping, dry mouth, mild stomach upset, headache, nervousness, dizziness, loss of appetite or thirst. These effects should subside as your body adjusts to the medication. If they persist or become bothersome, inform your doctor.

Loratadine does not usually cause drowsiness when used at recommended doses and under normal circumstances. However, be sure of the drug's effects before engaging in activities that require alertness.

Notify your doctor if you develop: heart pounding, irregular heartbeat, chest pain, ringing in the ears, difficulty urinating.

An allergic reaction to this drug is unlikely, but seek immediate medical attention if it occurs. Symptoms of an allergic reaction include: rash, itching, swelling, severe dizziness, trouble breathing.

If you notice other effects not listed above, contact your doctor or pharmacist.

Precautions

If you have glaucoma, diabetes, difficulty urinating, an enlarged prostate gland, heart, kidney, liver, or respiratory disease, high blood pressure, an overactive thyroid gland or have serious difficulty in swallowing, do not use this drug unless your doctor knows of your medical condition.

Limit alcohol intake, as it may intensify drug side effects, especially drowsiness.

Drug Interactions

Tell your doctor of any over-the-counter or prescription medication you may take, especially if you have: high blood pressure drugs, antidepressants, sleeping pills, sedatives, tranquilizers, muscle relaxants, other cold or allergy medicines.

Do not take this drug if you have taken an monoamine oxidase inhibitor (e.g., furazolidone, linezolid, phenelzine, selegiline, tranylcypromine) within the last two weeks.

Do not start or stop any medicine without first consulting your doctor or pharmacist.

Notes

Do not share this product with others.

Missed Dose

If you miss a dose, take it as soon as you remember. If it is near the time of the next dose, skip the missed dose and resume your usual dosing schedule. Do not double the dose to catch up.

Storage

Store at room temperature away from sunlight and moisture. Do not store in the bathroom.

LORAZEPAM TABLET

Common Brand Name: Ativan

Uses
Lorazepam is used to treat anxiety.

How to Use
Take as directed. The dose and frequency of use will depend on your condition and response.

Long-term or excessive use of this medication can cause physical or psychological dependence (habit forming).

Side Effects
This drug can cause drowsiness, dizziness, lack of coordination, grogginess, head-ache, nausea, dry mouth, blurred vision. If these effects continue or become severe, contact your doctor.

Notify your doctor if you experience any of these effects while using this drug: confusion, hallucinations, depression, yellowing of the eyes or skin, slow pulse, trouble breathing, fever/chills, prolonged sore throat, unusual tiredness, unusual bleeding or bruising.

If you notice other effects not listed above, contact your doctor or pharmacist.

Precautions
Tell your doctor your medical history, especially if you have: heart disease, kidney or liver disease, lung disease or trouble breathing, muscle disorders, glaucoma, de-pression or psychiatric conditions, drug dependency, any allergies.

Use caution driving or performing tasks requiring alertness.

Older adults may be more sensitive to the effects of this medication.

Drug Interactions
Tell your doctor of all nonprescription and prescription drugs you take especially: narcotic pain relievers, sedatives, tranquilizers, sleeping pills, antidepressants,

seizure medication, barbiturates, theophylline. This drug may increase the sedative effects of these medications.

It is recommended to limit the use of alcohol while using this medication as excessive drowsiness can occur.

Do not start or stop any medicine without first consulting your doctor or pharmacist.

Missed Dose

If you miss a dose, take it as soon as you remember. If it is near the time of the next dose, skip the missed dose and resume your usual dosing schedule. Do not double the dose to catch up.

Storage

Store at controlled room temperature away from sun and moisture. Do not store in the bathroom.

LOSARTAN

Common Brand Name: COZAAR

Uses
This drug is used to treat high blood pressure (hypertension) and heart failure. It works by preventing the narrowing of blood vessels. High blood pressure reduction helps prevent strokes, heart attacks, and kidney problems.

How to Use
Take this medication by mouth as prescribed, and learn proper usage. Consult your pharmacist.

Be sure to follow the dosing instructions closely. Do not increase your dose, skip any doses or stop taking this without first consulting your doctor.

Before using potassium supplements or salt substitutes, consult your doctor or pharmacist.

It is important to continue taking this medication even if you do not feel sick. Most people with high blood pressure do not have any symptoms.

Side Effects
Infrequent side effects such as dizziness, diarrhea, stomach upset, stuffed nose or dry mouth may occur the first several days as your body adjusts to the medication. If any of these effects persist or worsen, contact your doctor.

Unlikely to occur but report promptly: abdominal pain, persistent sore throat, muscle weakness, unusual fatigue, joint or muscle aches, fever, major change in the amount of urine eliminated.

In the unlikely event you have an allergic reaction to this drug, seek immediate medical attention. Symptoms of an allergic reaction include: rash, itching, swelling, dizziness, breathing trouble.

If you notice other effects not listed above, contact your doctor or pharmacist.

Precautions
Tell your doctor your medical history, including kidney or liver disease, congestive heart failure, diabetes, allergies (especially drug allergies).

To avoid dizziness and lightheadedness when rising from a seated or lying position, get up slowly. Also limit your intake of alcoholic beverages which will aggravate these effects.

Use caution performing tasks requiring alertness if this medication causes you to feel dizzy.

Drug Interactions

Tell your doctor of all over-the-counter or prescription medication you may take including: other drugs for blood pressure (e.g., diuretics-"water pills"), aspirin or aspirin-related pain or fever drugs, drugs that can cause kidney problems.

Do not take any over-the-counter medication for allergies or cough or colds without consulting your doctor or pharmacist. Many of the products contain ingredients which may interact with the effects of this medication.

Do not start or stop any medicine without first consulting your doctor or pharmacist.

Notes

Laboratory tests will be done periodically to be sure the drug is working properly and to monitor for possible side effects.

Learn how to monitor your pulse and blood pressure. Talk to your health care professional about this.

Missed Dose

If you miss a dose, take it as soon as you remember. If it is near the time of the next dose, skip the missed dose and resume your usual dosing schedule. Do not double the dose to catch up.

Storage

Store at room temperature between 59 and 86 degrees F (15 to 30 degrees C) away from heat and light. Do not store in the bathroom.

LOSARTAN/HCTZ

Common Brand Name: HYZAAR

Uses
This medication is used to treat high blood pressure (hypertension) and congestive heart failure.

How to Use
Take this medication by mouth as prescribed, usually once or twice a day. It may be taken with or without food. Your dosage depends on your medical condition and response to the drug.

Be sure to follow the dosing instructions closely. Do not increase your dose, skip any doses or stop taking this without first consulting your doctor.

It is important to continue taking this medication even if you do not feel sick. Many people with high blood pressure do not have any symptoms.

The full benefit of this drugs usually occurs within 4 weeks.

Before using potassium supplements or salt substitutes, consult your doctor or pharmacist.

Side Effects
Nausea or vomiting, dry mouth, headache, fatigue or diarrhea may occur. If these effects persist or worsen, notify your doctor promptly.

Report promptly: lightheadedness or dizziness, muscle weakness or cramping.

Unlikely but report promptly: stomach pain, unusual change in amount of urine (after the first several days), unusual thirst, fainting, mental/mood changes.

Very unlikely but report promptly: persistent sore throat or cough, fever, unusual bleeding or bruising, swelling of the lips and tongue, chest pain, rapid heartbeat, joint pain.

In the unlikely event you have an allergic reaction to this product, seek immediate medical attention. Symptoms of an allergic reaction include: rash, itching, swelling, dizziness, trouble breathing.

If you notice other effects not listed above, contact your doctor or pharmacist.

Precautions

Tell your doctor your medical history, especially if you have: kidney problems, heart disease, liver problems, diabetes, gout, high cholesterol or lipids (triglycerides), lupus, metabolic problems (e.g., potassium or sodium imbalances), allergies (especially to sulfa drugs).

Use caution performing tasks requiring alertness if this medication makes you dizzy.

To avoid dizziness and lightheadedness when rising from a seated or lying position, get up slowly. Also, limit your intake of alcoholic beverages which can intensify these effects.

Excessive loss of body fluids (e.g., sweating or diarrhea) can cause a drop in blood pressure and make you lightheaded. Avoid excessive exercise. Consult your doctor or pharmacist.

Hydrochlorothiazide may increase sensitivity to sunlight.

Avoid prolonged sun exposure. If you become sun sensitive, use a sunscreen and wear protective clothing when outdoors.

Caution is advised when this product is used with older people since this group may be more sensitive to drug side effects.

Drug Interactions

This drug is not recommended for use with dofetilide. Ask your doctor or pharmacist for more details.

Tell your doctor of all prescription and nonprescription medications you may use, especially if you have: potassium supplements (including salt substitutes with potassium), other blood pressure drugs, lithium, barbiturates (e.g., phenobarbital), drugs used for diabetes, colestipol, cholestyramine, NSAIDs (e.g., ibuprofen, naproxen, aspirin), ACTH, corticosteroids (e.g., prednisone), drugs that cause kidney problems, allergy or cough-and-cold products (e.g., pseudoephedrine).

Do not start or stop any medicine without first consulting your doctor or pharmacist.

Notes

Laboratory tests will be done periodically to check your progress and monitor for adverse effects.

Learn to monitor your pulse and blood pressure. Talk to your health care professional about this.

Do not share this medication with others.

Missed Dose

If you miss a dose, take it as soon as you remember. If it is near the time of the next dose, skip the missed dose and resume your usual dosing schedule. Do not double the dose to catch up.

Storage

Store at room temperature below 86 degrees F (30 degrees C) away from light and moisture.

MECLIZINE

Common Brand Name: Antivert

Uses
This medication is used to prevent or treat nausea, vomiting and dizziness caused by motion sickness or middle ear infections.

How to Use
For motion sickness, take the first dose 30 minutes before traveling. For other conditions, take exactly as directed by your doctor.

Chewable tablets must be chewed thoroughly before swallowing.

Side Effects
May cause drowsiness, blurred vision, stomach upset, constipation, confusion, urinary retention, headache or dry mouth. These effects should subside as your body adjusts to the medication. If they persist or become bothersome, inform your doctor.

Since this medication may cause drowsiness, use caution engaging in activities requiring alertness.

If you notice other effects not listed above, contact your doctor or pharmacist.

Precautions
Tell your doctor your medical history, especially if you have: glaucoma, prostate problems, urinary problems, asthma, any allergies you have.

Alcohol may intensify the drowsiness effect of this drug.

Limit alcohol intake and use caution performing tasks that require alertness such as driving and operating machinery.

Drug Interactions
Tell your doctor of all prescription and nonprescription drugs you may use, especially of drugs that have a drowsiness effect such as: medications for cough/colds and allergies, drugs used for sleep, anti-seizure medications, narcotic pain drugs (e.g., codeine), barbiturates (e.g., phenobarbital), tranquilizers.

Do not start or stop any medicine without first consulting your doctor or phar-macist.

Notes
Older adults are most sensitive to the adverse effects of this agent.

Missed Dose
If you miss a dose, take it as soon as you remember. If it is near the time of the next dose, skip the missed dose and resume your usual dosing schedule. Do not double the dose to catch up.

Storage
Store at room temperature away from sunlight and moisture.

MEDROXYPROGESTERONE

Common Brand Names: Provera, Cycrin

Uses
This medication is a female hormone. It is used to treat abnormal bleeding from the uterus, or endometriosis (a painful condition where the lining of the uterus is abnormal). It is also used to treat certain types of cancer, and menopausal symptoms as part of hormone replacement therapy (HRT). Progestins lower the risk of estrogen-related cancer of the uterus.

How to Use
May be taken with food or immediately after a meal to prevent stomach upset.

Take this medication as prescribed. It is usually taken for 5 to 13 days during the later end of month when estrogen is taken each day on days 1 through 25 of the month. Provera may also be taken every day without stopping. Your doctor will determine what regimen is best for you. For treatment of cancer, the medication is usually taken more often. Follow the dosing schedule carefully.

Be sure to ask your doctor if you have any questions.

Side Effects
This medication may cause nausea, vomiting, headache, dizziness, depression, sleeplessness, or irritability.

These effects should disappear as your body adjusts to the medication. If they persist or become severe, inform your doctor.

Notify your doctor promptly if you experience any of the following effects: dizziness or fainting, sudden severe headache, changes in vision, numbness or tingling in the arms or legs, swelling of the hands or feet, acute chest pain, shortness of breath, pain in the calves accompanied by swelling/warmth/ redness, changes in vaginal bleeding (spotting, breakthrough bleeding, prolonged or complete stoppage of bleeding).

If you notice other effects not listed above, contact your doctor or pharmacist.

Precautions
Before you take this medication, tell your doctor your medical history, including: high blood pressure, seizures, migraine headaches, diabetes, asthma, heart disease, liver or kidney disease, strokes, blood clots, heart attacks, cancer of the breast or genitals, high blood level of cholesterol or fats, depression, jaundice (yellowing of skin or eyes).

Drug Interactions
Tell your doctor what prescription and nonprescription drugs you are taking.

Do not start or stop any medicine without first consulting your doctor or pharmacist.

Notes
It is important to have an annual physical exam and do regular self breast examinations while taking this medication.

Patient information should be included with the medication. Some women may experience menstrual bleeding each month, 3 to 10 days after this drug is stopped.

Read it carefully and ask your doctor or pharmacist about any questions you may have.

Missed Dose
If you miss a dose, take it as soon as you remember. If it is near the time of the next dose, skip the missed dose and resume your usual dosing schedule. Do not double the dose to catch up.

Storage
Store at room temperature between 59 and 86 degrees F (between 15 and 30 degrees C) away from moisture and sunlight. Do not store in the bathroom.

METAXALONE

Common Brand Name: SKELAXIN

Uses
This medication relaxes muscles and relieves pain and discomfort associated with strains, sprains, spasms or other muscle injuries.

How to Use
May be taken with food or immediately after meals to prevent stomach upset.

Do not increase your dose, take it more frequently or take it for a longer period of time than prescribed by your doctor.

Side Effects
May cause stomach upset, heartburn, constipation, headache, dizziness or drowsiness the first few days as your body adjusts to the medication. If these symptoms persist or become severe, notify your doctor.

Inform your doctor if you develop: persistent stomach pain, skin rash, itching, rapid heart rate, yellowing of eyes or skin.

May discolor urine. This will disappear when the medication is stopped.

In the unlikely event you have an allergic reaction to this drug, seek immediate medical attention. Symptoms of an allergic reaction include: rash, itching, swelling, dizziness, trouble breathing.

If you notice other effects not listed above, contact your doctor or pharmacist.

Precautions
Tell your doctor your medical history, especially if you have: seizures, kidney or liver disease, any drug allergies.

Alcoholic beverages may increase the dizziness/drowsiness effects of this drug. Limit alcohol intake. Use caution engaging in activities requiring alertness such as driving or operating machinery.

When arising quickly from a sitting or lying position, this drug may cause dizziness/lightheadedness. Change positions slowly.

Drug Interactions

Tell your doctor of any over-the-counter or prescription medication you take including any medication such as: sedatives, tranquilizers, narcotics (pain medication), sleeping pills, medication for seizures, depression, allergies, hay fever, colds.

Do not start taking any of the drugs mentioned above without consulting your doctor.

Do not start or stop any medicine without first consulting your doctor or pharmacist.

Notes

This medication provides temporary relief and must be used in addition to rest, physical therapy and other measures as directed by your doctor.

Do not allow anyone else to take this medication.

Missed Dose

If you miss a dose, take it as soon as you remember. If it is near the time of the next dose, skip the missed dose and resume your usual dosing schedule. Do not double the dose to catch up.

Storage

Store at room temperature between 59 and 86 degrees F (between 15 and 30 degrees C) away from moisture and sunlight. Do not store in the bathroom.

METFORMIN

Common Brand Name: Glucophage

Uses

Metformin works by lowering the level of glucose (sugar) in the blood. Metformin is used along with diet and exercise programs to control high blood sugar in diabetic patients.

How to Use

This is best taken with meals. Try to take this medication at the same time(s) each day.

The long-acting form of this medication must be swallowed whole; do not crush or chew the tablets.

Side Effects

Nausea, stomach upset, diarrhea or metallic taste may occur as your body adjusts to the medication. If any of these effects persist or worsen, notify your doctor promptly.

Notify your doctor immediately if you develop: chills, weakness, change in heart rate, breathing problems, sleepiness, muscle pain, vomiting.

This medication may, but usually does not, cause low blood sugar (hypoglycemia) which manifests as dizziness, weakness, drowsiness, headache, sweating, nervousness, shaking, tingling of hands or feet, hunger, increased pulse rate or rapid heart rate.

However, should these symptoms occur, drink a glass of orange juice or non-diet soda or eat a piece of candy to raise your blood sugar level quickly. Report the incident to your doctor. To help prevent low blood sugar, eat meals on a regular schedule and do not skip meals.

Symptoms of high blood sugar (hyperglycemia) include confusion, drowsiness, flushing, rapid breathing or fruity breath odor. Notify your doctor if you experience any of these symptoms.

If you notice other effects not listed above, contact your doctor or pharmacist.

Precautions

Tell your doctor your medical history, especially if you have: liver disease, lung problems, kidney problems, heart disease, strokes, major surgery, allergies.

Notify your doctor if you become ill, are injured or acquire a severe infection.

Limit alcohol intake while using this medication as alcohol can increase the effect of metformin on lowering blood sugar.

Drug Interactions

Tell your doctor of any over-the-counter or prescription medication you may take. Certain drugs may increase your blood sugar. Inform your doctor if you are taking: diazoxide, beta-blockers, diuretics, corticosteroids (e.g., prednisone-like drugs), niacin, phenytoin, decongestants, diet pills.

If you are scheduled to undergo any diagnostic procedure using iodinated contrast material (contrast dye with x-rays), be sure to inform your doctor that you are taking metformin. Metformin may need to be stopped before the test is performed.

Do not start or stop any medicine without first consulting your doctor or pharmacist.

Notes

This medication is not a substitute for proper diet and exercise. It is recommended to attend a diabetes education program to understand diabetes and all aspects of its treatment including diet, exercise, personal hygiene, medications and getting regular eye exams.

While taking this medication, periodic laboratory tests will be done to monitor therapy and prevent side effects.

Controlling high blood sugar helps prevent heart disease, strokes, kidney disease and circulation problems.

Missed Dose

If you miss a dose, take it as soon as you remember. If it is near the time of the next dose, skip the missed dose and resume your usual dosing schedule. Do not double the dose to catch up.

Storage

Store this medication at room temperature between 59 and 86 degrees F (15 and 30 degrees C) away from heat, light and moisture. Do not store in the bathroom. Keep this and all medications out of the reach of children.

METHYLPHENIDATE

Common Brand Names: Ritalin, Concerta

Uses
Methylphenidate increases mental alertness. It is used in those who have problems staying awake (narcolepsy) and for attention-deficit hyperactivity disorder (ADHD).

How to Use
This medication is best taken 30 to 45 minutes before a meal or take as directed by your doctor. Dosage depends on your condition and response to this medication.

If loss of appetite occurs or if you experience stomach upset, it may be taken with or after meals or a snack. The last dose should be given several hours before bedtime.

Use this medication exactly as prescribed. Do not increase your dose, use it more frequently or use it for a longer period of time than prescribed because this drug can be habit-forming.

Also, if used for a long period of time, do not suddenly stop using this without first consulting your doctor.

When used for extended periods, this medication may not work as well and may require different dosing. Consult your doctor if the medication isn't working well.

Side Effects
Loss of appetite, blurred vision, dizziness, lightheadedness, dry mouth, stomach upset, sleeplessness, irritability or constipation may occur the first few days as your body adjusts to the medication. If these effects persist or worsen, inform your doctor.

Notify your doctor if you experience: weight loss, chest pain, nervousness, pounding heart, difficulty urinating, mood changes.

In the unlikely event you have an allergic reaction to this drug, seek immediate medical attention. Symptoms of an allergic reaction include: rash, itching, swelling, dizziness, trouble breathing.

If you notice other effects not listed above, contact your doctor or pharmacist.

Precautions

Tell your doctor your medical history, especially seizures or motor tics, Tourette's disorder, glaucoma, high blood pressure, severe anxiety, alcoholism, drug dependence, mental conditions, any allergies.

If this medication makes you dizzy or lightheaded, use caution driving or engaging in activities requiring alertness.

Drug Interactions

MAO inhibitors (e.g., furazolidone, phenelzine, selegiline, linezolid, tranylcypromine) taken with this medicine could result in serious, even fatal, interactions.

Tell your doctor of all nonprescription and prescription drugs you may use, especially: "blood thinners" (e.g., warfarin), medications for seizures, medicine for depression (tricyclics such as amitriptyline), high blood pressure medicine (e.g., guanethidine).

Do not start or stop any medicine without first consulting your doctor or pharmacist.

Notes

Do not allow anyone else to take this medication. Do not chew or crush the sustained release form. Methylphenidate is used with older people who are withdrawn, apathetic, and disinterested in their activities.

Missed Dose

If you miss a dose, take it as soon as you remember. If it is near the time of the next dose, skip the missed dose and resume your usual dosing schedule. Do not double the dose to catch up.

Storage

Store at room temperature between 59 and 86 degrees F (between 15 and 30 degrees C) away from moisture and sunlight. Do not store in the bathroom.

METHYLPREDNISOLONE

Common Brand Name: Medrol

Uses
This medication is a corticosteroid. It reduces swelling.

It is used for many conditions, among them: allergic reactions, hives, skin diseases (psoriasis) breathing problems; certain cancers, blood disorders, and eye problems; arthritis, digestive problems, and for hormone replacement.

How to Use
Take with food or immediately after a meal to prevent stomach upset.

Take this medication as prescribed. Follow the dosing schedule carefully. Be sure to ask your doctor if you have any questions.

If you are taking this medication only once a day, it should be taken in the morning before 9 a.m.

The liquid (suspension) form must be shaken well before each use. First use of suspension may require shaking for 5 to 7 minutes. After the first use, no more than 30 seconds of shaking should be required to mix all the ingredients well.

If you have been taking this medication for a long time, do not suddenly stop taking it without your doctor's approval. Your dose may need to be gradually reduced. You may experience extreme fatigue, weakness, stomach upset or dizziness when the medication is suddenly stopped.

Side Effects
May cause dizziness, nausea, indigestion, increased appetite, weight gain, weakness or sleep disturbances.

These effects should disappear as your body adjusts to the medication. If they persist or become bothersome, inform your doctor.

Notify your doctor if you experience: vomiting of blood, black or tarry stools, puffing of the face, swelling of the ankles or feet, unusual weight gain, prolonged sore throat or fever, muscle weakness, breathing difficulties, mood changes, vision changes.

In the unlikely event you have an allergic reaction to this drug, seek medical attention immediately. Symptoms of an allergic reaction include rash: itching, swelling, dizziness, trouble breathing.

If you notice other effects not listed above, contact your doctor or pharmacist.

Precautions

Before using this drug, tell your doctor your medical history, particularly if you have: liver or kidney disease, heart problems, intestinal problems, ulcers, diabetes, high blood pressure, an underactive thyroid gland, myasthenia gravis, herpes eye infection, a history of tuberculosis (TB), seizures, blood clots, osteoporosis (brittle bones), eye problems, any allergies.

Do not have a vaccination, other immunization or any skin test (e.g. tuberculosis) while you are using this drug unless your doctor specifically tells you that you may.

Avoid persons with chickenpox or measles infection while taking this drug. If you have a history of ulcers or take large doses of aspirin or other arthritis medication, limit your consumption of alcoholic beverages while taking this medication. It may make your stomach and intestines more susceptible to the irritating effects of alcohol, aspirin, and certain arthritis medications, increasing your risk of ulcers.

Report any injuries or signs of infection (fever, sore throat, pain during urination, and muscle aches) that occur during treatment and within 12 months after treatment with this drug.

Your dose may need to be adjusted or you may need to start taking the drug again.

If you have diabetes, this drug may increase your blood sugar level. Check your blood (or urine) glucose level frequently, as directed by your doctor. Promptly report any abnormal results as directed. Your medicine, exercise plan, or diet may be adjusted.

If the phlegm (sputum) you cough up when ill becomes thickened or changes color from clear white to yellow, green, or gray, contact your doctor; these changes may be signs of an infection.

Drug Interactions

Before you take this drug, tell your doctor of any over-the-counter or prescription medications you are taking especially: aspirin, arthritis medication, anticoagulants (warfarin) diuretics ("water pills"), rifampin, phenobarbital, estrogens, phenytoin, ketoconazole, neostigmine, pyridostigmine, ambenonium, drugs for diabetes.

Do not start or stop any medicine without first consulting your doctor or pharmacist.

Notes
Persons taking this medication for long-term therapy should wear or carry identification stating that they are taking a corticosteroid.

Missed Dose
If you miss a dose, take it as soon as you remember. If it is near the time of the next dose, skip the missed dose and resume your usual dosing schedule. Do not double the dose to catch up.

Storage
Store at room temperature between 59 and 86 degrees F (between 15 and 30 degrees C) away from moisture and sunlight. Do not store in the bathroom. Do not freeze liquid forms of this medication.

Certain liquid forms may require refrigeration. Consult your pharmacist.

METOCLOPRAMIDE 10MG TAB

Common Brand Name: Reglan

Uses
Metoclopramide is used to relieve certain stomach-and-esophagus problems such as diabetic gastroparesis and gastroesophageal reflux disorder (GERD).

How to Use
Take this medication by mouth as directed by your doctor. Metoclopramide works best when taken 30 minutes before a meal. Your dosage depends on your condition and response to the medication.

Do not take this more often or in larger doses than prescribed by your doctor.

Side Effects
Nausea, diarrhea, headache, dizziness, drowsiness, dry mouth, restlessness or sleeplessness may occur. If any of these effects persist or worsen, inform your doctor.

Notify your doctor if you experience: involuntary movements of the eyes/face/limbs, muscle spasms, trembling of the hands.

Also, notify your doctor if you experience the following: any personality changes such as depression.

In the unlikely event you have an allergic reaction to this drug, seek immediate medical attention. Symptoms of an allergic reaction include: rash, itching, swelling, dizziness, trouble breathing.

If you notice other effects not listed above, contact your doctor or pharmacist.

Precautions
Tell your doctor your medical history, especially adrenal tumors, seizure disorders, Parkinson's disease, high blood pressure, heart disease, liver disease, kidney disease, mental problems or depression, intestinal/stomach blockage or bleeding, diabetes, asthma, any allergies.

Use caution engaging in activities requiring alertness such as driving or using machinery.

Alcoholic beverages can add to the drowsiness effect caused by this drug. Avoid alcohol while taking this medication.

Drug Interactions
Tell your doctor of all medicines you may use (both prescription and nonprescription), especially: cimetidine, insulin, cabergoline, cyclosporine, digoxin, levodopa, MAO inhibitors (e.g., furazolidone, linezolid, moclobemide, phenelzine, procarbazine, selegiline), drugs that may add to the drowsiness effect of metoclopramide (narcotic pain medications, medications, tranquilizers, sleep medicines, antidepressants, drowsiness-causing antihistamines such as diphenhydramine), alcoholic beverages.

Before having surgery with a general anesthetic, including dental surgery, tell the doctor or dentist in charge you are taking metoclopramide.

Do not start or stop any medicine without first consulting your doctor or pharmacist.

Notes
Do not share this medication with others.

Missed Dose
If you miss a dose, take it as soon as you remember. If it is near the time of the next dose, skip the missed dose and resume your usual dosing schedule. Do not double the dose to catch up.

Storage
Store at room temperature between 68 and 78 degrees F (between 20 and 25 degrees C) away from moisture and sunlight. Do not store in the bathroom. Do not freeze liquid forms.

METOPROLOL

Common Brand Names: Toprol XL, Lopressor

Uses
This medication is used for chest pain (angina), high blood pressure and irregular heartbeats, and after a heart attack to help prevent another attack.

How to Use
Take this medication exactly as prescribed. Try to take it at the same time(s) each day.

Do not suddenly stop taking this medication without consulting your doctor. Your doctor many want you to reduce gradually the amount that your are taking before it is stopped completely. Some conditions may become worse when the drug is suddenly stopped.

Side Effects
You may experience dizziness, lightheadedness, fatigue, drowsiness, and blurred vision as your body adjusts to the medication. Use caution engaging in activities requiring alertness.

Because beta-blockers reduce blood circulation to the extremities, your hands and feet may be more susceptible to cold temperatures. Dress warm.

Inform your doctor if you develop: easy bruising or bleeding, shortness of breath, swollen hands or feet, confusion, depression, a prolonged sore throat.

In the unlikely event you have an allergic reaction to this drug, seek medical attention immediately. Symptoms of an allergic reaction include: rash, itching, swelling, dizziness, trouble breathing.

If you notice other effects not listed above, contact your doctor or pharmacist.

Precautions
Before taking this drug, tell your doctor if you have a history of: heart disease, kidney disease, liver disease, asthma, bronchitis, emphysema, any other lung disease, diabetes, overactive thyroid gland, any drug allergies.

Before having surgery, tell the doctor or dentist in charge that you are taking a beta-blocker.

In persons with diabetes, this medicine may cover up signs of low blood sugar (e.g., sweating, increased pulse rate).

Drug Interactions
Tell your doctor of all prescription and nonprescription drugs you may use, especially if you have: diuretics, cold preparations and nasal decongestants, reserpine, other heart or high blood pressure medications, St John's wort.

Do not start or stop any medicine without first consulting your doctor. or pharmacist.

Notes
Your doctor may want you to take your pulse each day while you take this medication. Learn how to monitor your pulse.

Missed Dose
If you miss a dose, take it as soon as you remember. If it is near the time of the next dose, skip the missed dose and resume your usual dosing schedule. Do not double the dose to catch up.

Storage
Store at room temperature between 59 and 86 degrees F (between 15 and 30 degrees C) away from moisture and sunlight. Do not store in the bathroom.

METRONIDAZOLE

Common Brand Name: Flagyl

Uses
Metronidazole is an antibiotic used to treat a variety of infections and in the treatment of peptic ulcers.

How to Use
This medication should be taken with food or a full glass of water or milk to prevent stomach upset.

Antibiotics work best when the amount of medicine in your body is kept at a constant level. Do this by taking the medication at evenly spaced intervals throughout the day and night.

Continue to take this medication until the full prescribed amount is finished even if symptoms disappear after a few days.

Stopping the medication too early may allow bacteria to continue to grow resulting in a relapse of the infection.

Side Effects
Dizziness, headache, diarrhea, nausea, stomach pain, change in taste sensation or dry mouth may occur. If these effects persist or worsen, contact your doctor.

Unlikely but report: seizures, loss of consciousness, metallic taste in the mouth, tingling of hands or feet.

Very unlikely but report: unsteadiness, mood/mental changes, rash, itching, sore throat, fever, severe stomach pain, vomiting, vaginal irritation.

This drug may cause urine to darken in color. This is not harmful.

In the unlikely event you have an allergic reaction to this drug, seek immediate medical attention. Symptoms of an allergic reaction include: rash, itching, swelling, dizziness, trouble breathing.

If you notice other effects not listed above, contact your doctor or pharmacist.

Precautions

Tell your doctor your medical history especially if you have: liver problems, seizure disorders, any allergies.

Use of this medication for prolonged or repeated periods may result in a secondary infection (e.g., oral or bladder infection).

Avoid alcoholic beverages or products containing alcohol (e.g., cough and cold preparations) while taking this medication and for at least 3 days after finishing this medicine because severe stomach upset, nausea, vomiting, headache, and flushing may occur.

Drug Interactions

Inform your doctor about all the medicines you may use (both prescription and nonprescription) especially if you take: phenobarbital, "blood thinners" (e.g., warfarin, phenytoin, lithium).

Do not take this medicine if you are currently taking disulfiram. Contact your doctor.

Do not start or stop any medicine without first consulting your doctor or pharmacist.

Notes

Treatment of certain infections (trichomoniasis), may require that sexual partners be treated as well to avoid reinfection. During therapy, refrain from sexual intercourse or wear a condom.

This medication has been prescribed for your current condition only. Do not use it later for another infection or give it to someone else. A different medication may be necessary in those cases.

Missed Dose

If you miss a dose, take it as soon as you remember. If it is near the time of the next dose, skip the missed dose and resume your usual dosing schedule. Do not double the dose to catch up.

Storage

Store at room temperature away from moisture and sunlight. Do not store in the bathroom.

MINOCYCLINE

Common Brand Name: Minocin

Uses
Minocycline is an antibiotic used to treat a wide variety of bacterial infections including acne.

How to Use
Take each dose by mouth with a full glass of water (4oz. or 120ml) or more. Food or milk taken with this medicine may reduce the amount of this drug reaching your bloodstream. This interaction is unlikely to affect your treatment but consult your doctor or pharmacist for advice (especially if you have stomach upset). Follow all directions exactly.

The liquid suspension form of this medicine must be shaken well before each dose.

Avoid taking antacids containing magnesium, aluminum and calcium, or iron products, zinc (including vitamins) and sucralfate within 2-3 hours of taking this medication. These products may bind with the medicine, preventing absorption.

Antibiotics work best when the amount of medicine in your body is kept at a constant level. Do this by taking the medication at evenly spaced intervals throughout the day and night.

Continue to take this medication until the full prescribed amount is finished even if symptoms disappear after a few days.

Stopping the medication too early may allow bacteria to continue to grow resulting in a relapse of the infection.

Side Effects
This medication may cause stomach upset, diarrhea, dizziness, unsteadiness, drowsiness, headache or vomiting. If these symptoms persist or worsen, notify your doctor.

Minocycline increases sensitivity to sunlight. Avoid prolonged sun exposure.

Very unlikely but report: fever, stomach pain, sore throat, vision changes, mental changes.

In the unlikely event you have an allergic reaction to this drug, seek immediate medical attention. Symptoms of an allergic reaction include: rash, itching, swelling, severe dizziness, trouble breathing.

If you notice other effects not listed above, contact your doctor or pharmacist.

Precautions

Tell your doctor your medical history, especially if you have: kidney or liver problems, any allergies, trouble swallowing or esophagus problems (e.g., hiatal hernia, GERD).

Use of this medication for prolonged or repeated periods may result in a secondary infection (e.g., oral or bladder infection).

To minimize dizziness and lightheadedness, get up slowly when rising from a seated or lying position.

This drug may make you dizzy or drowsy; use caution engaging in activities requiring alertness such as driving or using machinery. Limit alcoholic beverages.

Minocycline may make you more prone to sunburn. Wear protective clothing and a sunscreen.

Drug Interactions

Inform your doctor about all the medicines you may use (both prescription and nonprescription), especially if you have: penicillin-type antibiotics, warfarin, antacids, iron, vitamins (zinc), sucralfate.

Do not start or stop any medicine without first consulting your doctor or pharmacist.

Notes

This medication has been prescribed for your current condition only. Do not use it later for another infection or give it to someone else. A different medication may be necessary.

Missed Dose

If you miss a dose, take it as soon as you remember. If it is near the time of the next dose, skip the missed dose and resume your usual dosing schedule. Do not double the dose to catch up.

Storage

Store at room temperature away from sunlight and moisture.

MIRTAZAPINE

Common Brand Name: Remeron

Uses
Mirtazapine is used to treat depression.

How to Use
Take this medication by mouth once daily preferably at bedtime, or as directed by your doctor. The dosage is based on your medical condition and response to therapy.

It may take up to two weeks before the full benefit of this drug takes effect. Therefore, do not increase your dose or take it more frequently than prescribed. Consult your doctor.

Side Effects
Drowsiness, dizziness, dry mouth, constipation, increased appetite, or weight gain may occur. If any of these effects persist or worsen, notify your doctor.

Tell your doctor immediately if any of these serious side effects occur: swelling of hands or feet, muscle pain, mental/mood changes.

Tell your doctor immediately if any of these unlikely but serious side effects occur: back pain, shakiness (tremor), increased urination.

Tell your doctor immediately if any of these highly unlikely but very serious side effects occur: persistent sore throat or fever, chills, trouble breathing, chest pain.

If you notice other effects not listed above, contact your doctor or pharmacist.

Precautions
Tell your doctor your medical history, especially if you have: kidney problems, liver problems, other mental/mood conditions (e.g., bipolar disorder), seizures, heart disease, strokes, high cholesterol, any allergies.

This drug may make you dizzy or drowsy; use caution engaging in activities requiring alertness such as driving or using machinery. Limit alcoholic beverages.

To minimize dizziness and lightheadedness, get up slowly when rising from a seated or lying position.

Caution is advised when using this drug with older people because they may be more sensitive to the effects of the drug.

Drug Interactions

Tell your doctor of all prescription and nonprescription medication you may use.

Certain medications taken with this product could result in serious, even fatal, drug interactions. Do not take MAO inhibitors (e.g., furazolidone, linezolid, moclobemide, phenelzine, procarbazine, selegiline, isocarboxazid, tranylcypromine) for at least 14 days before or after taking this medication. Consult your pharmacist.

Tell your doctor if you take any drugs that cause drowsiness such as: medicine for sleep, tranquilizers, anti-anxiety drugs (e.g., diazepam), narcotic pain relievers (e.g., codeine), psychiatric medicines (e.g., phenothiazines such as chlorpromazine or tricyclics such as amitriptyline), anti-seizure drugs (e.g., carbamazepine), muscle relaxants, certain antihistamines (e.g., diphenhydramine).

Check the label on all your medicines (e.g., cough-and-cold products) because they may contain drowsiness-causing ingredients. Ask your pharmacist about the safe use of these products.

Do not start or stop any medicine without first consulting your doctor or pharmacist.

Notes

Do not share this medication with others.

Laboratory and/or medical tests may be performed to monitor your progress.

Missed Dose

If you miss a dose, take it as soon as you remember. If it is near the time of the next dose, skip the missed dose and resume your usual dosing schedule. Do not double the dose to catch up.

Storage

Store at room temperature between 59 and 86 degrees F (2 to 30 degrees C) away from light and moisture.

MOMETASONE

Common Brand Names: ELOCON, Nasonex

Uses
This medication is used to treat swelling, inflammation, or itching of skin conditions such as eczema, dermatitis, rashes, insect bites, poison ivy, allergies, and other irritations.

How to Use
Clean and dry the affected area before applying the medication.

To apply, gently massage a small amount of the medication into the affected area and surrounding skin.

Do not bandage, wrap, or cover the area treated unless you are instructed to do so by your doctor.

Avoid using this medication around the eyes unless directed to do so by your doctor.

Side Effects
This medication may cause burning, stinging, itching or redness when first applied to the skin. This should disappear in a few days as your body adjusts to the medication.

If these effects persist or worsen, inform your doctor.

Skin infections can become worse when using this medication.

Notify your doctor if redness, swelling or irritation does not improve.

Very unlikely to occur but report promptly the following side effects: unusual weakness, weight loss, nausea/vomiting, fainting, dizziness.

If you notice other effects not listed above, contact your doctor or pharmacist.

Precautions
Do not use this medication near the eyes if you have glaucoma.

Treatment with clobetasol, halobetasol propionate and augmented betamethasone dipropionate beyond two weeks consecutively is not recommended.

Do not use if there is an infection or sores present on the area to be treated.

Though very unlikely, it is possible this medication will be absorbed into your bloodstream. This may have undesirable consequences that may require additional corticosteroid treatment. This is especially if they also have serious medical problems such as serious infections, injuries or surgeries. This precaution applies for up to one year after stopping use of this drug. Consult your doctor or pharmacist for more details.

Drug Interactions
Tell your doctor of all medications you may use, (both prescription and nonprescription), especially if you have: prednisone (or similar drugs), other skin medicines.

Do not start or stop any medicine without first consulting your doctor or pharmacist.

Notes
Inform all your doctors you use (or have used) this medication.

Do not share this medication with others.

Missed Dose
If you miss a dose, take it as soon as you remember. If it is near the time of the next dose, skip the missed dose and resume your usual dosing schedule. Do not double the dose to catch up.

Storage
Store at room temperature away from sunlight. Avoid freezing.

MORPHINE SULFATE SUSTAINED-RELEASE

Common Brand Names: MS Contin, Oramorph SR

Uses
This medication is used to relieve moderate-to-severe pain.

How to Use
To prevent upset stomach, take with food or milk.

Swallow tablets whole. Do not chew or crush them or dissolve them in liquid.

Pain medications work best in preventing pain before it occurs. Take this medicine regularly to most effectively relieve pain.

Use this medication exactly as directed by your doctor. Do not increase your dose, use it more frequently or use it for a longer period of time than prescribed because this drug can be habit-forming. Also, if used for an extended period, do not suddenly stop using this drug without your doctor's approval.

Sudden discontinuation may cause withdrawal side effects.

Side Effects
May cause constipation, lightheadedness, dizziness, drowsiness, stomach upset, nausea, decrease in urination, and dryness of the mouth for the first few days as your body adjusts to the medication. If these symptoms persist or become bothersome, inform your doctor.

Notify your doctor if you develop: irregular heartbeat, anxiety, tremors, seizures or excessive drowsiness.

In the unlikely event you have an allergic reaction to this drug, seek immediate medical attention. Symptoms of an allergic reaction include: rash, itching, swelling, dizziness, trouble breathing.

If you notice other effects not listed above, contact your doctor or pharmacist.

Precautions

Tell your doctor your medical history, especially if you have: kidney or liver disease, breathing problems, history of alcohol and/or drug use, colitis or other intestinal/stomach problems, severe diarrhea, head injury, heart problems, drug allergies.

Use caution when engaging in activities requiring alertness such as driving. Limit alcohol intake because it may add to the dizziness/drowsiness effects of this medication. Older adults may be more sesitive to the effects of this drug.

Drug Interactions

Tell your doctor of all drugs you are taking, both prescription and nonprescription, especially if you have: alcohol-containing drugs, tranquilizers, antidepressants, buprenorphine, seizure medications, naltrexone, zidovudine, monoamine oxidase (MAO) inhibitors (e.g., furazolidone, linezolid, phenelzine, selegiline, tranylcypromine), cimetidine. The drug will add to the sedative effects of other drugs that you may be taking, including non-prescription allergy cough and cold and sleep medicines.

Do not start or stop any medicine without first consulting your doctor or pharmacist.

Notes

To prevent constipation increase your intake of fiber, drink plenty of water and exercise. Stool softeners may be helpful and laxatives may be needed to avoid constipation with this drug. Consult your doctor or pharmacist for more information.

Do not allow anyone else to take your medication: it is against the law.

Missed Dose

If you miss a dose, take it as soon as you remember. If it is near the time of the next dose, skip the missed dose and resume your usual dosing schedule. Do not double the dose to catch up.

Storage

Store at room temperature between 59 and 86 degrees F (between 15 and 30 degrees C) away from moisture and sunlight. Do not store in the bathroom.

MUPIROCIN

Common Brand Name: Bactroban

Uses
This medication is used to treat infections of the skin such as impetigo.

How to Use
Clean and dry the affected area before applying the medication.

To apply, gently massage a small amount of the medication into the affected area and surrounding skin three times daily or as directed by your doctor.

Cover with a loose fitting bandage if desired.

Continue to use the medication as prescribed for the full time prescribed. Stopping therapy too early can result in a re-infection.

If no improvement is seen in 3 to 5 days, consult your doctor.

Another medication may be necessary.

Avoid using this medication around the eyes, nose or mouth.

Side Effects
This medication may cause burning, stinging or itching when first applied to the skin. This should disappear in a few days as your body adjusts to the medication. If these effects persist or worsen, inform your doctor.

Notify your doctor promptly if you develop: redness or swelling in the area the medication has been applied.

If you notice other effects not listed above, contact your doctor or pharmacist.

Precautions
Tell your doctor your medical history, especially if you have: allergies (especially drug allergies).

Use of this medication for prolonged or repeated periods may result in a secondary infection (e.g., fungal infection).

Drug Interactions
Tell your doctor of all medicines you may use (both prescription and nonprescrip-

231

tion), especially if you have: chloramphenicol, other topical antibiotics, topical corticosteroids (e.g., hydrocortisone).

Do not start or stop any medicine without first consulting your doctor or pharmacist.

Notes
This medication is prescribed for your current condition only. Do not use it for another infection or share it with someone else. Another infection later on may require a different medication.

Missed Dose
If you miss a dose, take it as soon as you remember. If it is near the time of the next dose, skip the missed dose and resume your usual dosing schedule. Do not double the dose to catch up.

Storage
Store ointment at room temperature at or below 77 degrees F (25 degrees C) away from moisture and sunlight. Avoid freezing. Do not store in the bathroom.

NAPROXEN

Common Brand Names: Naprosyn, Anaprox

Uses
This medication is used to treat pain and reduce inflammation. It is used to treat headaches, muscle aches, dental pain, arthritis, or athletic injuries. Some NSAIDs are also used to reduce fever.

How to Use
Take this medication by mouth with a full glass of water (8oz. or 240ml) as directed by your doctor. The dosage is based on your medical condition and response to therapy.

   If stomach upset occurs while taking this medication, take it with food, milk, or an antacid.

   In certain conditions (e.g., arthritis), it may take up to two weeks, taken regularly, before the full benefit of this drug takes effect.

   If you use this for migraine headache, and the pain is not relieved or it worsens after the first dose, seek immediate medical attention.

Side Effects
Upset stomach, nausea, vomiting, heartburn, headache, diarrhea, constipation, drowsiness, and unusual fatigue may occur. If any of these effects persist or worsen, notify your doctor.

   Tell your doctor immediately if any of these serious side effects occur: stomach pain, swelling of the feet or ankles, ringing in the ears (tinnitus).

   Tell your doctor immediately if any of these unlikely but serious side effects occur: vision changes, joint pain, muscle pain or weakness, easy bruising or bleeding, persistent sore throat and fever.

   Tell your doctor immediately if any of these highly unlikely but very serious side effects occur: changes in amount or color of urine, yellowing of the eyes or skin.

   If you notice any of the following unlikely but serious side effects, stop taking this medication and consult your doctor or pharmacist immediately: black stools, persistent stomach/ abdominal pain, vomit that looks like coffee grounds.

An allergic reaction to this drug is unlikely, but seek immediate medical attention if it occurs. Symptoms of an allergic reaction include: rash, itching, swelling, dizziness, trouble breathing.

If you notice other effects not listed above, contact your doctor or pharmacist.

Precautions
Tell your doctor your medical history, especially if you have: kidney problems, liver problems, stomach problems (e.g., ulcers), heart disease (e.g., arrhythmias, heart failure), high blood pressure (hypertension), diabetes, blood problems (e.g., anemia, bleeding disorders, porphyria), asthma, eye problems, severe or long-lasting headaches, any allergies.

This drug may make you dizzy or drowsy. Use caution engaging in activities requiring alertness such as driving or using machinery. Limit alcoholic beverages.

This medication may make you more sensitive to the sun. Avoid prolonged sun exposure, use a sunscreen, and wear protective clothing when outdoors.

This medicine may cause stomach bleeding. Daily use of alcohol and this medicine may increase your risk for stomach bleeding.

Caution is advised when using this drug with older people because they may be more sensitive to the effects of the drug.

Drug Interactions
Tell your doctor of all prescription and nonprescription medication you may use, especially: "blood thinners" (e.g., warfarin), other medications for arthritis (e.g., aspirin, methotrexate), "water pills" (diuretics), lithium, anti-ulcer medication (e.g., cimetidine), high blood pressure medication such as ACE inhibitors (e.g., captopril, lisinopril), and beta-blockers (e.g., metoprolol, propranolol), probenecid, phenytoin, cyclosporine, sulfa drugs, medicine for diabetes (e.g., glipizide, glyburide), alendronate.

Check the labels on all your medicines because they may contain aspirin or other aspirin-like NSAIDs (e.g., ibuprofen, naproxen). Ask your pharmacist about the safe use of those products.

Do not start or stop any medicine without first consulting your doctor or pharmacist.

Notes
Do not share this medication with others.

Laboratory and/or medical tests may be performed to monitor your progress.

Missed Dose

If you miss a dose, take it as soon as you remember. If it is near the time of the next dose, skip the missed dose and resume your usual dosing schedule. Do not double the dose to catch up.

Storage

Store at room temperature between 36 and 86 degrees F (2 to 30 degrees C) away from light and moisture.

NITROFURANTOIN

Common Brand Name: Macrobid

Uses
Nitrofurantoin is an antibiotic used to treat or prevent urinary tract infections.

How to Use
Take with food or milk twice daily or as directed by your doctor. Swallow whole for maximum effect.

Antibiotics work best when the amount of medicine in your body is kept at a constant level. Do this by taking the medication at evenly spaced intervals throughout the day and night.

Continue to take this medication until the full prescribed amount is finished even if symptoms disappear after a few days.

Stopping the medication too early may allow bacteria to continue to grow resulting in a relapse of the infection.

Side Effects
May cause stomach upset, diarrhea, loss of appetite, nausea, dizziness and headache during the first few days as your body adjusts to the medication. If these symptoms persist or become severe, inform your doctor.

May cause urine to turn yellow-brown in color. This is not a cause for concern and will disappear when the drug is stopped.

Inform your doctor if you develop: unusual weakness, tingling of the hands or feet, chills, muscle aches, cough, yellowing of the eyes or skin.

In the unlikely event you have an allergic reaction to this drug, seek medical attention immediately. Symptoms of an allergic reaction include: rash, itching, swelling, fever, trouble breathing.

If you notice other effects not listed above, contact your doctor or pharmacist.

Precautions
Before using this drug, tell your doctor your medical history including: allergies

(drug allergies), kidney or liver problems, lung diseases, nerve disorders (peripheral neuropathy, anemia, diabetes, eye problems (optic neuritis).

Use of this medication for prolonged or repeated periods may result in a secondary infection (e.g., oral or bladder infection).

Drug Interactions

Inform your doctor about all the medicines you use (both prescription and nonprescription), especially if you have: probenecid, sulfinpyrazone, quinolone antibiotics (e.g., ciprofloxacin), magnesium trisilicate-containing antacids.

Do not start or stop any medicine without first consulting your doctor or pharmacist.

Notes

This medication has been prescribed for your current condition only. Do not use it later for another infection or give it to someone else. A different medication may be necessary in those cases.

Missed Dose

If you miss a dose, take it as soon as you remember. If it is near the time of the next dose, skip the missed dose and resume your usual dosing schedule. Do not double the dose to catch up.

Storage

Store at room temperature between 59 to 86 degrees F (15 to 30 degrees C) away from moisture and sunlight. Do not store in the bathroom.

NORTRIPTYLINE

Common Brand Names: Pamelor, Aventyl HCL

Uses
This medication is used to treat depression, obsessive-compulsive disorders, neuropathic pain, and prevention of migraines.

How to Use
Use this as prescribed. Try to use each dose at the same time(s) each day so you remember to routinely use it.

It may take 2 to 3 weeks before the full benefit of this medication becomes apparent.

Do not stop using this medication without your doctor's approval. Nausea, headache or fatigue can occur if the drug is suddenly stopped.

Side Effects
May cause drowsiness, dizziness, increased sun sensitivity or blurred vision.

May initially cause dizziness and lightheadedness when rising too quickly from a sitting or lying position.

Other side effects include heartburn, loss of appetite, dry mouth, strange taste in mouth, anxiety, restlessness or sweating.

If any side effects persist or worsen, notify your doctor.

Report promptly: chest pain, rapid or irregular heartbeat, difficulty urinating, nightmares, ringing in the ears, excessive drowsiness, uncoordinated movements, fainting.

Taking this medication at bedtime may help minimize side effects. Talk to your doctor about this.

In the unlikely event you have an allergic reaction to this drug, seek medical attention immediately. Symptoms of an allergic reaction include: rash, itching, swelling, dizziness, trouble breathing.

If you notice other effects not listed above, contact your doctor or pharmacist.

Precautions

Before using this drug tell your doctor your medical history, especially if you have: glaucoma, prostate problems, decreased urine output, thyroid disease, breathing problems, seizure problems, alcohol use, heart disease, mental/emotional problems, liver or kidney disease, any drug allergies.

Use caution when engaging in tasks requiring alertness such as driving or operating machinery.

Limit alcohol consumption as it may increase the drowsiness and dizziness effects of this drug.

Caution is advised when using this drug with older people, because they may be more sensitive to the effects of the drug (e.g., confusion may occur or worsen).

Drug Interactions

Inform your doctor about the medicines you take, especially if you take: clonidine, guanadrel, guanethidine, MAO inhibitors (e.g., furazolidone, linezolid, phenelzine, selegiline, tranylcypromine), cimetidine, SSRIs (e.g., fluoxetine, sertraline), warfarin, carbamazepine, adrenaline-type drugs (e.g., dopamine, ephedrine, epinephrine, pseudoephedrine, phenylephrine, isoproterenol-some of which may be found in cough-and-cold or asthma products), narcotic pain medications (e.g., codeine), cisapride, St John's wort, any other prescription or nonprescription drugs you take.

Do not start or stop any medicine without first consulting your doctor or pharmacist.

Notes

Do not allow anyone else to use this medication.

Missed Dose

If you miss a dose, take it as soon as you remember. If it is near the time of the next dose, skip the missed dose and resume your usual dosing schedule. Do not double the dose to catch up.

Storage

Store at room temperature away from moisture and sunlight. Do not store in the bathroom. Do not freeze liquid forms of this medication.

NYSTATIN

Common Brand Name: Mycostatin

Uses
This medication is used to treat fungal skin and oral cavity infections.

How to Use
Clean and dry the affected area before applying the medication.

To apply, gently massage a small amount of the medication to the affected area and surrounding skin.

Continue to use the medication as prescribed for the full time prescribed. Stopping therapy too early may not clear the infection, causing it to return. Cover with a bandage only if instructed to do so by your doctor.

It may take one week before any improvement is seen. If no improvement is seen after four weeks, consult your doctor.

Another medication may be necessary.

Do not apply this medication into the eyes, nose or mouth; use carefully when applying close to these areas.

Side Effects
This medication may cause burning, stinging or redness when first applied to the skin. This should disappear in a few days as your body adjusts to the medication. If these effects persist or worsen, inform your doctor promptly.

If you notice other effects not listed above, contact your doctor or pharmacist.

Precautions
Tell your doctor your medical history, especially if you have: other skin conditions, any allergies.

Drug Interactions
Tell your doctor of all prescription and nonprescription drugs you may use, especially if you have: other skin products.

Do not start or stop any medicine without first consulting your doctor or pharmacist.

Notes
For patients who wear dentures, remove dentures before administering nystatin suspension. This medication is prescribed for your current condition only. Do not use it for another infection or share it with someone else. Another infection later on may require a different medicine.

Missed Dose
If you miss a dose, take it as soon as you remember. If it is near the time of the next dose, skip the missed dose and resume your usual dosing schedule. Do not double the dose to catch up.

Storage
Store at room temperature away from moisture and sunlight. Avoid freezing. Keep powdered form from getting wet. Do not store in the bathroom. Keep out of the reach of children.

OLANZAPINE

Common Brand Name: Zyprexa

Uses
This medication is used for the treatment of certain mental disorders, and behavioral disturbances associated with dementia.

How to Use
Take as directed, usually once a day by mouth. Stand up slowly, especially when starting this medication, to avoid dizziness.

Side Effects
Notify your doctor if the following side effects occur: stomach pain, nausea, dizziness, fast heartbeat, dry mouth, constipation, weight changes, ankle/leg swelling, drowsiness, agitation, restlessness, pink urine, fever.

Unlikely but possible: confusion, thirst, muscle stiffness, facial or body muscle twitching, lip or tongue movements, tremor, weakness, rash, itching, trouble breathing, weakness on one side of your body, vision changes, headache, frequent or painful urination, painful or prolonged erection in men, difficulty swallowing.

If you notice other effects not listed above, contact your doctor or pharmacist.

Precautions
Before taking this medicine, tell your doctor if you have: other medical problems, liver or heart disease, low blood pressure, breast cancer, stroke, diabetes, seizures (any neurological problems), prostate problems, narrow angle glaucoma, intestinal disease, phenylketonuria, allergies (especially drug allergies).

This medication can reduce sweating, making you prone to heat stroke. Avoid activities that might cause you to overheat (e.g., doing strenuous work or exercising in hot weather; using hot tubs).

Alcohol use may add to the dizziness and drowsiness effect of this drug.

Use with caution with older people.

Drug Interactions

Tell your doctor of all prescription or nonprescription drugs you take, especially if you have: medicine for sleep, antidepressants, tranquilizers (such as diazepam), narcotic pain medicines, Parkinson's disease or seizure medicines, high blood pressure drugs, antihistamines, omeprazole, rifampin, anti-cholinergics (e.g., benztropine, hyoscyamine).

Do not start or stop any medicine without first consulting your doctor or pharmacist.

Notes

Obtain regular eye exams as part of your regular health care, and to check for any unlikely, but possible, eye problems. Your doctor should evaluate the use and effectiveness of olanzapine periodically (every 6-12 months).

Missed Dose

If you miss a dose, take it as soon as you remember. If it is near the time of the next dose, skip the missed dose and resume your usual dosing schedule. Do not double the dose to catch up.

Storage

Store at room temperature between 68 and 77 degrees F (20-25 degrees C) away from moisture and light as directed. Do not store in the bathroom.

OMEPRAZOLE

Common Brand Name: Prilosec

Uses
Omeprazole is used to treat various acid-related stomach and/or throat (esophagus) problems (e.g., GERD, ulcers, erosive esophagitis, or Zollinger-Ellison Syndrome). It works by blocking the production of acid in the stomach.

When using this medication to treat stomach ulcers caused by Helicobacter pylori, it may be prescribed along with certain antibiotics (e.g., amoxicillin, clarithromycin).

How to Use
Take this medication by mouth, usually once daily, 15 to 30 minutes before a meal; or as directed by your doctor.

The dosage and length of treatment is based on your medical condition and response to therapy.

Do not crush or chew the medication. Swallow the medication whole.

If you take sucralfate in addition to this medication, take your dose of omeprazole at least 30 minutes before your sucralfate.

Side Effects
Headache, diarrhea, gas, or constipation, may occur. If any of these effects persist or worsen, notify your doctor.

Tell your doctor immediately if any of these serious side effects occur: rash, stomach/abdominal pain, back pain, unusual tiredness, dizziness, vomiting.

Tell your doctor immediately if any of these unlikely but serious side effects occur: chest pain, dark urine, yellowing eyes or skin.

An allergic reaction to this drug is unlikely, but seek immediate medical attention if it occurs. Symptoms of an allergic reaction include: rash, itching, swelling, trouble breathing.

If you notice other effects not listed above, contact your doctor or pharmacist.

Precautions

Tell your doctor your medical history, especially if you have: liver problems, any allergies.

Drug Interactions

Tell your doctor of all prescription and nonprescription medication you may use, especially: diazepam, warfarin, phenytoin, azole antifungals (e.g., ketoconazole, itraconazole), ampicillin, iron supplements, sucralfate, cilostazol, diazepam.

Do not start or stop any medicine without first consulting your doctor or pharmacist.

Notes

Do not share this medication with others.

If your conditions worsens or does not improve, contact your doctor.

Missed Dose

If you miss a dose, take it as soon as you remember. If it is near the time of the next dose, skip the missed dose and resume your usual dosing schedule. Do not double the dose to catch up.

Storage

Store at room temperature between 59 and 86 degrees F (15 to 30 degrees C) away from light and moisture.

OXYBUTYNIN

Common Brand Name: Ditropan

Uses
This medication relaxes muscle spasms of the bladder. It is used to relieve certain bladder and urinary conditions.

How to Use
Take this medication as directed.

Side Effects
Dry mouth or eyes, headache, constipation, nausea, or drowsiness may occur. If these effects persist or worsen, notify your doctor promptly.

Report promptly: weakness, dizziness, vision problems, symptoms of urinary infection (e.g., urinary burning, urgent or frequent urination).

Unlikely but report promptly: eye pain, difficulty with urination, severe stomach pain, chest pain, fast or irregular heartbeat, fever, mental/mood changes, flushing hot or dry skin.

In the unlikely event you have an allergic reaction to this drug, seek immediate medical attention. Symptoms of an allergic reaction include: rash, itching, swelling, severe dizziness, trouble breathing.

To relieve dry mouth, suck on hard candy or ice chips, chew gum, drink water or use saliva substitute.

If you notice other effects not listed above, contact your doctor or pharmacist.

Precautions
Tell your doctor your medical history, especially heart problems, liver or kidney disease, stomach or intestine problems, glaucoma (narrow angle), overactive thyroid, difficulty urinating (e.g., enlarged prostate in men), muscle disease (myasthenia gravis), any allergies.

Because this medication may cause drowsiness or blurred vision, use caution when performing tasks requiring alertness such as driving or operating machinery. Limit alcohol consumption because it may add to these effects.

This medication reduces sweating, which can lead to heat stroke in hot weather or saunas. Avoid strenuous activity in hot weather.

Use with caution with older people, since they may be more sensitive to side effects of this medication.

Drug Interactions

Tell your doctor of all prescription and nonprescription medication you use, especially: bisphosphonate drugs (e.g., alendronate, etidronate), macrolide antibiotics (e.g., erythromycin), azole antifungals (e.g., ketoconazole, itraconazole), anti-Parkinson's drugs (e.g., benztropine, trihexyphenidyl), other anticholinergic drugs (e.g., scopolamine or tolterodine).

Also report other drugs which may cause drowsiness, such as: anti-anxiety or anti-seizure drugs, sedatives or tranquilizers, narcotic pain relievers (e.g., codeine), psychiatric medicines (e.g., chlorpromazine, amitriptyline), muscle relaxants, sedating antihistamines like diphenhydramine (this also includes anti-histamines found in nonprescription cough/cold products).

Do not start or stop any medicine without first consulting your doctor or pharmacist.

Notes

Do not allow anyone else to take this medication.

Missed Dose

If you miss a dose, take it as soon as you remember. If it is near the time of the next dose, skip the missed dose and resume your usual dosing schedule. Do not double the dose to catch up.

Storage

Store at room temperature and keep away from moisture and sunlight. Do not store in the bathroom. Do not freeze the liquid forms.

OXYCODONE

Common Brand Name: OxyContin

Uses

This drug is used to relieve moderate-to-severe chronic pain. It is very beneficial for pain relief (e.g., cancer pain).

Oxycontin is not used "as needed" for acute pain, nor is it indicated for acute pain after surgery.

How to Use

Take by mouth exactly as directed by your doctor.

Take with food or milk to minimize or prevent stomach upset.

Swallow tablet(s) whole. Do not crush, break or chew them.

This drug is usually taken every 12 hours (2 times daily). Do not increase your dose, take it more frequently or use it for a longer period of time than prescribed because this drug can be habit-forming. Also, if used for an extended period of time, do not suddenly stop using this drug without your doctor's approval.

Over time, this drug may not work as well as it did at the beginning. Consult your doctor if this medication isn't relieving the pain sufficiently.

Side Effects

May cause constipation, lightheadedness, stomach upset, dizziness, drowsiness, nausea, and flushing. If these effects persist or worsen, contact your doctor.

Notify your doctor if you develop: irregular heartbeat, anxiety, tremors, seizures, decreased respirations.

In the unlikely event you have an allergic reaction to this drug, seek medical attention immediately. Symptoms of an allergic reaction include: rash, itching, swelling, dizziness, trouble breathing.

If you notice other effects not listed above, contact your doctor or pharmacist.

Precautions

Before using this drug, tell your doctor your medical history, especially: severe diarrhea, stomach or intestinal disorders, breathing problems, kidney or liver disease, history of alcohol use, drug dependence, any allergies.

Alcoholic beverages may increase the effects of this drug causing dizziness or lightheadedness. Limit alcohol intake. Use caution engaging in activities requiring alertness such as driving.

Caution is advised when using this drug with older people because they may be more sensitive to the effects of this drug.

Excessive sedation (mental confusion) and cognitive impairment (memory) may be seen with low doses.

Drug Interactions

Before using this drug, tell your doctor of all the medications you may use, both prescription and nonprescription, especially: cimetidine, alcohol use.

Tell your doctor if you take drugs that cause drowsiness such as: medicine for sleep, sedatives, tranquilizers, anti-anxiety drugs (e.g., diazepam), other narcotic pain relievers (e.g., codeine), psychiatric medicines (e.g., phenothiazines or tricyclics), anti-seizure drugs (e.g., carbamazepine), muscle relaxants, antihistamines that cause drowsiness (e.g., diphenhydramine).

Many cough-and-cold preparations contain ingredients that may add to the drowsiness effects of oxycodone. Consult your doctor or pharmacist before using any such medications.

Do not start or stop any medicine without first consulting your doctor or pharmacist.

Notes

This medication is a controlled substance. It is illegal to share this medication with others. Regular release oxycodone is used in combination with other analgesics such as with acetaminophen or aspirin. The combination is used to reduce the amount of narcotic needed.

Missed Dose

If you miss a dose, take it as soon as you remember. If it is near the time of the next dose, skip the missed dose and resume your usual dosing schedule. Do not double the dose to catch up.

Storage

Store at room temperature between 59 and 86 degrees F (between 15 and 30 degrees C) away from moisture and sunlight. Do not store in the bathroom.

OXYCODONE/APAP

Common Brand Names: Percocet, Roxicet, Endocet, Tylox

Uses
This drug is used to relieve moderate-to-severe pain.

How to Use
Take by mouth exactly as directed by your doctor.

Take with food or milk to minimize or prevent stomach upset.

This drug is usually taken every 6 to 12 hours (2 to 4 times daily). Do not increase your dose, take it more frequently, or use it for a longer period of time than prescribed because this drug can be habit-forming. Also, if used for an extended period of time, do not suddenly stop using this drug without your doctor's approval.

Over time, this drug may not work as well as it did at the beginning. Consult your doctor if this medication isn't relieving the pain sufficiently.

Side Effects
May cause constipation, lightheadedness, stomach upset, dizziness, drowsiness, nausea and flushing. If these effects persist or worsen, contact your doctor.

Notify your doctor if you develop: irregular heartbeat, anxiety, tremors, seizures, decreased respirations.

In the unlikely event you have an allergic reaction to this drug, seek medical attention immediately. Symptoms of an allergic reaction include: rash, itching, swelling, dizziness, trouble breathing.

If you notice other effects not listed above, contact your doctor or pharmacist.

Precautions
Before using this drug, tell your doctor your medical history, especially if you have: severe diarrhea, stomach or intestinal disorders, breathing problems, kidney or liver disease, history of alcohol use, drug dependence, any drug allergies.

Alcoholic beverages may increase the effects of this drug causing dizziness or lightheadedness. Limit alcohol intake. Use caution engaging in activities requiring alertness such as driving.

Caution is advised when using this drug with older people because they may be more sensitive to the effects of this drug.

The medication should be used only when clearly needed during pregnancy. Discuss the risks and benefits with your doctor.

Drug Interactions

Before using this drug, tell your doctor of all the medications you may use, both prescription and nonprescription, especially if you have: cimetidine, other narcotic pain relievers, sleep medications, drugs for mental/mood conditions, alcohol use.

Many cough-and-cold preparations contain ingredients that may add to the drowsiness effects of oxycodone. Consult your doctor or pharmacist before using any such medications.

Do not start or stop any medicine without first consulting your doctor or pharmacist.

Notes

Do not share this medication with others. It is against the law.

Missed Dose

If you miss a dose, take it as soon as you remember. If it is near the time of the next dose, skip the missed dose and resume your usual dosing schedule. Do not double the dose to catch up.

Storage

Store at room temperature between 59 and 86 degrees F (between 15 and 30 degrees C) away from moisture and sunlight. Do not store in the bathroom.

PANTOPRAZOLE

Common Brand Name: Protonix

Uses
This medication is used to treat various acid-related stomach and/or throat problems (e.g., GERD, ulcers, esophagitis).

How to Use
Take this medication by mouth, usually once daily before a meal, as directed by your doctor. Take around the same time everyday.

The dosage and length of treatment is based on your medical condition and response to therapy.

Do not crush, chew, or split the medication. Swallow the medication whole.

If you take sucralfate in addition to this medication, take your dose of pantoprazole at least 30 minutes before your sucralfate.

Antacids may be taken along with this medication, if needed.

Side Effects
Diarrhea, gas, or headache may occur. If any of these effects persist or worsen, notify your doctor promptly.

Tell your doctor immediately if any of these very unlikely but serious side effects occur: mental/mood changes, vision problems, persistent stomach pain, black/bloody stools, yellowing eyes or skin, dark urine.

An allergic reactions to this drug is unlikely, but seek immediate medical attention if it occurs. Symptoms of an allergic reaction include: rash, itching, swelling, dizziness, trouble breathing.

If you notice other effects not listed above, contact your doctor or pharmacist.

Precautions
Tell your doctor your medical history, especially if you have: liver problems, any allergies.

Drug Interactions

Tell your doctor of all prescription and nonprescription medication you may use, especially if you have: azole antifungal medications (e.g., ketoconazole, itraconazole), ampicillin, digoxin, sucralfate, iron.

Do not start or stop any medicine without first consulting your doctor or pharmacist.

Notes

Do not share this medication with others.

Missed Dose

If you miss a dose, take it as soon as you remember. If it is near the time of the next dose, skip the missed dose and resume your usual dosing schedule. Do not double the dose to catch up.

Storage

Store at room temperature between 59 and 86 degrees F (15 to 30 degrees C) away from light and moisture.

PAROXETINE

Common Brand Name: Paxil

Uses
Paroxetine is used to treat depression, panic attacks, obsessive compulsive disorders (OCD), social anxiety disorder (social phobia), and generalized anxiety disorder.

This medication works by helping to restore the balance of certain natural chemicals in the brain.

How to Use
Take this medication by mouth usually once daily in the morning, with or without food; or as directed by your doctor.

The dosage is based on your medical condition and response to therapy.

It is important to continue taking this medication as prescribed even if you feel well. Also, do not stop taking this medication without consulting your doctor.

It may take up to several weeks before the full benefit of this drug takes effect.

Side Effects
Nausea, drowsiness, dizziness, diarrhea, trouble sleeping, constipation, or dry mouth may occur. If any of these effects persist or worsen, notify your doctor promptly.

Tell your doctor immediately if any of these serious side effects occur: loss of appetite, unusual or severe mental/mood changes, increased sweating/flushing, unusual fatigue, uncontrolled movements (tremor), decreased interest in sex.

Tell your doctor immediately if any of these unlikely but serious side effects occur: blurred vision, changes in sexual ability, painful and/or prolonged erection, change in amount of urine.

Tell your doctor immediately if any of these highly unlikely but very serious side effects occur: fainting, irregular heartbeat, muscle pain, trouble swallowing, unusual swelling, seizures, easy bruising or bleeding, tingling or numbness of the hands/feet.

An allergic reaction to this drug is unlikely, but seek immediate medical attention if it occurs. Symptoms of an allergic reaction include: rash, itching, swelling, severe dizziness, trouble breathing.

If you notice other effects not listed above, contact your doctor or pharmacist.

Precautions

Tell your doctor your medical history, especially if you have: liver problems, kidney problems, seizures, heart problems, other mental/mood disorders (e.g., bipolar disorder), thyroid problems, any allergies.

This drug may make you dizzy or drowsy; use caution engaging in activities requiring alertness such as driving or using machinery. Limit alcoholic beverages.

Older adults may need a lower dose of this drug because it may be removed from their body more slowly.

Drug Interactions

Certain medications taken with this product could result in serious, even fatal, drug interactions. Avoid taking MAO (monoamine oxidase) inhibitors (e.g., furazolidone, isocarboxazid, linezolid, moclobemide, phenelzine, procarbazine, selegiline, tranylcypromine) within 2 weeks, and avoid taking thioridazine within 5 weeks, before or after treatment with this medication.

Consult your doctor or pharmacist for additional information.

This drug is not recommended for use with: weight loss drugs (e.g., sibutramine, phentermine), thioridazine, terfenadine, astemizole.

Ask your doctor or pharmacist for more details.

Tell your doctor of all prescription and nonprescription medication you may use, especially: other SSRI antidepressants (e.g., citalopram, fluoxetine), nefazodone, trazodone, tramadol, venlafaxine, "triptan" migraine drugs (e.g., sumatriptan, zolmitriptan), tricyclic antidepressants (e.g., amitriptyline, nortriptyline), cimetidine, digoxin, flecainide, propafenone, clozapine, lithium, tryptophan, warfarin, theophylline, herbal/natural products (e.g., melatonin, ayahuasca, St John's wort).

Tell your doctor if you take any drugs that cause drowsiness such as: medicine for sleep, sedatives, tranquilizers, anti-anxiety drugs (e.g., diazepam), narcotic pain relievers (e.g., codeine), phenothiazines (e.g., chlorpromazine), anti-seizure drugs (e.g., carbamazepine), muscle relaxants, non-prescription antihistamines (e.g., diphenhydramine). Use of paroxetine with certain drugs may cause abnormal heart rhythm, including: dofetilide, pimozide, sotalol, quinidine, procainamide, sparfloxacin.

Ask your doctor or pharmacist for more details.

Do not start or stop any medicine without first consulting your doctor or pharmacist.

Notes

Do not share this medication with others.

Laboratory and/or medical tests may be performed to monitor your progress.

Missed Dose

If you miss a dose, take it as soon as you remember. If it is near the time of the next dose, skip the missed dose and resume your usual dosing schedule. Do not double the dose to catch up.

Storage

Store at room temperature between 59 and 86 degrees F (15 and 30 degrees C) away from light and moisture.

PENICILLIN VK

Common Brand Names: Pen-Vee K, Veetids

Uses
Penicillins are antibiotics used to treat a wide variety of bacterial infections (respiratory tract, sinusitis, skin and urinary tract infections).

How to Use
This medication may be taken without regard to meals. However, absorption is best if medication is taken on an empty stomach (1 hour before or 2 to 3 hours after meals).

Antibiotics work best when the amount of medicine in your body is kept at a constant level. Do this by taking the medication at evenly spaced intervals throughout the day and night.

Continue to take this medication until the full prescribed amount is finished even if symptoms disappear after a few days.

Stopping the medication too early may allow bacteria to continue to grow resulting in a relapse of the infection.

Side Effects
This medication may cause stomach upset, diarrhea, nausea, and vomiting during the first few days as your body adjusts to the medication. If these symptoms persist or become severe, inform your doctor.

Notify your doctor immediately if an allergic reaction occurs while taking this medication. Symptoms include: difficulty breathing, skin rash, hives, itching.

Use of this medication for prolonged or repeated periods may result in a secondary infection (e.g., oral, bladder or vaginal yeast infection).

If you notice other effects not listed above, contact your doctor or pharmacist.

Precautions
Tell your doctor if you have any allergies (especially to penicillin or other antibiotics).

Drug Interactions
Tell your doctor of all prescription and nonprescription drugs you may use, especially of tetracycline, probenacid.

Do not start or stop any medicine without first consulting your doctor or pharmacist.

Notes
This medication has been prescribed for your current condition only. Different medication may be necessary in those cases.

Missed Dose
If you miss a dose, take it as soon as you remember. If it is near the time of the next dose, skip the missed dose and resume your usual dosing schedule. Do not double the dose to catch up.

Storage
Store medication at room temperature away from moisture and sunlight. Do not store in the bathroom.

PHENOBARBITAL

Uses
This medication is used for seizure disorders. It is also used as a short-term sleep aid (for insomnia), and for tension relief (e.g., before a medical procedure).

How to Use
Take with food or milk if stomach upset occurs.

For insomnia, take 30 to 60 minutes prior to bedtime.

Take this medication exactly as prescribed. Do not increase your dose or take it more often than prescribed because this drug can be habit-forming. Also, if used for a longer period of time, do not suddenly stop using this without first consulting your doctor.

When used for extended periods, this medication may not work as well and may require different dosing. Consult your doctor if the medication is not working well.

Side Effects
This medication causes drowsiness and dizziness.

Other side effects may include stomach upset, headache, weakness, grogginess or dreaming. If these effects persist or worsen, inform your doctor.

Notify your doctor if you develop: chest pain, rapid heart rate, nosebleeds, confusion, hallucinations.

In the unlikely event you have an allergic reaction to this drug, seek immediate medical attention. Symptoms of an allergic reaction include: rash, itching, swelling, dizziness, trouble breathing.

If you notice other effects not listed above, contact your doctor or pharmacist.

Precautions
Tell your doctor your medical history, especially about: liver problems, blood disorders (porphyria), asthma, any allergies.

Avoid alcohol while taking this as it can lead to extreme drowsiness.

Use caution performing tasks requiring alertness such as driving or using machinery.

Older adults are usually more sensitive to the effects of this medication. Use cautiously.

Drug Interactions

Inform your doctor about all the medicines you use (both prescription and nonprescription), especially: "blood thinners" (e.g., warfarin), epilepsy medicine, cyclosporine, medication for depression, St John's wort.

Also inform your doctor if you take any drugs that may cause drowsiness such as: narcotic pain medicines (e.g., codeine), antihistamines (e.g., diphenhydramine), muscle relaxants, alcoholic beverages.

Do not start or stop any medicine without first consulting your doctor or pharmacist.

Notes

Do not share this medication with others.

Missed Dose

If you miss a dose, take it as soon as you remember. If it is near the time of the next dose, skip the missed dose and resume your usual dosing schedule. Do not double the dose to catch up.

Storage

Store at room temperature away from moisture and sunlight. Do not store in the bathroom. Do not freeze liquid forms of this medication.

PHENYTOIN

Common Brand Name: Dilantin

Uses
This medication is used to treat seizures, epilepsy, trigeminal neuralgia, arrhythmias.

How to Use
Take with food or milk if stomach upset occurs. Take this medication with a full glass (8 oz/240 ml) of water, unless directed otherwise.

Capsules should be swallowed whole unless otherwise directed.

Chewable tablets must be chewed thoroughly before swallowing.

The suspension must be shaken well before measuring each dose.

This medication must be taken as prescribed. Do not stop taking this drug suddenly without consulting your doctor as seizures may occur.

It is important to take all doses on time to keep the level of medication in your blood constant. Do this by taking doses at the same time(s) each day. Do not skip doses.

Side Effects
Constipation, dizziness and drowsiness may occur.

If these effects continue or worsen, inform your doctor.

Unlikely but report: blurred vision, unsteadiness, nausea, mood changes or confusion, slurred speech, rash, insomnia, headache.

Very unlikely but report: vomiting, stomach pain, uncoordinated movements, tingling in hands or feet, fever, yellowing of the eyes or skin, swollen glands, sore throat, unusual bleeding or bruising.

May cause enlargement of the gums. This can be minimized by maintaining good oral hygiene with regular brushing, flossing and massaging of the gums.

In the unlikely event you have an allergic reaction to this drug, seek immediate medical attention. Symptoms of an allergic reaction include: rash, itching, swelling, dizziness, trouble breathing.

If you notice other effects not listed above, contact your doctor or pharmacist.

Precautions

Tell your doctor your medical history, especially if you have: blood disorders (e.g., porphyria), allergies (especially drug allergies), liver disease, patients with low serumalbumin.

Use caution operating machinery or performing tasks requiring alertness if this medication makes you dizzy or drowsy.

Limit alcohol use as it may increase the drowsiness effect of this medication.

Limit your caffeine usage.

Drug Interactions

Inform your doctor of all the medicines you may use (both prescription and non-prescription), especially if you have: warfarin, cimetidine, omeprazole, sucralfate, disulfiram, oral antifungal medication (azoles), xanthine drugs (e.g., theophylline), isoniazid, folic acid, sulfa antibiotics, rifampin, trimethoprim, amiodarone, fluoxetine, anticancer drugs, valproic acid or divalproex, estrogens, disopyramide, levodopa, felodipine, primidone, felbamate, digoxin, dopamine, St John's wort, chloramphenicol, phenylbutazone, quinidine, doxycycline, cyclosporine, corticosteroids (e.g., prednisone, hydrocortisone), narcotic pain medicines (e.g., codeine), aspirin.

Do not start or stop any medicine without first consulting your doctor or pharmacist.

Notes

Do not change from one brand of this product to another without consulting your doctor or pharmacist. Products made by different companies may not be equally effective.

Lab tests may be done to monitor your progress.

Missed Dose

If you miss a dose, take it as soon as you remember. If it is near the time of the next dose, skip the missed dose and resume your usual dosing schedule. Do not double the dose to catch up.

Storage

Store at room temperature away from moisture and sunlight. Do not store in the bathroom.

PIOGLITAZONE

Common Brand Name: Actos

Uses
This medication is used to treat diabetes. It works by helping to restore your body's proper response to insulin, thereby lowering your blood sugar.

How to Use
Take by mouth, with or without food, once daily as directed by your doctor. Dosage is based on your medical condition and response to therapy.

This medication may be used in addition to other medications to treat diabetes. Take all other medication as directed by your doctor.

Side Effects
Headache may occur. If this effect persists or worsens, notify your doctor promptly.

Tell your doctor immediately if you have any of these unlikely but serious side effects: prolonged sore throat, cough, unusual tiredness or weakness, dizziness, tremors, rapid pulse, muscle ache, swelling, unusual thirst, unusual amount of urine, increased shortness of breath, trouble breathing, sudden weight gain.

Tell your doctor immediately if you have any of these very unlikely but serious side effects: vomiting, stomach pain, dark urine, yellowing eyes/skin.

If you notice other effects not listed above, contact your doctor or pharmacist.

Precautions
Use of this medication is not recommended if you have newly diagnosed or worsening heart failure (acute congestive heart failure).

Tell your doctor your medical history, including: any allergies, swelling (edema), heart problems (e.g., chronic congestive heart failure), very high blood glucose (diabetic ketoacidosis), blood problems (e.g., anemia), liver disease.

Consult your doctor or pharmacist to learn the symptoms of high or low blood sugar. Some symptoms of high blood sugar include thirst and increased urination. Low blood sugar may cause you to feel shaky, sweaty, hungry or have an increased pulse.

Carry glucose tablets or gel to treat low blood sugar. Consult your pharmacist.

During times of stress, such as fever, infection, injury or surgery, it may be more difficult to control your blood sugar.

Consult your doctor, as additional medication may be required.

Drug Interactions

Tell your doctor of all prescription and nonprescription medication you may use, especially if you have: drugs for diabetes (e.g., rosiglitazone, insulin, glipizide, glyburide), ketoconazole.

Do not start or stop any medicine without first consulting your doctor or pharmacist.

Notes

Do not share this medication with others.

It is recommended you attend a diabetes education program to understand diabetes and all important aspects of its treatment including meals, exercise, personal hygiene, medication and getting regular eye and medical exams. Consult your doctor or pharmacist.

Keep all medical appointments. Laboratory and/or medical tests (e.g., liver function tests) will be performed to monitor for side effects and response to therapy. Regularly check your blood or urine for sugar, as directed by your doctor or pharmacist.

Controlling high blood sugar helps prevent heart disease, strokes, kidney disease, circulation problems, and blindness.

Missed Dose

If you miss a dose, take it as soon as you remember. If it is near the time of the next dose, skip the missed dose and resume your usual dosing schedule. Do not double the dose to catch up.

Storage

Store at room temperature between 59 and 86 degrees F (15 to 30 degrees C) away from light and moisture.

POTASSIUM CHLORIDE

Common Brand Names: K-Dur, Klor-Con, Micro-K

Uses
Potassium supplements are used to prevent or treat low potassium blood levels. Certain diuretics and illnesses are known to lower potassium levels in the body.

How to Use
Take this by mouth as directed. You should swallow the tablets whole or, if you have trouble swallowing tablets, dissolve the tablet coating in a glass of cool water. It may take a few minutes to dissolve. After the tablet has dissolved, stir for a minute, swirl the glass and drink. Fill the glass with water (8oz or 240ml) and drink it to assure all the medication is taken.

Take this medication with meals to prevent stomach upset. Do not take on an empty stomach.

Do not lie down for 30 minutes after taking this medication to decrease irritation to your esophagus.

Side Effects
Nausea, stomach upset, vomiting or diarrhea may occur the first several days as your body adjusts to this. If these symptoms continue or become severe, inform your doctor.

Notify your doctor if you experience: breathing trouble, chest pain, an irregular heartbeat, dark or tarry stools, confusion, tingling of the hands or feet, stomach pain.

If you notice other effects not listed above, contact your doctor or pharmacist.

Precautions
Before taking this, tell your doctor if you have kidney disease, heart disease, a history of ulcers, allergies.

Symptoms of low potassium include fatigue, weakness, muscle twitching or cramps, dry mouth and excessive thirst.

Symptoms of high potassium levels include irregular heartbeat or muscle weakness.

Drug Interactions
Inform your doctor about all the medicines you use (both prescription and nonprescription) especially if you take: "water pills" (diuretics such as furosemide or amiloride), ACE inhibitors (e.g., lisinopril), digoxin, salt substitutes containing potassium.

Do not start or stop any medicine without first consulting your doctor or pharmacist.

Notes
Salt substitutes contain potassium instead of sodium.

Talk to your doctor or pharmacist about using a salt substitute.

Good sources of potassium-containing foods include bananas, citrus fruits, watermelon, cantaloupe, raisins, dates, prunes, avocados, apricots, beans, lentils, fish, chicken, turkey, ham, beef and milk.

Missed Dose
If you miss a dose, take it as soon as you remember. If it is near the time of the next dose, skip the missed dose and resume your usual dosing schedule. Do not double the dose to catch up.

Storage
Store at room temperature between 59 and 86 degrees F (15 to 30 degrees C) away from heat and light as directed. Do not store in the bathroom.

PRAMIPEXOLE

Common Brand Name: MIRAPEX

Uses
This medication is used to treat Parkinson's disease. It replaces the brain chemical called dopamine, which is low in persons with Parkinson's disease.

How to Use
Take this medication as prescribed. Do not increase your dose or take it more often than directed.

Do not stop taking this medication without your doctor's approval. Stopping this drug suddenly may cause you to experience unwanted side effects.

Dose is adjusted based on your condition, any side effects, and renal function.

Side Effects
Nausea, dizziness, drowsiness, trouble sleeping, constipation, unusual weakness, stomach upset and pain, headache or dry mouth may occur. If these effects persist or worsen, notify your doctor promptly.

To relieve dry mouth, drink water, suck on hard candy or ice chips, chew gum, or use saliva substitute.

Report promptly any of these serious side effects: hallucinations, difficulty moving or walking, trouble breathing.

Unlikely but report promptly any of these effects: twitching, confusion, fainting, leg/foot swelling, restlessness, chest pain. Very unlikely but report promptly any: muscle pain, vision problems, fever, severe muscle stiffness.

If you notice other effects not listed above, contact your doctor or pharmacist.

Precautions
Tell your doctor your medical history, especially if you have: heart disease, heart arrhythmias (abnormal rhythms), mental confusion, hallucinations, difficulty walking, low blood pressure, kidney or liver disease, any allergies or other medications for Parkinson's disease.

To avoid dizziness and lightheadedness when rising from a seated or lying position, get up slowly.

Use caution when performing tasks requiring mental alertness such as driving or using machinery. Limit alcohol use because it may intensify the drowsiness and dizziness effects of this drug.

Drug Interactions

Tell your doctor of any over-the-counter or prescription medication you may take including: metoclopramide, psychiatric medicine, drugs for depression, medicine for Parkinson's disease, cimetidine, sleep medication, muscle relaxants, tranquilizers, narcotic pain relievers, anti-seizure drugs, certain antihistamines (e.g., diphenhydramine).

Do not start or stop any medicine without first consulting your doctor or pharmacist.

Notes

Do not share this medication with others.

Missed Dose

If you miss a dose, take it as soon as you remember. If it is near the time of the next dose, skip the missed dose and resume your usual dosing schedule. Do not double the dose to catch up.

Storage

Store at controlled room temperature away from moisture and sunlight. Do not store in the bathroom.

PRAVASTATIN

Common Brand Name: Pravachol

Uses
Pravastatin is used, along with a cholesterol-lowering diet, to help lower cholesterol and fats (triglycerides) in the blood. Reducing cholesterol and triglycerides helps prevent strokes and heart attacks. Progesterone works by decreasing the amount of cholesterol that is made in the body.

How to Use
Take this medication by mouth usually once daily with or without food; or as directed by your doctor. The dosage is based on your medical condition and response to therapy.

If you take this medication in combination with other cholesterol-lowering treatments (e.g., bile acid-binding resins such as cholestyramine or colestipol), take your pravastatin at least 1 hour before or 4 hours after these drugs.

It may take up to 4 weeks before the full benefit of this drug takes effect.

It is important to continue taking this medication even if you feel well. Most people with high cholesterol or triglycerides do not feel sick.

Side Effects
Headache, nausea, diarrhea, constipation, gas, or stomach upset/pain may occur. If any of these effects persist or worsen, notify your doctor promptly.

Tell your doctor immediately if any of these unlikely but serious side effects occur: joint pain, muscle pain or weakness, fever, unusual tiredness, chest pain, swelling in the arms or legs, dizziness.

Tell your doctor immediately if any of these highly unlikely but very serious side effects occur: yellowing eyes and skin, dark urine, change in the amount of urine, vision problems, black stool, severe stomach pain.

An allergic reaction to this drug is unlikely, but seek immediate medical attention if it occurs. Symptoms of an allergic reaction include: rash, itching, swelling, severe dizziness, trouble breathing.

If you notice other effects not listed above, contact your doctor or pharmacist.

Precautions

This medication is not recommended for use if you have the following medical conditions: liver problems.

Tell your doctor your medical history, especially if you have: heart disease, kidney problems, eye problems (e.g., cataracts), thyroid problems, uncontrolled seizures, recent serious infection, recent major surgery, low blood pressure, alcohol use, any allergies (especially to other "statin" drugs).

Daily use of alcohol may increase your chance for serious side effects. Limit alcoholic beverages while using this medication.

Drug Interactions

Tell your doctor of all prescription and nonprescription medication you may use, especially: colestipol, cholestyramine, cyclosporine, macrolide antibiotics (e.g., clarithromycin, erythromycin), fibrates (e.g., gemfibrozil), azole antifungals (e.g., itraconazole, ketoconazole), mibefradil, niacin (nicotinic acid), "blood thinners" (e.g., warfarin).

Do not start or stop any medicine without first consulting your doctor or pharmacist.

Notes

Do not share this medication with others.

Laboratory and/or medical tests (e.g., liver function tests) should be performed before starting this drug, then should be performed periodically to monitor your progress.

For best results, this medication should be used along with exercise and a low-cholesterol/low-fat diet. Consult your doctor.

Missed Dose

If you miss a dose, take it as soon as you remember. If it is near the time of the next dose, skip the missed dose and resume your usual dosing schedule. Do not double the dose to catch up.

Storage

Store at room temperature between 56 and 86 degrees F (13 to 30 degrees C) away from light and moisture.

PREDNISONE

Common Brand Name: Deltasone

Uses
This medication is a corticosteroid. It reduces swelling and inflammation.

It is used for many conditions, among them: allergic reactions, skin diseases (psoriasis, hives), breathing problems; certain cancers, blood disorders, and eye problems; arthritis, digestive problems, and for corticosteroid replacement.

How to Use
Take with food or immediately after a meal to prevent stomach upset.

Take this medication as prescribed. Follow the dosing schedule carefully. Be sure to ask your doctor if you have any questions.

If you are taking this medication only once a day, it should be taken in the morning before 9 a.m.

If you have been taking this medication for a long time, do not suddenly stop taking it without your doctor's approval. Your dose may need to be gradually reduced. You may experience extreme fatigue, weakness, stomach upset or dizziness if the medication is suddenly stopped.

Side Effects
May cause dizziness, nausea, indigestion, increased appetite, weight gain, increased blood sugar, weakness or sleep disturbances.

These effects should disappear as your body adjusts to the medication. If they persist or become bothersome, inform your doctor.

Notify your doctor if you experience: vomiting of blood, black or tarry stools, puffing of the face, swelling of the ankles or feet, unusual weight gain, prolonged sore throat or fever, muscle weakness, breathing difficulties, mood changes, vision changes.

In the unlikely event you have an allergic reaction to this drug, seek medical attention immediately. Symptoms of an allergic reaction include rash: itching, swelling, dizziness, trouble breathing.

If you notice other effects not listed above, contact your doctor or pharmacist.

Precautions

Before using this drug, tell your doctor your medical history, particularly if you have: liver or kidney disease, heart problems, intestinal problems, ulcers, high blood pressure, an underactive thyroid gland, myasthenia gravis, herpes eye infection, a history of tuberculosis (TB), seizures, blood clots, osteoporosis (brittle bones), eye problems, any allergies.

Do not have a vaccination, other immunization or any skin test while you are using this drug unless your doctor specifically tells you that you may.

If you have a history of ulcers or take large doses of aspirin or other arthritis medication, limit your consumption of alcoholic beverages while taking this medication. It may make your stomach and intestines more susceptible to the irritating effects of alcohol, aspirin, and certain arthritis medications, increasing your risk of ulcers.

Report any injuries or signs of infection (fever, sore throat, pain during urination, and muscle aches) that occur during treatment and within 12 months after treatment with this drug.

Your dose may need to be adjusted or you may need to start taking the drug again.

If you have diabetes, this drug may increase your blood sugar level. Check your blood (or urine) glucose level frequently, as directed by your doctor. Promptly report any abnormal results as directed. Your medicine, exercise plan, or diet may be adjusted.

If the phlegm (sputum) you cough up when ill becomes thickened or changes color from clear white to yellow, green, or gray, contact your doctor; these changes may be signs of an infection.

Consult your doctor or pharmacist for more details.

Drug Interactions

Before you take this drug, tell your doctor of any over-the-counter or prescription medications you are taking especially: aspirin, arthritis medication, warfarin, diuretics ("water pills"), rifampin, phenobarbital, estrogen (e.g., birth control pills), phenytoin, ketoconazole, neostigmine, pyridostigmine, ambenonium, drugs for diabetes.

Do not start or stop any medicine without first consulting your doctor or pharmacist.

Notes

Persons taking this medication for long-term therapy should wear or carry identification stating that they are taking a corticosteroid.

Do not allow anyone else to take this medication.

Missed Dose
If you miss a dose, take it as soon as you remember. If it is near the time of the next dose, skip the missed dose and resume your usual dosing schedule. Do not double the dose to catch up.

Storage
Store at room temperature between 59 and 86 degrees F (between 15 and 30 degrees C) away from moisture and sunlight. Do not store in the bathroom. Do not freeze liquid forms of this medication.

PROMETHAZINE

Common Brand Name: Phenergan

Uses
Promethazine is used to prevent nausea and vomiting. It is also used for sedation, allergy symptoms (runny nose, itchy eyes) and motion sickness (prevention and treatment).

How to Use
May be taken with food or milk to lessen stomach irritation. Do not take more medication than is prescribed. For motion sickness, medication should be taken 30-60 minutes before travel.

Side Effects
Constipation, drowsiness, vision changes or dry mouth may occur. If any of these effects persist or worsen, notify your doctor.

Unlikely to occur but report promptly: restlessness, muscle stiffness, weakness, difficulty speaking, loss of balance, mask-like facial expression, trembling or shaking, dizziness, lip smacking or other uncontrollable movements, difficulty urinating, skin rash/discoloration.

Very unlikely to occur but report promptly: sore throat, unusual bleeding or bruising, stomach pain, dark urine, hot dry skin, vomiting.

Though very unlikely to occur, notify your doctor immediately if you experience any of the following effects: severe muscle stiffness, confusion, fever, seizures, irregular/fast heartbeat, increased sweating, prolonged/painful erection.

In the unlikely event you have an allergic reaction to this drug, seek immediate medical attention. Symptoms of an allergic reaction include: rash, itching, swelling, dizziness, trouble breathing.

If you notice other effects not listed above, contact your doctor or pharmacist.

Precautions
Tell your doctor your medical history, especially if you have: very high or very low

blood pressure, liver or heart disease, Reye's syndrome, alcohol or drug dependencies, nervous system problems, blood disorders, allergies (especially drug allergies).

Use caution performing tasks that require alertness, such as driving or using machinery.

Use of alcohol can cause extreme drowsiness. Avoid alcohol use.

This medication may increase sensitivity to sunlight. Avoid prolonged sun exposure and wear a sunscreen and protective clothing when you are exposed to the sun.

This medication can reduce sweating making you more susceptible to heat stroke. Avoid strenuous work or exercise in hot weather.

Drug Interactions

Inform your doctor of all the medications you may use (both prescription and nonprescription), especially if you have: anti-depressant/anti-anxiety drugs, lithium, metrizamide, cabergoline, tranquilizers, barbiturates, sleeping pills, narcotic pain medication (e.g., codeine), other medicines that make you drowsy.

Many cough-and-cold products contain ingredients that may add a drowsiness effect. Before you use cough-and-cold medications, ask your doctor or pharmacist about the safe use of those products.

Do not start or stop any medicine without first consulting your doctor or pharmacist.

Notes

Do not share this medication with others.

Missed Dose

If you miss a dose, take it as soon as you remember. If it is near the time of the next dose, skip the missed dose and resume your usual dosing schedule. Do not double the dose to catch up.

Storage

Store at room temperature away from sunlight and moisture.

PROMETHAZINE/CODEINE

Common Brand Name: Codeine

Uses
This combination medication is used to relieve symptoms associated with a cold, allergies or respiratory tract illness.

How to Use
Take this medication with food if stomach upset occurs.

Take this medication as directed. Do not increase the dose or take it more often or longer than prescribed.

This is a strong medication and must only be used for the condition for which it is prescribed. It should not be used for just any cough or cold.

It is helpful to drink plenty of fluids (6-8 glasses a day) to help relieve congestion.

Side Effects
Stomach upset, nausea, vomiting, constipation, dizziness, drowsiness or headache may occur. If these effects persist or worsen, inform your doctor promptly.

Unlikely but notify your doctor promptly if you develop: rapid heart rate.

In the unlikely event you have an allergic reaction to this drug, seek immediate medical attention. Symptoms of an allergic reaction include: rash, itching, swelling, dizziness, trouble breathing.

If you notice other effects not listed above, contact your doctor or pharmacist.

Precautions
Tell your doctor your medical history, especially heart disease, kidney or liver disease, lung disease, asthma, ulcers, glaucoma, difficulty urinating, stomach/intestinal problems, diarrhea, enlarged prostate, allergies, history of seizures, history of drug dependency.

Because this medication may cause dizziness or drowsiness, use caution performing tasks requiring alertness and limit alcohol intake, which can aggravate this effect.

Drug Interactions
Tell your doctor of all over-the-counter and prescription medication you may use including: sleeping pills, sedatives, tranquilizers, muscle relaxants, medication for depression, seizure medicine, narcotic pain medication, quinolone antibiotics (e.g., sparfloxacin), metrizamide, glaucoma eye medicines, antihistamines, guanethidine, guanadrel, quinidine, cimetidine, cabergoline.

Do not start or stop any medicine without first consulting your doctor or pharmacist.

Notes
Do not share this medication with others.

Missed Dose
If you miss a dose, take it as soon as you remember. If it is near the time of the next dose, skip the missed dose and resume your usual dosing schedule. Do not double the dose to catch up.

Storage
Store at room temperature away from sunlight and moisture. Do not freeze.

PROPOXYPHENE
WITH ACETAMINOPHEN (APAP)

Common Brand Name: Darvocet

Uses
This is an analgesic medication is used to relieve moderate-to-severe pain.

How to Use
To prevent upset stomach, take with food or milk.

Use this medication exactly as directed by your doctor. Do not increase your dose; use it more frequently or use it for a longer period of time than prescribed because this drug can cause physical and psychological dependence. Also, if used for an extended period, do not suddenly stop using this drug without your doctor's approval.

Over time, this drug may not work as well. Consult your doctor if this medication is not relieving the pain sufficiently.

Side Effects
May cause constipation, lightheadedness, dizziness, drowsiness, stomach upset, nausea, flushing or vision changes. If any of these effects persist or worsen, inform your doctor.

Notify your doctor immediately if you develop: irregular heartbeat, anxiety, tremors, confusion, depression, low blood pressure, fainting, yellowing of the eyes or skin, stomach pain, dark urine.

In the unlikely event you have an allergic reaction to this drug, seek immediate medical attention. Symptoms of an allergic reaction include: rash, itching, swelling, severe dizziness, trouble breathing.

If you notice other effects not listed above, contact your doctor or pharmacist.

Precautions
Tell your doctor your medical history, especially if you have: kidney or liver disease,

breathing problems, seizures, alcohol and/or drug use, colitis or other intestinal/stomach problems, severe diarrhea, head injury, heart problems, drug allergies.

Use caution when engaging in activities requiring alertness such as driving. Limit alcohol intake because it may add to the dizziness/drowsiness effects of this medication.

Acetaminophen may cause liver damage. Daily use of alcohol, especially when combined with acetaminophen, may increase your risk for liver damage. Check with your doctor or pharmacist for more information.

Older adults may be more sensitive to the effects of this drug, especially drowsiness and confusion.

Drug Interactions

Tell your doctor of all the medicines you may use both prescription and nonprescription, especially if you have: carbamazepine, cimetidine, ritonavir, other narcotic pain medications, sedatives, tranquilizers, drugs used for anxiety or depression, warfarin.

Before taking over-the-counter pain relievers or cold, cough and allergy products, read their labels to be sure they do not also contain acetaminophen. This medication contains acetaminophen and too much acetaminophen can cause liver problems.

Do not start or stop any medicine without first consulting your doctor or pharmacist.

Notes

Do not share this medication with others.

Missed Dose

If you miss a dose, take it as soon as you remember. If it is near the time of the next dose, skip the missed dose and resume your usual dosing schedule. Do not double the dose to catch up.

Storage

Store at room temperature away from sunlight and moisture.

PROPRANOLOL

Common Brand Name: Inderal

Uses
This medication belongs to a class of drugs called beta-blockers. Propranolol slows the heart and reduces hypertension (high blood pressure). It is used in the treatment of angina (chest pain), hypertension, arrhythmias (irregular heartbeats), migraine headaches, tremors, and certain medical problems.

How to Use
Take this medication exactly as prescribed. Try to take it at the same time(s) each day.

Do not suddenly stop taking this medication without consulting your doctor. Some conditions may become worse when the drug is suddenly stopped.

Side Effects
You may experience dizziness, lightheadedness, drowsiness, and blurred vision as your body adjusts to the medication. Use caution engaging in activities requiring alertness.

Because propranolol reduces blood circulation to the extremities, your hands and feet may be more susceptible to the cold temperatures. Dress warm.

Inform your doctor if you develop: breathing difficulties, increasing shortness of breath, easy bruising or bleeding, swollen hands or feet, confusion or depression, sore throat.

If you notice other effects not listed above, contact your doctor or pharmacist.

Precautions
Tell your doctor your medical history, especially if you have: heart disease, kidney problems, liver disease, asthma, bronchitis, emphysema or other lung disease, diabetes, an over-active thyroid gland, allergies (especially drug allergies).

You may want to check your pulse every day while taking this medication. Discuss with your doctor what changes in your pulse rate mean.

Before having surgery, tell the doctor or dentist in charge that you are taking propranolol.

Drug Interactions
Tell your doctor of all prescription and nonprescription drugs you may use, especially if you have: diuretics, cold preparations and nasal decongestants, reserpine, other heart medications, high blood pressure medications, St John's wort.

Do not start or stop any medicine without first consulting your doctor or pharmacist approval.

Notes
Do not share this product with others.

Missed Dose
If you miss a dose, take it as soon as you remember. If it is near the time of the next dose, skip the missed dose and resume your usual dosing schedule. Do not double the dose to catch up.

Storage
Store at room temperature between 59 and 86 degrees F (between 15 and 30 degrees C) away from moisture and sunlight. Do not store in the bathroom.

QUINAPRIL

Common Brand Name: Accupril

Uses
Quinapril prevents certain enzymes in the body from narrowing blood vessels. This helps to lower blood pressure and makes the heart beat stronger. This medication is used to treat high blood pressure or heart failure and may prevent kidney problems in persons with diabetes.

How to Use
This medication may be taken without regard to meals. Take it exactly as prescribed and try to take it at the same time each day.

If you are taking a tetracycline antibiotic or a quinolone (e.g., ciprofloxacin, levofloxacin) antibiotic, take it at least 3 hours apart from this medicine. This product contains magnesium, which can interfere with absorption of these antibiotics.

Do not stop taking this medication without consulting your doctor. Some conditions may become worse when the drug is abruptly stopped. Your dose may need to be gradually decreased before it is stopped completely.

Side Effects
Headache, diarrhea, constipation, nausea, fatigue or dry cough may occur the first several days as your body adjusts to the medication.

Unlikely but report promptly: chest pain, tingling or swelling around the face, throat and mouth, hands or feet, yellowing eyes or skin, difficulty breathing, sore throat, dizziness.

In the unlikely event you have an allergic reaction to this drug, seek immediate medical attention. Symptoms of an allergic reaction include: rash, itching, swelling, dizziness, trouble breathing.

If you notice other effects not listed above, contact your doctor or pharmacist.

Precautions
Before taking this drug tell your doctor your medical history, especially if you have:

angioedema, high blood levels of potassium, kidney disease or kidney dialysis, salt restrictive diet, liver disease, allergies (especially drug allergies).

Consult your doctor before using salt substitutes or low salt milk.

To avoid dizziness and lightheadedness when rising from a seated or lying position, get up slowly.

Limit your intake of alcohol and use caution when exercising or during hot weather as these can aggravate dizziness and lightheadedness.

Drug Interactions
Inform your doctor about all the medicine you use (both prescription and nonprescription), especially if you take: lithium, potassium supplements, potassium-sparing water pills or other water pills (diuretics), high blood pressure drugs, NSAID (aspirin-like drugs), quinidine, azole antifungals (e.g., ketoconazole), quinolones (e.g., ciprofloxacin), tetracyclines, sodium polystyrene sulfonate.

Do not start or stop any medicine without first consulting your doctor or pharmacist.

Notes
It is important to have your blood pressure checked regularly while taking this medication. Learn how to monitor your blood pressure. Discuss this with your doctor.

Lab tests may be performed periodically to monitor your progress and to make sure there are no unwanted side effects.

Missed Dose
If you miss a dose, take it as soon as you remember. If it is near the time of the next dose, skip the missed dose and resume your usual dosing schedule. Do not double the dose to catch up.

Storage
Store at room temperature away from sunlight and moisture. Do not store in the bathroom.

RABEPRAZOLE

Common Brand Name: Aciphex

Uses
Rabeprazole is used to treat various acid-related stomach and/or throat (esophagus) problems (e.g., GERD, ulcers, or Zollinger-Ellison Syndrome). It works by blocking the production of acid in the stomach.

How to Use
Take this medication by mouth, usually once daily before a meal; or as directed by your doctor.

The dosage and length of treatment is based on your medical condition and response to therapy.

Do not crush, chew, or split this medication. Swallow the medication whole.

If you take sucralfate in addition to this medication, take your dose of rabeprazole at least 30 minutes before your sucralfate.

Antacids may be taken along with this medication, if needed.

Side Effects
Headache, diarrhea, nausea, gas, upset stomach, dizziness, or constipation may occur. If any of these effects persist or worsen, notify your doctor.

Tell your doctor immediately if any of these serious side effects occur: rash, stomach/abdominal pain, back pain, unusual tiredness, vomiting.

Tell your doctor immediately if any of these unlikely but serious side effects occur: ringing in the ears, fever, swelling, unusual weight gain or weight loss, trouble breathing, vision problems, change in amount of urine.

Tell your doctor immediately if any of these highly unlikely but very serious side effects occur: chest pain, unusually fast or slow heartbeat, dark urine, yellowing eyes or skin, seizures.

An allergic reaction to this drug is unlikely, but seek immediate medical attention if it occurs. Symptoms of an allergic reaction include: rash, itching, swelling, trouble breathing.

If you notice other effects not listed above, contact your doctor or pharmacist.

Precautions

Tell your doctor your medical history, especially if you have: liver problems, other stomach problems (e.g., tumors), any allergies.

Drug Interactions

Tell your doctor of all prescription and nonprescription medication you may use, especially: digoxin, azole antifungals (e.g., ketoconazole, itraconazole), ampicillin, iron supplements, sucralfate.

Do not start or stop any medicine without first consulting your doctor or pharmacist.

Notes

Do not share this medication with others.

Medical tests may be performed to monitor your progress.

Missed Dose

If you miss a dose, take it as soon as you remember. If it is near the time of the next dose, skip the missed dose and resume your usual dosing schedule. Do not double the dose to catch up.

Storage

Store at room temperature between 59 and 86 degrees F (15 to 30 degrees C) away from light and moisture.

RALOXIFENE

Common Brand Name: Evista

Uses
This medication is used after menopause to prevent bone weakening (osteoporosis).

How to Use
Take this medication by mouth, generally one tablet (60mg) daily with or without food.

Calcium supplements and vitamin D are recommended if daily intake is not adequate. Consult your doctor or pharmacist.

Side Effects
Hot flashes, stomach upset, trouble sleeping or sweating may occur. If these effects persist or worsen, notify your doctor promptly.

Report promptly: muscle aches, flu-like symptoms nasal stuffiness/pain.

Unlikely but notify your doctor promptly if you experience: persistent fever, rash, lumps in breast, breast pain, abnormal vaginal bleeding or discomfort, chest pain.

Very unlikely but notify your doctor promptly if you experience: calf pain, sudden severe headache, one-sided weakness, slurred speech, weakness or tingling in arm or leg, trouble breathing, or vision changes.

If you notice other effects not listed above, contact your doctor or pharmacist.

Precautions
Before using this drug, tell your doctor your medical history, including: any allergies (especially drug allergies), blood clots, heart failure, cancer, liver disease.

If your cholesterol levels have ever increased because you took estrogens, inform your doctor.

This drug should be stopped at least 3 days before and during long periods of inactivity (e.g., bed rest). Blood clots, though unlikely, are more common when not moving. Avoid long periods of sitting or lying down during travel.

Drug Interactions

Tell your doctor of all nonprescription and prescription medication you may use, especially if you have: bile-acid resin drugs (such as cholestyramine), warfarin, clofibrate, diazepam, diazoxide, estrogens (e.g., conjugated estrogens).

This drug may alter certain laboratory tests, including cholesterol, thyroid, corticosteroid or other hormone tests.

Do not start or stop any medicine without first consulting your doctor or pharmacist.

Notes

Do not share this medication with others.

Smoking, alcohol use and lack of exercise have been linked to bone loss. Discuss these risk factors with your doctor.

Missed Dose

If you miss a dose, take it as soon as you remember. If it is near the time of the next dose, skip the missed dose and resume your usual dosing schedule. Do not double the dose to catch up.

Storage

Store at room temperature between 68-77 degrees F (20-25 degrees C) away from light and moisture.

RAMIPRIL

Common Brand Name: Altace

Uses
This medication belongs to a group of drugs called ACE inhibitors. ACE inhibitors prevent certain substances in the body from narrowing the blood vessels. This helps to lower blood pressure and makes the heart beat stronger.

Ramipril is used to treat high blood pressure, heart failure and, in certain cases, to prevent heart problems (such as heart attacks), strokes, and protection from kidney problems associted with diabetes.

How to Use
This medication may be taken without regard to meals. Take it exactly as prescribed and try to take it at the same time each day.

Swallow capsules whole, or the contents of the capsule may be sprinkled on a small amount of soft food such as applesauce or mixed in apple juice or water. Swallow or drink the entire mixture.

Do not stop taking this medication without consulting your doctor. Some conditions may become worse when the drug is abruptly stopped. Your dose may need to be gradually decreased.

It is important to continue taking this medication even if you feel well. Most people with high blood pressure do not feel sick.

Side Effects
Dizziness, headache, diarrhea, constipation (swelling of the neck/lips), nausea, fatigue or dry cough may occur the first several days as your body adjusts to the medication.

Inform your doctor if you develop: chest pain, tingling of the hands or feet, persistent sore throat and fever.

In the unlikely event you have an allergic reaction to this drug, seek immediate medical attention. Symptoms of an allergic reaction include: rash, itching, swelling, dizziness, trouble breathing.

If you notice other effects not listed above, contact your doctor or pharmacist.

Precautions

Before taking this drug tell your doctor your medical history, especially if you have: swelling, high blood levels of potassium, kidney disease or kidney dialysis, salt restrictive diets, liver disease, heart problems, any allergies you may have.

Consult your doctor before using salt substitutes or low salt milk.

To avoid dizziness and lightheadedness when rising from a seated or lying position, get up slowly.

Limit your intake of alcohol and use caution when exercising or during hot weather as these can aggravate dizziness and lightheadedness.

Caution is advised when this medication is used with older people.

Drug Interactions

Inform your doctor about all the medicine you use (both prescription and nonprescription) especially: lithium, potassium supplements, potassium-sparing "water pills" (e.g. aldosterone), anti-inflammatory drugs (NSAIDs), digoxin.

Avoid "stimulant" drugs that may increase your heart rate such as decongestants or caffeine. Decongestants are commonly found in over-the-counter cough-and-cold medicine.

Do not start or stop any medicine without first consulting your doctor or pharmacist.

Notes

It is important to have your blood pressure checked regularly while taking this medication. Learn how to monitor your blood pressure. Discuss this with your doctor.

Missed Dose

If you miss a dose, take it as soon as you remember. If it is near the time of the next dose, skip the missed dose and resume your usual dosing schedule. Do not double the dose to catch up.

Storage

Store the capsule at room temperature away from sunlight and moisture. Do not store in the bathroom. The medication mixture of food or liquid can be kept at room temperature for 24 hours or refrigerated for 48 hours.

RANITIDINE

Uses

This medication reduces the amount of acid in your stomach. It is used to treat and prevent ulcers, to treat gastroesophageal reflux disorder (GERD), and to treat conditions associated with excessive acid secretion.

How to Use

This medication is best taken with or immediately after meals. Antacids and sucralfate can block the effect of this medication. If you are taking an antacid in addition to this medication, separate the doses of each medication by at least one half hour. If you are taking sucralfate in addition to this medication, take the ranitidine 2 hours before the sucralfate. Do not stop taking this medication without your doctor's approval.

Stopping therapy too soon may delay healing of the ulcer.

Side Effects

Nausea, diarrhea, headache, or dizziness may occur at first as your body adjusts to the medication. If these effects persist or become bothersome, inform your doctor.

Notify your doctor if you experience: unusual bleeding or bruising, rash, difficulty sleeping, mental changes, extreme weakness, fast/slow/irregular heartbeat.

An allergic reaction to this drug is unlikely, but seek immediate medical attention if it occurs. Symptoms of an allergic reaction include: rash, itching, swelling, dizziness, trouble breathing.

If you notice other effects not listed above, contact your doctor or pharmacist.

Precautions

Tell your doctor your full medical history, especially if you have: kidney or liver disease, porphyria, any allergies.

Smoking helps cause ulcers and can prevent healing. Smoking should be avoided. Alcohol can irritate the stomach and cause bleeding. Consult your doctor.

Drug Interactions
Tell your doctor of all over-the-counter and prescription medication you may use, especially if you have: ketoconazole, itraconazole, triazolam.

This medication is available in both prescription and over-the-counter formulations. Do not take both at the same time.

Do not start or stop any medicine without first consulting your doctor or pharmacist.

Notes
Your doctor may recommend some lifestyle changes such as stop-smoking programs, diet changes and exercise to assist in the treatment and prevention of ulcers. Ranitidine may affect the results of tests for urine protein. Be sure to tell your doctor you are taking ranitidine.

Remember that all nonprescription/prescription aspirin or aspirin-like medicine can cause stomach irritation/ulcers.

Consult your doctor or pharmacist.

Missed Dose
If you miss a dose, take it as soon as you remember. If it is near the time of the next dose, skip the missed dose and resume your usual dosing schedule. Do not double the dose to catch up.

Storage
Store between 59 and 86 degrees F (between 15 and 30 degrees C) away from moisture and sunlight. Do not store in the bathroom.

RISPERIDONE

Common Brand Name: Risperdal

Uses
This medication is used in the treatment of psychotic or mental or psychiatric conditions.

How to Use
Take this medication exactly as prescribed. During the first few days your doctor may gradually increase your dose to allow your body to adjust to the medication.

Do not take this more often or increase your dose without consulting your doctor. Your condition will not improve any faster but the risk of serious side effects will be increased. Do not stop taking this drug without your doctor's approval.

Side Effects
Dizziness, drowsiness, nausea, increased dreaming, nervousness, loss of appetite, dry mouth or fatigue may occur the first several days as your body adjusts to the medication. Weight gain, vision changes, decreased sexual desire and insomnia have also been reported. If any of these effects continue or become bothersome, inform your doctor.

Notify your doctor if you develop: rapid/pounding/irregular heartbeat, skin rash, itching, difficulty moving, muscle stiffness, muscle spasms or twitching, sweating, involuntary movements (especially about the face or tongue), drooling, tremors, trouble swallowing, mental confusion, seizures.

If you notice other effects not listed above, contact your doctor or pharmacist.

Precautions
Tell your doctor your medical history, especially if you have: kidney disease, liver disease, heart disease, diabetes, seizures, blood disorders, breast cancer, swallowing difficulty, allergies (especially drug allergies).

Because this medication may cause drowsiness or dizziness, use caution operating machinery or engaging in activities requiring alertness such as driving.

Dizziness on standing may occur. To avoid dizziness or lightheadedness when rising from a seated or lying position, get up slowly.

This medication may make you more sensitive to the sun. Avoid prolonged sun exposure. Wear protective clothing and use a sunscreen containing an SPF of at least 15 when outdoors.

Older adults may be more sensitive to the effects of the drug, especially the side effects.

Drug Interactions
Tell your doctor of any over-the-counter or prescription medication you may take, especially if you have: sedatives, narcotic pain relievers (e.g., codeine), anti-anxiety agents, antidepressants, muscle relaxers, medication for seizures.

It is recommended you avoid consuming alcohol while taking this medication.

Do not start or stop any medicine without first consulting your doctor or pharmacist.

Notes
Laboratory tests may be done periodically while taking this medication to monitor the effects. See your doctor regularly.

Missed Dose
If you miss a dose, take it as soon as you remember. If it is near the time of the next dose, skip the missed dose and resume your usual dosing schedule. Do not double the dose to catch up.

Storage
Store this medication at room temperature between 59 and 86 degrees F (between 15 and 30 degrees C) away from heat and light. Do not store in the bathroom. Keep this and all medications out of the reach of children.

RIVASTIGMINE

Common Brand Name: Exelon

Uses
Rivastigmine is used to treat the memory and behavioral symptoms of Alzheimer's disease.

How to Use
Take this medication by mouth, usually twice daily in the morning and evening with food, or take as directed by your doctor. The dose depends on your condition and your response to the drug.

If you stop taking rivastigmine for several days, consult your doctor or pharmacist before restarting the medication. Your dosage should be reduced to minimize the chance of developing very severe gastrointestinal effects. It may take several weeks before before the full benefit of the drug is seen. Your dosage should then be increased gradually. Follow all your doctor's dosing instructions exactly.

Side Effects
Nausea, vomiting, stomach pain, diarrhea, dizziness, or drowsiness may occur. If any of these effects persist or worsen, contact your doctor or pharmacist promptly.

Tell your doctor immediately if any of these serious side effects occur: weight loss or loss of appetite.

Tell your doctor immediately if any of these unlikely but serious side effects occur: unusual sweating, weakness, chest pain, swelling, mental/mood changes.

If you notice other effects not listed above, contact your doctor or pharmacist.

Precautions
Tell your doctor your medical history, especially if you have: stomach or intestinal problems (e.g., ulcers, bleeding), eating disorders (e.g., anorexia nervosa), heart problems (e.g., sick sinus syndrome), lung problems (e.g., asthma, obstructive pulmonary disease), seizures, urinary tract problems (e.g., obstruction), allergies and other medications to treat (especially drug allergies) alzheimers disease.

This drug may make you dizzy or drowsy. Use caution engaging in activities requiring alertness such as driving or using machinery. Avoid alcoholic beverages.

Drug Interactions
Tell your doctor of all prescription and nonprescription drugs you may use, especially if you have: anticholinergic drugs (e.g., tolterodine, atropine, scopolamine, benztropine, oxybutynin, diphenhydramine), succinylcholine, neostigmine, bethanechol.

Do not start or stop any medicine without first consulting your doctor or pharmacist.

Notes
Do not share this medication with others.

Missed Dose
If you miss a dose, use it as soon as you remember.

If it is near the time of the next dose, skip the missed dose and resume your usual dosing schedule. Do not double the dose to catch up.

Storage
Store at room temperature below 77 degrees F (25 degrees C) away from light and moisture.

ROFECOXIB

Common Brand Name: Vioxx

Uses
This medication is a nonsteroidal anti-inflammatory drug (NSAID) which relieves pain and swelling (inflammation). It is used to treat arthritis or other acute pain.

This drug works by blocking the production of prostaglandins in your body. Decreasing prostaglandins helps to reduce pain and swelling.

How to Use
Take this drug by mouth, generally once daily as directed. To decrease the chance of stomach upset, this drug is best taken with food. Dosage is based on your medical condition and response to therapy.

Take this medication with 6 to 8 ounces (180-240ml) of water.

Do not lie down for at least 30 minutes after taking this drug.

Side Effects
Stomach upset or tiredness may occur. If these effects persist or worsen, notify your doctor promptly.

Unlikely but report promptly: severe headache, change in the amount of urine, mental/mood changes, very stiff neck.

Very unlikely but report promptly: dark urine, yellowing eyes or skin.

If you notice any of the following unlikely but very serious side effects, stop taking this drug and consult your doctor immediately: black stools, persistent stomach/ abdominal pain, vomit that looks like coffee grounds.

In the unlikely event you have an allergic reaction to this drug, seek immediate medical attention. Symptoms of an allergic reaction include: rash, itching, swelling, dizziness, trouble breathing.

If you notice other effects not listed above, contact your doctor or pharmacist.

Precautions
Tell your doctor your medical history, including allergies (especially to aspirin/other NSAIDs), liver problems, kidney problems, heart disease, stomach/intestinal ulcers

or bleeding, history of smoking, alcoholism, asthma, high blood pressure, growths in the nose (e.g., nasal polyps), serious infections, swelling (edema), blood disorders (anemia), poorly controlled diabetes, dehydration.

This medicine may cause stomach bleeding. Daily use of alcohol, especially when combined with this medicine, may increase your risk for stomach bleeding. Check with your doctor or pharmacist for more information. Caution is advised when this drug is used with older people, as this group may be more sensitive to drug side effects, especially stomach bleeding.

Drug Interactions
Tell your doctor of all prescription and nonprescription medication you may use, especially if you have: high blood pressure drugs, (e.g., ACE inhibitors such as lisinopril), water pills (diuretics such as furosemide or thiazides), aspirin or other NSAID (e.g., ibuprofen), lithium, methotrexate, corticosteroids (e.g., prednisone), rifampin.

Check all prescription and nonprescription medicine labels carefully since many contain pain relievers/fever reducers (NSAIDs such as ibuprofen, naproxen, or aspirin) which are similar to this drug. Aspirin, as prescribed by your doctor for reasons such as heart attack or stroke prevention (usually these dosages are 81-325 mg per day), should be continued. Take the dose of aspirin each day before the dose of rofecoxib. Consult your doctor or pharmacist for more details.

Do not start or stop any medicine without first consulting your doctor or pharmacist.

Notes
Do not share this medication with others.

Laboratory or medical tests may be performed to monitor your progress.

Missed Dose
If you miss a dose, take it as soon as you remember. If it is near the time of the next dose, skip the missed dose and resume your usual dosing schedule. Do not double the dose to catch up.

Storage
Store at room temperature (77 degrees F or 25 degrees C) away from light and moisture.

ROPINIROLE

Common Brand Name: Requip

Uses
This medication is used to treat Parkinson's disease. It replaces the brain chemical called dopamine, which is low in Parkinson's disease.

How to Use
Take this medication as prescribed. Do not increase your dose or take it more often than directed.

Do not stop taking this medication without your doctor's approval. Stopping this drug suddenly may cause you to experience unwanted side effects.

Dosing is based on your condition and this drug's side effects.

It may take a few weeks for this medication to take full effect.

Side Effects
Nausea, dizziness, drowsiness, trouble sleeping, constipation, unusual weakness, stomach upset and pain, headache or dry mouth may occur. If these effects persist or worsen, notify your doctor promptly.

To relieve dry mouth, drink water, suck on hard candy or ice chips, chew gum, or use saliva substitute.

Report promptly: hallucinations, difficulty moving or walking, difficulty breathing.

Unlikely but report promptly: confusion, restlessness, leg or foot swelling, fainting, twitching, chest pain. Very unlikely but report promptly: muscle pain, vision problems, fever, severe muscle stiffness.

If you notice other effects not listed above, contact your doctor or pharmacist.

Precautions
Tell your doctor if you have a history of disease or heart arrhythmias (abnormal rhythms), hallucinations, mental confusion, difficulty walking, any allergies, kidney problems, liver disease, low blood pressure or taking other medications for Parkinson's disease.

To avoid dizziness and lightheadedness when rising from a seated or lying position, get up slowly.

Use caution when performing tasks requiring mental alertness such as driving or using machinery. Limit alcohol use because it may intensify the drowsiness and dizziness effects of this drug.

Drug Interactions

Tell your doctor of any over-the-counter or prescription medication you may take, including: metoclopramide, medication for psychosis/anxiety/depression, other drugs used for Parkinson's, cimetidine, sleep medication, certain muscle relaxants, tranquilizers, narcotic pain relievers, anti-seizure drugs, certain antihistamines (e.g., diphenhydramine), ciprofloxacin.

Do not start or stop any medicine without first consulting your doctor or pharmacist.

Notes

Do not share this medication with others.

Missed Dose

If you miss a dose, take it as soon as you remember. If it is near the time of the next dose, skip the missed dose and resume your usual dosing schedule. Do not double the dose to catch up.

Storage

Store at controlled room temperature away from moisture and sunlight. Do not store in the bathroom.

ROSIGLITAZONE MALEATE

Common Brand Name: Avandia

Uses
This medication is used to treat diabetes. It works by helping to restore your body's proper response to insulin, thereby lowering your blood sugar.

Rosiglitazone is used either alone or in combination with other anti-diabetes medicines (e.g., metformin), as part of a diet and exercise program.

How to Use
Take by mouth, with or without food, as directed.

Dosage is based on your medical condition and response to therapy.

This medication may be used in addition to other medications to treat diabetes. Take all other medication as directed by your doctor.

Side Effects
Headache may occur. If this effect persists or worsens, notify your doctor promptly.

Unlikely but report promptly: back pain, cough, unusual tiredness or weakness, swelling, in hands or feet sudden weight gain, shortness of breath, trouble breathing, unusual thirst or urination.

Very unlikely but report promptly: dizziness, tremors, rapid pulse, vomiting, stomach pain, dark urine, yellowing eyes or skin.

If you notice other effects not listed above, contact your doctor or pharmacist.

Precautions
Use of this medication is not recommended if you have newly diagnosed or worsening heart failure (acute congestive heart failure).

Tell your doctor your medical history, including: allergies, high cholesterol, swelling (edema), heart problems (e.g., chronic congestive heart failure), very high blood glucose (diabetic ketoacidosis), blood problems (e.g., anemia), liver disease.

Consult your doctor or pharmacist to learn the symptoms of high or low blood sugar. Some symptoms of high blood sugar include thirst and increased urination.

Low blood sugar may cause you to feel shaky, sweaty, hungry or have an increased pulse.

Carry glucose tablets or gel to treat low blood sugar. Consult your pharmacist.

During times of stress, such as fever, infection, injury or surgery, it may be more difficult to control your blood sugar.

Consult your doctor, as additional medication may be required.

Drug Interactions
Tell your doctor of all prescription and nonprescription medication you may use, especially if you have: diabetes drugs.

Do not start or stop any medicine without first consulting your doctor or pharmacist.

Notes
Do not share this medication with others.

It is recommended you attend a diabetes education program to understand diabetes and all important aspects of its treatment including meals, exercise, personal hygiene, medication and getting regular eye and medical exams. Consult your doctor or pharmacist.

Keep all medical appointments. Laboratory and/or medical tests (e.g., liver function tests) will be performed to monitor for side effects and response to therapy. Regularly check your blood or urine for sugar, as directed by your doctor or pharmacist.

Controlling high blood sugar helps prevent heart disease, strokes, kidney disease, circulation problems, and blindness.

Missed Dose
If you miss a dose, take it as soon as you remember. If it is near the time of the next dose, skip the missed dose and resume your usual dosing schedule. Do not double the dose to catch up.

Storage
Store at room temperature between 59 and 86 degrees F (15 to 30 degrees C) away from light and moisture.

SALMETEROL

Common Brand Name: Serevent

Uses

Salmeterol opens air passages in the lungs to improve breathing. It is used to prevent/minimize problems in persons with breathing difficulties (e.g., asthma or chronic obstructive pulmonary disease).

This medication is not for use in an acute asthma attack.

How to Use

Make sure you understand how to use the inhaler properly. Shake the canister well before using. Place the mouthpiece of the canister near your mouth and exhale. Put your mouth tightly around the mouthpiece and depress the spray as you inhale deeply. Hold your breath for a few seconds to allow the drug to be absorbed.

If more than one inhalation is prescribed, wait at least one full minute between inhalations.

Rinse your mouth after using to help prevent dryness and relieve throat irritation.

Use this medication exactly as prescribed. Do not use it more frequently without your doctor's approval. This medication should not be used more frequently than every 12 hours. Excessive use may result in a decrease in drug's effectiveness and an increase in its side effects.

You should use this medication 30 to 60 minutes before exercise when using it to prevent exercise-induced asthma.

If you need to use 4 or more puffs daily or more than 1 inhaler every 8 weeks of a different, shorter-acting inhaler, tell your doctor or pharmacist.

If symptoms do not improve or if they worsen after using this medication, call your doctor immediately.

Side Effects

Dry mouth, irritated throat, dizziness, headache, lightheadedness, heartburn, loss of appetite, restlessness, anxiety, nervousness, trembling, and sweating may occur but should subside as your body adjusts to the medication. If these symptoms persist or worsen, inform your doctor.

To relieve dry mouth, suck on (sugarless) hard candy or ice chips, chew (sugarless) gum, drink water or use saliva substitute.

Inform your doctor if you experience: chest pain, pounding heartbeat, muscle tremors, flushing or if breathing difficulty persists.

In the unlikely event you have an allergic reaction to this drug, seek medical attention immediately. Symptoms of an allergic reaction include: rash, itching, swelling, dizziness, trouble breathing.

If you notice other effects not listed above, contact your doctor or pharmacist.

Precautions
Before using this drug, tell your doctor your medical history, especially if you have: heart disease, high blood pressure, an overactive thyroid gland, epilepsy, diabetes, enlarged prostate gland, drug allergies.

Drug Interactions
Tell your doctor of all drugs you may use, (both prescription and nonprescription) including: beta-blockers (e.g., propranolol, labetalol, timolol), drugs used for asthma, antidepressants, diuretics (e.g., hydrochlorothiazide), MAO inhibitors (tranylcypromine).

It is important to read carefully all labels on over-the-counter preparations, especially those used to treat colds or allergies. Do not use these without first consulting your doctor.

Do not start or stop any medicine without first consulting your doctor or pharmacist.

Notes
Do not share this medication with others.

If you need to use 4 or more puffs of a shorter acting inhaler (such as albuterol) on a regular basis or if your need to use more than 1 of these shorter acting inhalers every 8 weeks, tell your doctor or pharmacist. A spacer may be utilized to enhance maximal effectiveness. Do not use a spacer with the dry powder disus inhaler. Keep mouthpiece of powder diskus dry.

Missed Dose
If you miss a dose, take it as soon as you remember. If it is near the time of the next dose, skip the missed dose and resume your usual dosing schedule. Do not double the dose to catch up.

Storage
Store at room temperature between 59 and 86 degrees F (between 15 and 30 degrees C) away from moisture and sunlight. Do not store in the bathroom. Do not puncture.

SALMETEROL/FLUTICASONE

Common Brand Name: Advair Diskus

Uses

This combination medication is used as long-term treatment to prevent or decrease, the symptoms of asthma (e.g., wheezing, trouble breathing). It works by decreasing the inflammation and increasing the airway space in the lungs.

This medication does not work immediately and should not be used for asthma attacks. Use other quick-relief medicines/inhalers for sudden shortness of breath or asthma attacks.

How to Use

Learn all preparation and usage instructions in the product package. If any of the information is unclear, consult your doctor or pharmacist.

Inhale this medication by mouth usually twice daily, in the morning and the evening (12 hours apart); or use as directed by your doctor. Your dosage is based on your condition and response to treatment.

Use this medication exactly as prescribed; do not use it more frequently or use more inhalations than prescribed. Doing so would decrease the effectiveness of the drug and increase the risk of side effects.

Gargle and rinse your mouth after using this medication to help prevent dryness, relieve throat irritation, and to prevent mouth infections (e.g., thrush). Do not swallow the rinse solution.

If you find that your fast-acting inhaler is not working as well or if you need to use it more often than usual (i.e., using 4 or more puffs daily, or using more than 1 inhaler every 8 weeks), tell your doctor or pharmacist promptly. It may be a sign of worsening asthma which is a serious condition.

Do not breath into (exhale into) the inhaler, take the inhaler apart, or wash the mouthpiece of the inhaler. Keep the inhaler dry at all times and always use the inhaler in a level (horizontal) position.

Side Effects

Headache, cough, diarrhea, nausea, vomiting, dry mouth or mouth/throat or sinus irritation may occur. If any of these effects persist or worsen, notify your doctor or pharmacist promptly.

Tell your doctor immediately if any of these serious side effects occur: congestion, sinus infection, white and/or swollen mouth or tongue, muscle pain, stomach pain, weight gain.

Tell your doctor immediately if any of these unlikely but serious side effects occur: swelling, vision changes, joint pain, trouble sleeping, rash, tremors.

Tell your doctor immediately if any of these highly unlikely but very serious side effects occur: seizures, severe muscle weakness, irregular heartbeat, unusually fast heartbeat, numbness/tingling of the hands and feet, chest pain, muscle cramps, worsening of breathing symptoms (e.g., wheezing, choking).

Contact your doctor if you experience any of the following signs of low steroid levels: unusual weakness, weight loss, fainting, dizziness.

If you had been taking oral steroids (e.g., prednisone) for conditions other than asthma (e.g., sinus, eye, skin problems), these conditions may return or worsen.

To relieve dry mouth, suck on (sugarless) hard candy, ice chips, chew (sugarless) gum, drink water, or use a saliva substitute.

In the unlikely event you have an allergic reaction to this drug, seek medical attention immediately. Symptoms of an allergic reaction include: rash, itching, swelling, dizziness, trouble breathing.

If you notice other effects not listed above, contact your doctor or pharmacist.

Precautions

Tell your doctor your medical history, especially if you have: heart problems (e.g., arrhythmias), liver problems, diabetes, high blood pressure, low potassium levels (hypokalemia), eye problems (e.g., cataracts, glaucoma), depression, recent infections, exposure to contagious disease (e.g., chickenpox), seizures, thyroid problems (e.g., hyperthyroid), any allergies you may have.

This product may make you dizzy; use caution engaging in activities requiring alertness such as driving or using machinery. Limit alcoholic beverages.

Though very unlikely, it is possible this medication will be absorbed into your bloodstream. This may have undesirable consequences that may require additional corticosteroid treatment.

Drug Interactions

Tell your doctor of all prescription and nonprescription medication you may use, especially: oral corticosteroids (e.g., dexamethasone, prednisone), beta-blockers (e.g., metoprolol, propranolol), MAO inhibitors (e.g., furazolidone, linezolid, phenelzine, selegiline, tranylcypromine), tricyclic antidepressants (e.g., amitriptyline, nortriptyline), diuretics (e.g., furosemide, hydrochlorothiazide), macrolide antibiotics (e.g., clarithromycin, erythromycin), cimetidine, protease inhibitors (e.g., lopinavir, ritonavir), azole antifungals (e.g., itraconazole, ketoconazole).

Check the labels on all your medicines (e.g., cough-and-cold products, diet aids) because they may contain ingredients that could increase your heart rate or blood pressure. Ask your pharmacist about the safe use of those products.

Do not start or stop any medicine without first consulting your doctor or pharmacist.

Notes
Do not share this medication with others.

Laboratory and/or medical tests may be performed to monitor your progress.

Inform all your doctors you use (or have used) this medication. This product will not treat an acute attack of asthma quickly. Use of shorter acting albuterol is necessary for acute shortness of breath.

Missed Dose
If you miss a dose, take it as soon as you remember. If it is near the time of the next dose, skip the missed dose and resume your usual dosing schedule. Do not double the dose to catch up.

Storage
Store this medicine exactly as directed on the package.

SELEGILINE

Common Brand Name: Eldepryl

Uses
This medication is used to treat Parkinson's disease. It is used along with levodopa or levodopa/carbidopa.

How to Use
Take this medication as prescribed. This medication is usually taken 2 times a day, in the morning or early afternoon. Take the second dose in the early afternoon to avoid bedtime insomnia. Do not increase your dose or take it more often than directed.

It may take a few weeks for the full benefits of the drug to be noticed. Do not stop taking this drug without first consulting your doctor.

Side Effects
This medication may cause stomach upset, loss of appetite, nausea, heartburn or dry mouth. These effects should subside as your body adjusts to the medication. If they continue or become bothersome, inform your doctor.

To relieve dry mouth, drink water, suck on hard candy or ice chips, chew gum, or use saliva substitute.

Infrequently, this medication may increase the skin's sensitivity to sunlight. If this happens to you, avoid prolonged sun exposure, wear protective clothing and use a sunscreen.

This medication can cause dizziness and lightheadedness especially during the first few days of therapy. Avoid tasks requiring alertness if you experience these effects.

Notify your doctor promptly if you develop any of the following side effects: severe headache, chest pain, irregular heartbeat, tremors, clumsiness, confusion, involuntary movements (especially of the hands or face), nightmares, hallucinations, insomnia, difficulty breathing, difficulty urinating.

If you notice other effects not listed above, contact your doctor or pharmacist.

Precautions
Before using this drug, tell your doctor your medical history, especially if you have: peptic ulcer, allergies (especially drug allergies).

Drug Interactions
This drug should not be used with the following medications because very serious interactions may occur: apraclonidine, brimonidine, bethanidine, bupropion, buspirone, carbamazepine, dextromethorphan, entacapone, herbal products (e.g., ma huang), indoramin, meperidine, papaverine, sibutramine, SSRI antidepressants (e.g., fluoxetine, citalopram), sympathomimetics (e.g., methylphenidate, ephedrine), tolcapone, tricyclic antidepressants (e.g., amitriptyline, doxepin), "triptans" (e.g., sumatriptan, zolmitriptan).

If you are currently using any of these medications, tell your doctor or pharmacist before starting selegiline.

Before using this medication, be sure to tell your doctor what medicines (both prescription and nonprescription) you are taking, including: levodopa, insulin and oral antidiabetic drugs, other MAO inhibitors (e.g., furazolidone, linezolid, moclobemide, phenelzine), tryptophan, sedatives and drugs used to aid sleep, drugs used for blood pressure.

Consult your doctor about the need to watch your intake of foods containing tyramine. At doses higher than 10mg a day. It is possible consuming tyramine-containing foods while using this medication could cause headache and/or increased blood pressure and could lead to a medical emergency. Tyramine food precautions should be observed for at least 2 weeks after you stop using this medication.

The following is a partial list of tyramine-containing foods:

- Meat or fish: pickled herring/liver/dry sausage/salami/meats prepared with tenderizer
- Dairy: yogurt/sour cream/aged cheeses (cream or cottage cheese are okay) Beverages: beer/red wine/sherry Avoid excessive amount of caffeine-containing colas/coffee/tea
- Fruits and Vegetables: avocado/bananas/figs/raisins/broad beans/sauerkraut
- Other: yeast extract/soy sauce/large amounts of chocolate.

Do not start or stop any medicine without first consulting your doctor or pharmacist.

Notes
Do not share this medication with others.

Missed Dose

If you miss a dose, take it as soon as you remember. If it is near the time of the next dose, skip the missed dose and resume your usual dosing schedule. Do not double the dose to catch up.

Storage

Store at room temperature away from sunlight and moisture.

SERTRALINE

Common Brand Name: Zoloft

Uses
Sertraline is used to treat depression, panic attacks, obsessive compulsive disorders (OCD), and post-traumatic stress disorder (PTSD).

This medication works by helping to restore the balance of certain natural chemicals in the brain.

How to Use
Take this medication by mouth usually once daily with or without food; or as directed by your doctor. It is recommended that you take your dosage at the same time each day, either in the morning or in the evening.

The dosage is based on your medical condition and response to therapy.

It is important to continue taking this medication as prescribed even if you feel well. Also, do not stop taking this medication without consulting your doctor.

It may take up to 4 weeks before the full benefit of this drug takes effect.

Side Effects
Nausea, headache, diarrhea, trouble sleeping, dry mouth, drowsiness, dizziness, or upset stomach may occur. If any of these effects persist or worsen, notify your doctor promptly.

Tell your doctor immediately if any of these serious side effects occur: loss of appetite, unusual weight loss, unusual or severe mental/mood changes, increased sweating/flushing, uncontrolled movements (tremor), decreased interest in sex.

Tell your doctor immediately if any of these unlikely but serious side effects occur: vision changes, changes in sexual ability, painful and/or prolonged erection.

Tell your doctor immediately if any of these highly unlikely but very serious side effects occur: fainting, irregular heartbeat, chest pain, muscle pain, trouble swallowing, ringing in in the ears, seizures.

An allergic reaction to this drug is unlikely, but seek immediate medical attention if it occurs. Symptoms of an allergic reaction include: rash, itching, swelling, severe dizziness, trouble breathing.

If you notice other effects not listed above, contact your doctor or pharmacist.

Precautions

Tell your doctor your medical history, especially if you have: liver problems, kidney disease, seizures, heart problems, any allergies.

This drug may make you dizzy or drowsy; use caution engaging in activities requiring alertness such as driving or using machinery. Limit alcoholic beverages.

Older adults may need a lower dose of this drug, especially when starting therapy, because sertraline may be removed from their body more slowly.

Drug Interactions

Certain medications taken with this product could result in serious, even fatal, drug interactions. Avoid taking MAO (monoamine oxidase) inhibitors (e.g., furazolidone, isocarboxazid, linezolid, moclobemide, phenelzine, procarbazine, selegiline, tranylcypromine) within 2 weeks before or after treatment with this medication. Consult your doctor or pharmacist for additional information.

This drug is not recommended for use with: weight loss drugs (e.g., sibutramine, phentermine), terfenadine, astemizole.

Ask your doctor or pharmacist for more details.

Tell your doctor of all prescription and nonprescription medication you may use, especially: other SSRI antidepressants (e.g., citalopram, fluoxetine), nefazodone, venlafaxine, "triptan" migraine drugs (e.g., sumatriptan, zolmitriptan), tramadol, tricyclic antidepressants (e.g., amitriptyline, nortriptyline), cimetidine, flecainide, propafenone, clozapine, trazodone, lithium, tryptophan, warfarin, any herbal/natural products (e.g., melatonin, St John's wort, ayahuasca).

Tell your doctor if you take any drugs that cause drowsiness such as: medicine for sleep, sedatives, tranquilizers, anti- anxiety drugs (e.g., diazepam), narcotic pain relievers (e.g., codeine), phenothiazines (e.g., chlorpromazine), anti-seizure drugs (e.g., carbamazepine), muscle relaxants, non-prescription antihistamines (e.g., diphenhydramine).

Use sertraline with certain medicines may cause abnormal heart rhythm including: dofetilide, pimozide, sotalol, quinidine, procainamide, sparfloxacin.

Ask your doctor or pharmacist for more details.

Do not start or stop any medicine without first consulting your doctor or pharmacist.

Notes

Do not share this medication with others.

Laboratory and/or medical tests may be performed to monitor your progress.

Missed Dose

If you miss a dose, take it as soon as you remember. If it is near the time of the next dose, skip the missed dose and resume your usual dosing schedule. Do not double the dose to catch up.

Storage

Store at room temperature between 59 and 86 degrees F (15 and 30 degrees C) away from light and moisture.

SILDENAFIL CITRATE

Common Brand Name: Viagra

Uses
This medication is used to treat male sexual function problems (erection problems).

How to Use
This drug is taken by mouth as needed between four hours and one-half hour before sexual activity (about one hour before is most effective). Take only as directed, usually once daily as needed.

Sildenafil works along with sexual stimulation to help achieve an erection.

Side Effects
Headache, flushing, stomach upset, nasal stuffiness, diarrhea and dizziness might occur. If these effects persist or worsen, notify your doctor promptly.

Unlikely but report promptly: painful or other urination problems, vision problems, skin rash.

Very unlikely but report promptly: chest pain, fainting, foot or ankle swelling.

If you experience a painful or prolonged erection (lasting longer than 4 hours), stop using this drug and seek immediate medical attention.

If you notice other effects not listed above, contact your doctor or pharmacist.

Precautions
Before using this drug, tell your doctor your medical history, including: allergies (especially drug allergies), penis conditions such as fibrosis/scarring (e.g., Peyronie's disease), history of painful/prolonged erection (priapism), sickle cell anemia, blood system cancers (such as leukemia or myeloma), eye problems (retina diseases), kidney or liver disease, bleeding disorders, active stomach ulcers, heart disease, stroke, very high or low blood pressure.

Limit alcohol intake, as it may aggravate side effects of this drug.

Since this drug may cause dizziness, caution is advised when performing tasks requiring alertness (e.g., driving). To avoid dizziness and lightheadedness when rising from a seated or lying position, get up slowly.

This drug is not to be used in women or children.

Older adults may be more sensitive to the side effects of this drug, therefore a lower starting dose should be used.

Drug Interactions

This drug is not recommended for use with nitrates (e.g., nitroglycerin, isosorbide). Ask your doctor or pharmacist for more details.

Tell your doctor of all nonprescription and prescription medication you may use, especially if you have: cimetidine, erythromycin, azole antifungals (e.g., itraconazole, ketoconazole), mibefradil, rifamycins (e.g., rifampin), high blood pressure medicines, certain HIV protease inhibitors (such as saquinavir, ritonavir, amprenavir), delavirdine.

Do not start or stop any medicine without first consulting your doctor or pharmacist approval.

Notes

Do not share this medication with others, since they may have a problem that is not effectively treated by this drug.

Use of this drug does not protect against sexually transmitted diseases (e.g., HIV, Hepatitis B, gonorrhea, syphilis).

Missed Dose

Not applicable.

Storage

Store at room temperature between 59 and 86 degrees F (15-30 degrees C) away from light and moisture.

SIMVASTATIN

Common Brand Name: Zocor

Uses
Simvastatin works by decreasing the amount of cholesterol made by the body. Simvastatin is used, along with a cholesterol-lowering diet, to help lower cholesterol and fats (triglycerides) in the blood. Reducing cholesterol and triglycerides helps prevent strokes and heart attacks. Simvastatin is one of several drugs that are referred to as "statins."

How to Use
Take this medication by mouth usually once daily in the evening, with or without food. Certain medical conditions (e.g., familial hypercholesterolemia) may require more frequent dosage instructions as directed by your doctor. The dosage is based on your medical condition and response to therapy.

It may take up to 4 weeks before the full benefit of this drug takes effect.

It is important to continue taking this medication even if you feel well. Most people with high cholesterol or triglycerides do not feel sick.

Side Effects
Headache, nausea, diarrhea, constipation, gas, or stomach upset/pain may occur. If any of these effects persist or worsen, notify your doctor promptly.

Tell your doctor immediately if any of these unlikely but serious side effects occur: joint pain, muscle pain or weakness, fever, unusual tiredness, chest pain, swelling in the arms or legs, dizziness.

Tell your doctor immediately if any of these highly unlikely but very serious side effects occur: yellowing eyes and skin, dark urine, change in amount of urine, vision problems, black stool, severe stomach pain.

An allergic reaction to this drug is unlikely, but seek immediate medical attention if it occurs. Symptoms of an allergic reaction include: rash, itching, swelling, severe dizziness, trouble breathing.

If you notice other effects not listed above, contact your doctor or pharmacist.

Precautions

This medication is not recommended for use if you have the following medical conditions: liver problems.

Tell your doctor your medical history, especially if you have: heart disease, kidney problems, eye problems (e.g., cataracts), thyroid problems, uncontrolled seizures, recent serious infection, recent major surgery, low blood pressure, alcohol use, any allergies (especially to other "statin" drugs).

Daily use of alcohol may increase your chance for serious side effects. Limit alcoholic beverages.

Drug Interactions

This drug is not recommended for use with mibefradil, protease inhibitors (e.g., ritonavir, amprenavir, lopinavir), azole antifungals (e.g., itraconazole, ketoconazole).

Ask your doctor or pharmacist for more details.

Tell your doctor of all prescription and nonprescription medication you may use, especially: amiodarone, colestipol, cholestyramine, niacin (nicotinic acid) or niacin-containing products, cyclosporine, macrolide antibiotics (e.g., clarithromycin, erythromycin, troleandomycin), fibrates (e.g., gemfibrozil), nefazodone, digoxin, verapamil, "blood thinners" (e.g., warfarin), diltiazem, rifampin.

Do not start or stop any medicine without first consulting your doctor or pharmacist.

Notes

Do not share this medication with others.

Laboratory and/or medical tests may be performed to monitor your cholestrol levels and to see if the medicine is causing unwanted side effects.

For best results, this medication should be used along with exercise and a low-cholesterol/low-fat diet. Consult your doctor.

Missed Dose

If you miss a dose, take it as soon as you remember. If it is near the time of the next dose, skip the missed dose and resume your usual dosing schedule. Do not double the dose to catch up.

Storage

Store at room temperature between 59 and 86 degrees F (15 and 30 degrees C) away from light and moisture.

SPIRONOLACTONE

Common Brand Name: Aldactone

Uses
This drug is a diuretic or "water pill". It reduces the amount of water and sodium retained by the body. It is used to lower blood pressure, treat fluid retention (edema) and heart disease (congestive heart failure), and raise low potassium levels.

How to Use
Take this exactly as prescribed. Do not skip doses or increase the dose without your doctor's approval.

Take with food or milk to minimize stomach upset.

Because this drug may increase urination, avoid taking a dose right before bedtime.

Side Effects
This drug may cause dizziness or blurred vision.

Watch for signs of dehydration such as dry mouth or thirst.

You may experience nausea, vomiting, loss of appetite, fatigue, sleeplessness or nasal congestion the first few days as your body adjusts to the medication. If any of these effects persist or worsen, inform your doctor promptly.

Unlikely, but report promptly if you develop: deepening of the voice, sore throat, weakness, irregular pulse, persistent cough, decreased sexual ability, change in the amount of urine, increased breast size, breast soreness.

In the unlikely event you have an allergic reaction to this drug, seek immediate medical attention. Symptoms of an allergic reaction include: rash, itching, swelling, dizziness, breathing trouble.

If you notice other effects not listed above, contact your doctor or pharmacist.

Precautions
Tell your doctor your medical history especially if you have: kidney or liver disease, urinary problems, diabetes, sodium or potassium imbalances, any allergies.

Because this drug changes your fluid balance, you may feel dizzy if you change from a lying to a standing position too rapidly. Avoid this by rising slowly.

If this drug makes you dizzy, use caution while engaging in activities that require alertness such as driving or using machinery.

Before having surgery, including dental surgery, tell the doctor you take spirono-lactone.

Drug Interactions

Tell your doctor of all medications you may use (both prescription and nonprescrip-tion) especially if you have: other diuretics ("water pills" such as amiloride, tri-amterene, and furosenude), lithium, digoxin, potassium supplements, cyclosporine, mitotane, ACE inhibitors (e.g., lisinopril, captopril, enalapril), NSAIDs (e.g., ibuprofen, naproxen).

Aspirin may decrease the effects of spironolactone. Many nonprescription products contain aspirin. Consult your pharmacist if you are uncertain your nonprescription medicines contain aspirin.

This medication may increase your potassium levels. Consult your doctor or pharmacist before using potassium-containing products (salt substitutes or potassium supplements) or large amounts of potassium-containing foods (e.g., bananas, potatoes).

Do not start or stop any medicine without first consulting your doctor or phar-macist.

Notes

Do not share this medication with others.

Missed Dose

If you miss a dose, take it as soon as you remember. If it is near the time of the next dose, skip the missed dose and resume your usual dosing schedule. Do not double the dose to catch up.

Storage

Store at room temperature between 59 and 86 degrees F (between 15 and 30 degrees C) away from moisture and sunlight. Do not store in the bathroom.

SUMATRIPTAN

Common Brand Name: Imitrex

Uses
This medication is used to treat migraine and cluster headache attacks once they occur. It is not effective in preventing migraines.

How to Use
One dose is taken by mouth at the first signs of a migraine attack. If you must take a second dose, do so exactly as instructed by your doctor.

Do not take more than 200mg in a 24 hour period.

Tablets are to be swallowed whole with a glass of water. Do not crush or chew them.

Side Effects
This medication may initially cause flushing, pain at the injection site, dizziness, weakness, nausea, drowsiness, stiffness, or feelings of tingling, heat, fatigue. If any of these effects continue or become bothersome, inform your doctor.

In the unlikely event you have an allergic reaction to this drug, seek immediate medical attention. Symptoms of an allergic reaction include: rash, itching, swelling, dizziness, trouble breathing.

If you notice other effects not listed above, contact your doctor or pharmacist.

Precautions
Tell your doctor if you have coronary artery disease, high blood pressure, stroke, kidney disease, liver disease, allergies (especially drug allergies).

Since this medication may cause drowsiness, use caution operating machinery or engaging in activities requiring alertness and avoid alcohol because it may increase drowsiness/dizziness effects.

The manufacturer does not recommend use of sumatriptan with older people, because they may be more sensitive to its side effects.

Drug Interactions

Tell your doctor of all over-the-counter and prescription medication you take, especially if you have: ergotamine- containing medication, all headache drugs, MAO inhibitors (e.g., phenelzine, tranylcypromine).

Do not take MAO inhibitors with sumatriptan or use sumatriptan within 2 weeks of stopping use of MAO inhibitors.

Do not take any ergotamine-containing medication and sumatriptan within 24 hours of each other.

Also, report the use of all antidepressants or any medications used for weight control. If you are unsure about the types of medications you take, ask your care provider or pharmacist.

It is recommended to avoid consumption of alcohol while taking this medication.

Do not start or stop any medicine without first consulting your doctor or pharmacist.

Notes

This medication is used to relieve a migraine attack in progress. It is not effective in preventing migraine attacks.

Missed Dose

Take this medication only when a migraine attack occurs as directed. This is not taken routinely. Never the dose.

Storage

Store this medication at 15 to 30 degrees C (59 to 86 degrees F) away from heat and light. Do not store in the bathroom. Keep this and all medications out of the reach of children.

TAMOXIFEN

Common Brand Name: Nolvadex

Uses
Tamoxifen is a drug that blocks the action of the hormone estrogen. It is used in the treatment and prevention of breast cancer in women.

How to Use
Take this drug by mouth exactly as prescribed for the full treatment period.

Side Effects
Nausea, hot flashes, weight gain or headache may occur. If these effects persist or worsen, notify your doctor promptly.

Report promptly: abnormal vaginal bleeding or irregular periods, vaginal discharge, groin pain, vision changes.

Unlikely but report promptly: vomiting, rash.

Tell your doctor immediately if any of these highly unlikely but very serious side effects occur: dark urine, yellowing eyes and skin, easy bruising, persistent sore throat, fever, mental or mood changes, trouble breathing, unusual tiredness, leg pain or swelling, dizziness.

If you notice other effects not listed above, contact your doctor or pharmacist.

Precautions
Tell your doctor your medical history, especially if you have: eye problems, blood disorders, cancers, liver disease, allergies (especially drug allergies).

Drug Interactions
This drug is not recommended for use with mibefradil. Ask your doctor or pharmacist for more details.

Tell your doctor or pharmacist of all prescription and nonprescription drugs you may use, especially if you have: warfarin, St John's wort.

Report other drugs which affect the heart rhythm (QTc prolongation), such as:

dofetilide, pimozide, quinidine, sotalol, procainamide, sparfloxacin, "water pills" (diuretics such as furosemide or hydrochlorothiazide).

Ask your doctor or pharmacist for more details.

Do not start or stop any medicine without first consulting your doctor or pharmacist.

Notes

Keep all doctor and lab visits (e.g., yearly pelvic/gynecology exams) because it is important to have your progress monitored.

Missed Dose

If you miss a dose, take it as soon as you remember. If it is near the time of the next dose, skip the missed dose and resume your usual dosing schedule. Do not double the dose to catch up.

Storage

Store at room temperature away from sunlight and moisture.

TAMSULOSIN

Common Brand Name: Flomax

Uses
This medication is used to treat the symptoms of prostate enlargement (BPH), such as urinary hesitancy or urgency.

How to Use
This drug is generally taken once daily. Take the first dose at bedtime to minimize the chances of getting dizzy or fainting. After the first dose, take your regularly scheduled dose 30 minutes after the same meal each day. Or take exactly as directed by your doctor.

Do not crush, chew or open the capsules. Do not increase the dose without your doctor's approval.

Side Effects
Headache, dizziness, unusual weakness, back pain, drowsiness or sleeplessness could occur. If these persist or worsen, notify your doctor.

Notify your doctor promptly if any of these effects occur: ejaculation problems, dizziness.

Unlikely but report promptly: vision problems.

Very unlikely but report promptly any fainting episodes. Seek immediate medical attention if painful, prolonged erection occurs.

In the unlikely event you have an allergic reaction to this drug, seek immediate medical attention. Symptoms of an allergic reaction include: rash, itching, swelling, severe dizziness, trouble breathing.

If you notice other effects not listed above, contact your doctor or pharmacist.

Precautions
Tell your doctor your medical history, especially if you have: blood pressure problems, drug allergies.

To avoid dizziness or fainting, get up slowly from a lying or seated position; especially when you first start using this drug or if your doctor changes your dosing.

Limit your intake of alcohol and avoid getting overheated because they may increase the dizziness and drowsiness effects of this drug. Use caution performing tasks requiring alertness such as driving or using machinery.

This drug is not recommended for use in women.

Drug Interactions

Tell your doctor of all nonprescription or prescription medication you may use, especially: other alpha- blocker drugs (e.g., prazosin, doxazosin), blood pressure drugs (including "water pills" or diuretics), cimetidine, "blood thinners" (e.g., warfarin), drugs that can make you drowsy (e.g., sleep medicines, tranquilizers, sedatives, narcotic pain relievers like codeine, psychiatric medications, muscle relaxants, certain antihistamines like diphenhydramine, and anti-seizure drugs).

Do not start or stop any medicine without first consulting your doctor or pharmacist.

Notes

Do not share this medication with others.

Missed Dose

If you miss a dose, take it as soon as you remember. If it is near the time of the next dose, skip the missed dose and resume your usual dosing schedule. Do not double the dose to catch up.

Storage

Store at room temperature between 68 and 77 degrees F (20-25 degrees C) away from sunlight and moisture.

TEMAZEPAM

Common Brand Name: Restoril

Uses
This medication is used for the short term treatment of insomnia (sleeping disorders).

How to Use
Take this medication 15 to 30 minutes before bedtime as directed.

Take this with food or milk if stomach upset occurs.

Do not suddenly stop taking this medication without first consulting your doctor if you have been taking this for some time. It may be necessary to gradually decrease the dose.

Take this exactly as prescribed. Do not increase the dose or take this for longer than prescribed. Tolerance may develop with long-term or excessive use making it less effective.

Side Effects
Stomach upset, blurred vision, headache, constipation, confusion dizziness, depression, impaired coordination, trembling, nightmares, weakness, memory loss, hangover effect (grogginess) or clouded thinking may occur. If any of these effects persist or worsen, inform your doctor promptly.

Report promptly: mental confusion, seizures.

Very unlikely but report promptly: rapid heartbeat, fever.

In the unlikely event you have an allergic reaction to this drug, seek medical attention immediately. Symptoms of an allergic reaction include: rash, itching, swelling, dizziness, trouble breathing.

To avoid dizziness and lightheadedness when rising from a seated or lying position, get up slowly. Also limit your intake of alcoholic beverages which will aggravate these effects.

If you notice other effects not listed above, contact your doctor or pharmacist.

Precautions

Tell your doctor if you have disease, a history of drug dependence, history of depression, breathing problems, apnea, seizures, any allergies.

Caution is advised when using this drug with older people because they may be more sensitive to the affects of the drug.

Drug Interactions

Tell your doctor of any over-the-counter or prescription medication you may take including: medication for depression, anti-seizure drugs, narcotic pain relievers (e.g., codeine), sedatives. Sedative effects are enhanced with depressant drugs. Avoid alcohol with use.

Do not start or stop any medicine without first consulting your doctor or pharmacist.

Notes

You may experience sleeping difficulties the first one or two nights after stopping this medication. Be aware of this effect. If the problem continues, contact your doctor.

Older adults are usually more sensitive to the effects of this medication. Use cautiously.

Missed Dose

Take your dose at or near bedtime. If you miss a dose, skip the missed dose and resume your usual dosing schedule. Do not double the dose to catch up.

Storage

Store at room temperature between 59 and 86 degrees F (15 to 30 degrees C) away from heat and light. Do not store in the bathroom.

TERAZOSIN

Common Brand Name: Hytrin

Uses
This medication relaxes and dilates (expands) blood vessels resulting in lowered blood pressure. It is used to treat hypertension (high blood pressure).

In males, this drug is used for symptoms of prostate enlargement such as urinary hesitancy and/or urgency.

How to Use
Take this medication exactly as prescribed. Try to take it at the same time each day. Take the first dose at bedtime to minimize the chances of getting dizzy or fainting.

Tablets may be taken with food or milk to avoid stomach upset.

It is important to continue taking this medication even if you feel well. Most people with high blood pressure do not feel sick.

Do not stop taking this medication without consulting your doctor. Some conditions may become worse when the drug is abruptly stopped. Your dose may need to be gradually decreased.

Side Effects
Dizziness, drowsiness, headache, incontinence, constipation, dry mouth, loss of appetite, fatigue, nasal congestion or dry eyes may occur the first several days as your body adjusts to the medication.

This medication may rarely cause impotence.

Inform your doctor if you develop: chest pain, difficulty breathing, skin rash, swelling of the hands or feet, ringing in the ears.

If you notice other effects not listed above, contact your doctor or pharmacist.

Precautions
Tell your doctor your medical history, especially if you have: liver disease, kidney disease, allergies (especially drug allergies).

To avoid dizziness or fainting, get up slowly from a lying or seated position (especially when you first start using this drug or if your doctor changes your dosing).

Limit your intake of alcohol and avoid getting overheated because they may increase the dizziness and drowsiness effects of this drug. Use caution performing tasks requiring alertness such as driving or using machinery.

Drug Interactions
Inform your doctor about all the medicines you use (both prescription and nonprescription). Avoid any drugs that increase your heart rate or make you excited like decongestants because it may counteract your blood pressure medicine. Decongestants are commonly found in over-the-counter cough and cold products.

Do not start or stop any medicine without first consulting your doctor or pharmacist.

Notes
It is important to have your blood pressure checked regularly while taking this medication. Learn how to monitor your blood pressure. Discuss this with your doctor or pharmacist. Rise from sitting to standing very carefully.

Missed Dose
If you miss a dose, take it as soon as you remember. If it is near the time of the next dose, skip the missed dose and resume your usual dosing schedule. Do not double the dose to catch up.

Storage
Store at room temperature away from sunlight and moisture.

TETRACYCLINE

Common Brand Name: Achromycin V

Uses
This medication is used to treat a wide variety of bacterial infections. It is also used to treat acne.

How to Use
This medication works best if taken on an empty stomach one hour before or two hours after meals. Take each dose with a full glass of water (4oz. or 120ml) or more. Do not lie down for 30 minutes after taking this drug. May take with food if stomach upset occurs unless your doctor directs you otherwise.

The liquid suspension form of this medicine must be shaken well before using.

Avoid consuming dairy products or taking antacids containing aluminum, magnesium or calcium, sucralfate, zinc (e.g., vitamins) or iron preparations within 2-3 hours of taking this drug. These products bind with this antibiotic preventing its absorption.

Antibiotics work best when the amount of medicine in your body is kept at a constant level. Do this by taking the medication at evenly spaced intervals throughout the day and night.

Continue to take this medication until the full prescribed amount is finished even if symptoms disappear after a few days.

Stopping the medication too early may allow bacteria to continue to grow resulting in a relapse of the infection.

Side Effects
This medication may cause stomach upset, diarrhea, nausea, headache or vomiting. If these symptoms persist or worsen, notify your doctor.

Very unlikely, but report promptly: stomach pain, yellowing eyes or skin, vision problems, mental changes.

Tetracyclines increase sensitivity to sunlight.

Use of this medication for prolonged or repeated periods may result in a secondary infection (e.g., oral or infection) or sore throat while taking this medication.

In the unlikely event you have an allergic reaction to this drug, seek immediate medical attention. Symptoms of an allergic reaction include: rash, itching, swelling, dizziness, trouble breathing.

If you notice other effects not listed above, contact your doctor or pharmacist.

Precautions

Tell your doctor your medical history, especially if you have: kidney or liver problems, any allergies, trouble swallowing, esophagus problems (e.g., hiatal hernia, GERD).

This medication may make you more prone to sunburn. Wear protective clothing and a sunscreen if needed.

Drug Interactions

Inform your doctor or pharmacist about all the medicines you may use (prescription and nonprescription), especially: digoxin, penicillin-related drugs, live vaccines, antacids, cimetidine, warfarin, methoxyflurane, iron.

Do not start or stop any medicine without first consulting your doctor or pharmacist.

Notes

This medication has been prescribed for your current condition only. Do not use it later for another infection or give it to someone else. A different medication may be necessary.

Missed Dose

If you miss a dose, take it as soon as you remember. If it is near the time of the next dose, skip the missed dose and resume your usual dosing schedule. Do not double the dose to catch up.

Storage

Store at room temperature away from moisture and sunlight. Do not freeze liquid forms. Do not store in the bathroom. Discard any unused drug. Check the drug's expiration date.

Taking outdated tetracycline (or a related drug) can result in serious illness.

THEOPHYLLINE

Common Brand Names: Theo-Dur, Theo-24, Theolair, Uniphyl

Uses
This medication improves breathing by opening air passages in the lungs. It is used in the treatment of asthma, COPD (chronic bronchitis, and emphysema.).

How to Use
This medication works best when taken on an empty stomach one hour before or two hours after meals. If stomach upset occurs, it may be taken with food.

Long acting capsules and tablets must be swallowed whole.

Crushing or chewing them may destroy the long action and increase the possibility of side effects.

If capsules are too large to swallow, open the capsule and mix the contents with jelly or applesauce and swallow without chewing.

This medication works best if a constant level is maintained in the body. Do this by taking doses at evenly spaced intervals.

Side Effects
Dizziness, headache, lightheadedness, heartburn, stomach pain, loss of appetite, restlessness, nervousness, sleeplessness or increased urination may occur as your body adjusts to the medication. If these symptoms persist or worsen, inform your doctor.

Inform your doctor if you experience: chest pain, rapid or irregular heartbeat, confusion, severe stomach pain, breathing difficulties.

If you notice other effects not listed above, contact your doctor or pharmacist.

Precautions
Avoid drinking large amounts of beverages containing caffeine (coffee, tea, colas) or eating large amounts of chocolate. Caffeine can increase side effects of this medication.

Smoking affects this medication. Be sure to tell your doctor if you smoke or use nicotine. Inform your doctor if you stop smoking. Your dose may need to be adjusted.

Drug Interactions
Inform your doctor about all the medicines you use (both prescription and nonprescription), especially if you take: cimetidine, erythromycin, troleandomycin, mexiletine, tacrine, barbiturates, disulfiram, rifampin, thiabendazole, rifabutin, ticlopidine, quinolone antibiotics, beta-blockers, phenytoin, fluvoxamine (an SSRI antidepressant), St John's wort.

Do not start or stop any medicine without first consulting your doctor or pharmacist.

Notes
Don't change your diet without first checking with your doctor. Large amounts of char-broiled foods or a high protein, low carbohydrate diet can affect the action of this medication.

Do not change brands of this medication without consulting your doctor or pharmacist. Not all brands are identical in action.

Missed Dose
If you miss a dose, take it as soon as you remember. If it is near the time of the next dose, skip the missed dose and resume your usual dosing schedule. Do not double the dose to catch up.

Storage
Store at room temperature away from moisture and sunlight. Do not store in the bathroom. Do not freeze liquid forms of this medication.

TOLTERODINE

Common Brand Name: Detrol

Uses
This medication is used to treat an overactive bladder.

How to Use
Take this product by mouth exactly as directed by you doctor. Your dosage depends on your condition and response to therapy. This medication may be taken with or without food. The sustained release form must be swallowed whole. Do not crush or chew them.

Side Effects
Dry mouth, dry eyes, headache, constipation, nausea, dizziness or drowsiness may occur. If these effects persist or worsen, notify your doctor promptly.

To relieve dry mouth, suck on (sugarless) hard candy or ice chips, chew (sugarless) gum, drink water or use saliva substitute.

Report promptly: symptoms of urinary infection (e.g., urinary burning, urgent and frequent urination).

Unlikely but report promptly: vision problems, eye pain, difficulty with urination, severe stomach pain, chest pain, fast heartbeat, hot/dry skin, mental or mood changes.

If you notice other effects not listed above, contact your doctor or pharmacist.

Precautions
Tell your doctor your medical history, including any allergies, difficulty with urination (urinary retention or prostate enlargement in males), stomach/intestinal disorders (e.g., gastric retention), glaucoma (narrow angle), liver problems, kidney problems.

Limit alcohol intake, as it may aggravate certain side effects of this drug. Caution is advised when performing tasks requiring mental alertness (e.g., driving).

This medication may reduce sweating which can lead to heat stroke in hot weather. Consult your doctor or pharmacist.

Caution is advised with older people, who may be more sensitive to side effects should they occur.

Drug Interactions
Tell your doctor of all nonprescription and prescription medication you may use, especially if you have: macrolide antibiotics (e.g., erythromycin, clarithromycin), azole antifungals (e.g., ketoconazole, itraconazole), anti-Parkinson's drugs (e.g., benztropine, trihexyphenidyl, other antimuscarinic drugs (e.g., scopolamine, dicyclomine), oxybutynin, cyclosporine, vinblastine.

Also report other drugs which may cause drowsiness, such as: anti-anxiety or anti-seizure drugs, sedatives, tranquilizers, narcotic pain relievers, psychiatric medicines (e.g., chlorpromazine or amitriptyline), muscle relaxants, antihistamines that cause drowsiness (e.g., diphenhydramine).

Check the labels on all your medicines (e.g., cough-and-cold products) because they may contain drowsiness-causing ingredients. Ask your pharmacist about the safe use of those products.

Do not start or stop any medicine without first consulting your doctor or pharmacist.

Notes
Do not share this medication with others.

Missed Dose
If you miss a dose, take it as soon as you remember. If it is near the time of the next dose, skip the missed dose and resume your usual dosing schedule. Do not double the dose to catch up.

Storage
Store at room temperature between 66 and 77 degrees F (20-25 degrees C) away from light and moisture.

TRAMADOL

Common Brand Name: Ultram

Uses
Tramadol is used for pain relief.

How to Use
Take this medication by mouth as prescribed. It is usually taken every 4 to 6 hours as needed.

Use this medication exactly as prescribed. Do not increase your dose, use it more frequently or use it for a longer period of time than prescribed because this drug can be habit-forming.

Also, if used for an extended period of time, do not suddenly stop using this drug without your doctor's approval.

If this medicine does not provide effective pain relief, contact your doctor.

Side Effects
This medication may cause dizziness, weakness, incoordination, nausea or vomiting, stomach upset, constipation, headache, drowsiness, anxiety, irritability, dry mouth, or increased sweating. If any of these effects persist or worsen, inform your doctor.

Notify your doctor if you develop any of these serious effects while taking this medication: chest pain, rapid heart rate, skin rash or itching, mental confusion, disorientation, seizures, tingling of the hands or feet, trouble breathing.

In the unlikely event you have an allergic reaction to this drug, seek immediate medical attention. Symptoms of an allergic reaction include: rash, itching, swelling, dizziness, breathing trouble.

If you notice other effects not listed above, contact your doctor or pharmacist.

Precautions
Tell your doctor your medical history, especially if you have: kidney disease, liver disease, seizure disorder, lung disease, history of drug or alcohol dependency, any allergies you may have.

Limit alcohol as it may add to the dizziness or drowsiness effects caused by the medication.

Because this drug may make you dizzy/drowsy, use caution performing tasks requiring alertness such as driving.

Older adults may be more sensitive to the effects of the drug, especially the side effects.

Drug Interactions

Tell your doctor of all prescription and nonprescription medications you may use, especially if you have: carbamazepine, narcotic pain relievers (e.g., codeine), drugs used to aid sleep, antidepressants (e.g., SSRI-types such as fluoxetine or fluvoxamine), monoamine oxidase, inhibitors (e.g., furazolidone, linezolid, phenelzine, procarbazine, selegiline, tranylcypromine), psychiatric medicine (e.g., nefazodone), "triptan"-type drugs, anti-anxiety drugs (e.g., diazepam), sibutramine.

Also, report use of certain antihistamines (e.g., diphenhydramine) which are also present in many cough-and-cold products.

Do not start or stop any medicine without first consulting your doctor or pharmacist.

Notes

Do not share this medication with others.

Missed Dose

If you miss a dose, take it as soon as you remember. If it is near the time of the next dose, skip the missed dose and resume your usual dosing schedule. Do not double the dose to catch up.

Storage

Store this medication at room temperature between 59 and 86 degrees F (15 to 30 degrees C) away from heat and light.

Do not store in the bathroom. Keep this and all medications out of the reach of children.

TRAZODONE

Common Brand Name: Desyrel

Uses
This medication is used to treat depression. It may take 2 to 3 weeks before the full effects of this medication are noticed. This medicine is also used for short periods to treat sleep disorders (insomnia).

How to Use
May be taken with food to prevent stomach upset.

Take this as prescribed. Try to take each dose at the same time(s) each day so you remember to routinely take it. Since this drug can cause drowsiness, it is best taken at bedtime.

Do not stop taking this medication without your doctor's approval. Nausea, headache or fatigue can occur if the drug is suddenly stopped.

Side Effects
This drug may cause drowsiness, dizziness, blurred vision, loss of appetite, dry mouth, strange taste in mouth, anxiety, restlessness or sweating. If these effects persist or worsen, notify your doctor promptly.

Notify your doctor promptly if you develop: chest pain, rapid heart rate, shortness of breath, difficulty urinating, blood in the urine, nightmares, uncoordinated movements.

Males: if you experience painful and prolonged erections, stop using this drug and seek immediate medical attention.

In the unlikely event you have an allergic reaction to this drug, seek immediate medical attention. Symptoms of an allergic reaction include: rash, itching, swelling, dizziness, trouble breathing.

If you notice other effects not listed above, contact your doctor or pharmacist.

Precautions
Tell your doctor your medical history, especially if you have: heart disease, liver

disease, kidney disease, blood pressure problems, any allergies (including nefazodone).

Use caution performing tasks requiring alertness such as driving or using machinery.

To avoid dizziness and lightheadedness when rising from a seated or lying position, get up slowly.

Alcoholic beverages can add to the drowsiness caused by this drug. Limit alcohol intake.

Older adults may be more sensitive to the effects of trazodone. Especially side effects.

Drug Interactions

Tell your doctor of any over-the-counter or prescription drugs you are taking, especially: digoxin, phenytoin or other anti-seizure drugs, antihistamines, medicine for allergies or colds, sedatives, tranquilizers, barbiturates (e.g., phenobarbital), narcotic pain relievers, other medicine for depression (e.g., SSRIs such as fluoxetine), sleeping aids, drugs for high blood pressure, ginkgo.

Before you have surgery with a general anesthetic, including dental surgery, tell the doctor or dentist you are taking trazodone.

Do not start or stop any medicine without first consulting your doctor or pharmacist.

Missed Dose

If you miss a dose, take it as soon as you remember. If it is near the time of the next dose, skip the missed dose and resume your usual dosing schedule. Do not double the dose to catch up.

Storage

Store at room temperature between 59 and 86 degrees F (between 15 and 30 degrees C) away from moisture and sunlight. Do not store in the bathroom.

TRIAMCINOLONE

Common Brand Name: Azmacort

Uses
This medication is used to treat swelling, inflammation, or itching of skin conditions such as eczema, dermatitis, rashes, insect bites, poison ivy, allergies and other irritations.

How to Use
Clean and dry the affected area before applying the medication.

To apply, gently massage a small amount of the medication into the affected area and surrounding skin.

Do not bandage, wrap or cover the area treated unless you are instructed to do so by your doctor.

Do not use plastic pants or tight fitting diapers on children being treated with this medication in the diaper area.

Avoid using this medication around the eyes unless directed to do so by your doctor.

Side Effects
This medication may cause burning, stinging, itching or redness when first applied to the skin. This should disappear in a few days as your body adjusts to the medication.

If these effects persist or worsen, inform your doctor.

Skin infections can become worse when using this medication.

Notify your doctor if redness, swelling or irritation does not improve.

Very unlikely to occur but report promptly the following side effects: unusual weakness, weight loss, nausea/vomiting, fainting, dizziness.

If you notice other effects not listed above, contact your doctor or pharmacist.

Precautions
Do not use this medication near the eyes if you have glaucoma.

Treatment with clobetasol, halobetasol propionate and augmented betamethasone dipropionate beyond two weeks consecutively is not recommended.

Do not use if there is an infection or sores present on the area to be treated.

Though very unlikely, it is possible this medication will be absorbed into your bloodstream. This may have undesirable consequences that may require additional corticosteroid treatment. This is especially true for children and for those who have used this for an extended period if they also have serious medical problems such as serious infections, injuries or surgeries. This precaution applies for up to one year after stopping use of this drug. Consult your doctor or pharmacist for more details.

Drug Interactions

Tell your doctor of all medications you may use, (both prescription and nonprescription), especially if you have: prednisone (or similar drugs), other skin medicines.

Do not start or stop any medicine without first consulting your doctor or pharmacist.

Notes

Inform all your doctors you use (or have used) this medication. Do not use an y other steroid cream/ointment in conjunction with this product.

Do not share this medication with others.

Missed Dose

If you miss a dose, take it as soon as you remember. If it is near the time of the next dose, skip the missed dose and resume your usual dosing schedule. Do not double the dose to catch up.

Storage

Store at room temperature away from sunlight. Avoid freezing.

TRIAMCINOLONE ACETONIDE

Common Brand Name: Nasacort AQ

Uses
This is a nasal steroid that works directly on nasal tissue to reduce swelling and inflammation. It is used to treat nasal itching, runny nose, postnasal drip, nasal congestion and sneezing associated with allergic rhinitis.

How to Use
To get the most benefit from this medication, make sure you understand how to use the nasal spray properly. Ask your doctor or pharmacist to demonstrate the correct way to use a nasal spray. Shake well before using.

The medication must reach the nasal tissue to be effective.

Therefore, blow your nose to clear the nasal passage before using the medication. If passages are blocked, a nasal decongestant may be used first (for a maximum of 3 to 5 days) to open the passages allowing proper penetration of the medication.

Be sure to aim spray away from the middle of the nose, that is, away from the nasal septum and toward the inflamed areas inside the nasal passages.

Use this medication exactly as prescribed. It must be used routinely to be effective. Do not increase your dose or use this more frequently than directed without your doctor's approval. It may take a few days before the benefits of the medication are noticed. If after 2 to 3 weeks no improvement in symptoms is noticed, consult your doctor.

Use this medication with caution if sores or injuries are present in the nasal passages.

Side Effects
This medication may cause irritation, stinging, burning, or dryness of the nasal passages. Sneezing, nosebleed, headache, lightheadedness, loss of taste, throat irritation or nausea may also occur. If these effects continue or become bothersome, inform your doctor.

Unlikely but report promptly: persistent nose or throat irritation/soreness, white patchy areas.

Very unlikely but report promptly: broken or damaged nasal membranes, unusual weakness, weight loss, nausea/vomiting, fainting, dizziness, vision changes.

If you notice other effects not listed above, contact your doctor or pharmacist.

Precautions

This medication should be used with caution if the following medical conditions exist: glaucoma, herpes-type infection of the eye, infection, recent nasal surgery or existing nasal sores, liver disease, tuberculosis, underactive thyroid, or allergies to corticosteroids.

Though very unlikely, it is possible this medication will be absorbed into your bloodstream. This may have undesirable consequences that may require additional corticosteroid treatment. This is especially true for children and for those who have used this for an extended period if they also have serious medical problems such as serious infections, injuries or surgeries. This precaution applies for up to one year after stopping use of this drug. Consult your doctor or pharmacist for more details.

Drug Interactions

Tell your doctor of all prescription and nonprescription medication you use, especially if you have: other nasal products.

Do not start or stop any medicine without first consulting your doctor or pharmacist.

Notes

If no improvement in your symptoms is noted after 3 weeks of using this medication, notify your doctor. Another medication may be needed or the dose may need adjusting.

Inform all your doctors you use, or have used, this medication.

Watering or itching eyes often associated with allergies are not significantly relieved by this medication.

Each canister contains approximately 100-120 sprays.

Missed Dose

If you miss a dose, take it as soon as you remember. If it is near the time of the next dose, skip the missed dose and resume your usual dosing schedule. Do not double the dose to catch up.

Storage

Store at room temperature away from sunlight and moisture. Avoid freezing.

TRIAMTERENE/HCTZ

Common Brand Names: Maxzide, Dyazide

Uses
This drug is a diuretic or "water pill". It reduces the amount of water and sodium retained by the body. It is used to treat high blood pressure and to treat edema (fluid retention).

How to Use
Take with food or milk to minimize stomach upset.

Take this drug exactly as prescribed. Do not skip doses or increase the dose without your doctor's approval.

Because this drug may increase urination, avoid taking a dose late in the day.

Side Effects
This drug may cause dizziness or blurred vision.

Use caution engaging in activities requiring alertness.

Because this drug changes your fluid balance, you may feel dizzy if you change from a lying to a standing position too rapidly. Avoid this by sitting up a few minutes before rising.

Also avoid drinking alcohol, which will aggravate these effects.

This drug may cause nausea, vomiting, loss of appetite, headache, dizziness and drowsiness the first few days as your body adjusts to the medication.

This medication increases sensitivity to the sun.

Inform your doctor if you develop: muscle cramps, irregular heartbeat, tingling of the hands and feet, easy bleeding or bruising, breathing difficulties, difficulty urinating.

If you notice other effects not listed above, contact your doctor or pharmacist.

Precautions
Tell your doctor your medical history, especially if you have: diabetes, liver or kidney problems, allergies (especially allergies to sulfa drugs).

Thiazides can make you more prone to sunburn. Avoid prolonged sun exposure.

343

Use a sunblock with skin protection factor (SPF) of at least 15 and wear protective clothing if this drug makes you sun-sensitive.

The use of alcohol can increase dizziness or lightheadedness.

Ask your doctor about its use.

Drug Interactions

This drug is not recommended for use with dofetilide. Ask your doctor or pharmacist for more details.

Tell your doctor of all prescription and nonprescription drugs you may use, especially if you have: lithium, ACE inhibitors (e.g., captopril), indomethacin or other NSAIDs.

If your medicine contains a thiazide and you take colestipol or cholestyramine, take the diuretic 1 hour before or 4 hours after the cholesterol-lowering medicine because these drugs may decrease the amount of diuretic absorbed into your body.

If you are using this medicine for high blood pressure, avoid drugs that increase your heart rate or blood pressure like decongestants because they may counteract the blood pressure effect. Decongestants are commonly found in over the counter cough and cold products.

Do not start or stop any medicine without first consulting your doctor or pharmacist.

Notes

Triamterene and hydrochlorothiazide diuretics can change the amount of potassium in your body. Potassium supplements should be used only when directed to do so by your doctor.

Missed Dose

If you miss a dose, take it as soon as you remember. If it is near the time of the next dose, skip the missed dose and resume your usual dosing schedule. Do not double the dose to catch up.

Storage

Store at room temperature away from moisture and sunlight. Do not store in the bathroom.

TRIMETH/SULFAMETH

Common Brand Names: Cotrim, Bactrim, Septra

Uses
This antibiotic is used to treat a wide variety of infections including urinary tract infections, middle ear infections, and respiratory tract infections, including pneumocystis pneumonia.

How to Use
Take each dose with a full glass of water. If stomach upset occurs, it may be taken with food or milk.

The liquid suspension form of this medicine must be shaken well before each dose.

Drink plenty of fluids while taking this medication unless your doctor directs you otherwise.

Antibiotics work best when the amount of medicine in your body is kept at a constant level. Do this by taking the medication at evenly spaced intervals throughout the day and night.

Continue to take this medication until the full prescribed amount is finished. Stopping the medication too early may result in a relapse of the infection.

Side Effects
This medication may cause stomach upset, diarrhea, nausea, headache or vomiting. If any of these effects persist or become severe, inform your doctor.

The sulfa in this combination drug may increase sensitivity to sunlight.

Notify your doctor if you develop: chills, fever, sore throat, easy bleeding or bruising, yellowing of the eyes or skin.

In the unlikely event you have an allergic reaction to this drug, seek immediate medical attention. Symptoms of an allergic reaction include: rash, itching, swelling, dizziness, breathing trouble.

If you notice other effects not listed above, contact your doctor or pharmacist.

Precautions

Tell your doctor your medical history, especially if you have: liver or kidney problems, asthma or other breathing problems, blood disorders, allergies (especially drug allergies).

Because this medication may make you prone to sunburn, wear protective clothing and a sunscreen.

This medication is not recommended for use in infants younger than 2 months.

Drug Interactions

Tell your doctor of all the medicines you may use (both prescription and nonprescription), especially if you have: warfarin, oral drugs to treat diabetes, methotrexate, oral PABA, phenytoin, methenamine, cyclosporine.

Do not start or stop any medicine without first consulting your doctor or pharmacist approval.

Notes

This medication has been prescribed for your current condition only. Do not use it later for another infection or give it to someone else. A different medication may be necessary.

Missed Dose

If you miss a dose, take it as soon as you remember. If it is near the time of the next dose, skip the missed dose and resume your usual dosing schedule. Do not double the dose to catch up.

Storage

Store at room temperature away from sunlight and moisture.

VALACYCLOVIR

Common Brand Name: Valtrex

Uses
Valacyclovir is an antiviral agent used in the treatment of shingles (herpes zoster) or genital herpes.

How to Use
Take this medication by mouth as directed.

Take all this medication as prescribed. Do not skip doses or stop taking this without your doctor's approval. Stopping therapy too soon may result in ineffective treatment.

For best results, take this medication at evenly spaced intervals throughout the day and night.

Side Effects
Nausea, vomiting, headache, loss of appetite, weakness, stomach pain, or dizziness may occur the first several days as your body adjusts to the medication. If any of these effects continue or become bothersome, inform your doctor.

Notify your doctor if your condition does not appear to improve or you experience a worsening of symptoms while taking this medication.

Use caution operating machinery or participating in activities requiring alertness if this medication makes you feel dizzy.

If you notice other effects not listed above, contact your doctor or pharmacist.

Drug Interactions
Tell your doctor of any over-the-counter or prescription medication you may take including: cimetidine, probenecid.

Do not start or stop any medicine without first consulting your doctor or pharmacist.

Notes
This medication is most effective if it is started within 48 hours of when the rash

first appears. This medication will accelerate the resolution of the herpes. The dose of this medication must be adjusted for kidney problems.

Missed Dose

If you miss a dose, take it as soon as you remember. If it is near the time of the next dose, skip the missed dose and resume your usual dosing schedule. Do not double the dose to catch up.

Storage

Store this medication at room temperature between 59 and 77 degrees F (15 to 25 degrees C) away from heat and light.

Do not store in the bathroom.

Keep this and all medications out of the reach of children.

VALSARTAN

Common Brand Name: Diovan

Uses
This drug is used to treat high blood pressure (hypertension) and heart failure. It works by preventing the narrowing of blood vessels. High blood pressure reduction helps prevent strokes, heart attacks, and kidney problems.

How to Use
Take this medication by mouth as prescribed, and learn proper usage. Consult your pharmacist.

Be sure to follow the dosing instructions closely. Do not increase your dose, skip any doses or stop taking this without first consulting your doctor.

Before using potassium supplements or salt substitutes, consult your doctor or pharmacist.

It is important to continue taking this medication even if you do not feel sick. Most people with high blood pressure do not have any symptoms.

Side Effects
Infrequent side effects such as dizziness, diarrhea, stomach upset, stuffed nose or dry mouth may occur the first several days as your body adjusts to the medication. If any of these effects persist or worsen, contact your doctor.

Unlikely to occur but report promptly: abdominal pain, persistent sore throat, muscle weakness, unusual fatigue, joint or muscle aches, fever, major change in the amount of urine eliminated.

In the unlikely event you have an allergic reaction to this drug, seek immediate medical attention. Symptoms of an allergic reaction include: rash, itching, swelling, dizziness, breathing trouble.

If you notice other effects not listed above, contact your doctor or pharmacist.

Precautions
Tell your doctor your medical history, including kidney or liver disease, congestive heart failure, diabetes, allergies (especially drug allergies).

To avoid dizziness and lightheadedness when rising from a seated or lying position, get up slowly. Also limit your intake of alcoholic beverages which will aggravate these effects.

Use caution performing tasks requiring alertness if this medication causes you to feel dizzy.

Drug Interactions

Tell your doctor of all over-the-counter or prescription medication you may take including: other drugs for blood pressure (e.g., diuretics-"water pills"), aspirin or aspirin-related pain or fever drugs, drugs that can cause kidney problems.

Do not take any over-the-counter medication for allergies or cough or colds without consulting your doctor or pharmacist. Many of the products contain ingredients which may interact with the effects of this medication.

Do not start or stop any medicine without first consulting your doctor or pharmacist.

Notes

Laboratory tests will be done periodically to be sure the drug is working properly and to monitor for possible side effects.

Learn how to monitor your pulse and blood pressure. Talk to your health care professional about this.

Missed Dose

If you miss a dose, take it as soon as you remember. If it is near the time of the next dose, skip the missed dose and resume your usual dosing schedule. Do not double the dose to catch up.

Storage

Store at room temperature between 59 and 86 degrees F (15 to 30 degrees C) away from heat and light. Do not store in the bathroom.

Common Brand Name: Diovan HCT

Uses
This medication is used to treat high blood pressure (hypertension).

How to Use
Take this medication by mouth as prescribed, usually once a day. It may be taken with or without food. Your dosage depends on your medical condition and response to the drug.

Be sure to follow the dosing instructions closely. Do not increase your dose, skip any doses or stop taking this without first consulting your doctor.

It is important to continue taking this medication even if you do not feel sick. Many people with high blood pressure do not have any symptoms.

Before using potassium supplements or salt substitutes, consult your doctor or pharmacist.

Side Effects
Nausea or vomiting, dry mouth, headache, fatigue or diarrhea may occur. If these effects persist or worsen, notify your doctor promptly.

Report promptly: lightheadedness or dizziness, muscle weakness or cramping.

Unlikely but report promptly: stomach pain, unusual change in amount of urine (after the first several days), unusual thirst, fainting, mental/mood changes.

Very unlikely but report promptly: persistent sore throat or cough, fever, unusual bleeding or bruising, dark urine, chest pain, rapid heartbeat, joint pain.

In the unlikely event you have an allergic reaction to this product, seek immediate medical attention. Symptoms of an allergic reaction include: rash, itching, swelling, dizziness, trouble breathing.

If you notice other effects not listed above, contact your doctor or pharmacist.

Precautions
Tell your doctor your medical history, especially if you have: kidney problems, heart disease, liver problems, diabetes, gout, high cholesterol or lipids (triglycerides),

lupus, metabolic problems (e.g., potassium or sodium imbalances), allergies (especially to sulfa drugs).

Use caution performing tasks requiring alertness if this medication makes you dizzy.

To avoid dizziness and lightheadedness when rising from a seated or lying position, get up slowly. Also, limit your intake of alcoholic beverages which can intensify these effects.

Excessive loss of body fluids (e.g., sweating or diarrhea) can cause a drop in blood pressure and make you lightheaded. Consult your doctor or pharmacist.

Hydrochlorothiazide may increase sensitivity to sunlight.

Avoid prolonged sun exposure. If you become sun sensitive, use a sunscreen and wear protective clothing when outdoors.

Caution is advised when this product is used with older people since this group may be more sensitive to drug side effects.

Drug Interactions
This drug is not recommended for use with dofetilide. Ask your doctor or pharmacist for more details.

Tell your doctor of all prescription and nonprescription medications you may use, especially if you have: potassium supplements (including salt substitutes with potassium), other blood pressure drugs, lithium, barbiturates (e.g., phenobarbital), drugs used for diabetes, colestipol, cholestyramine, NSAIDs (e.g., ibuprofen, naproxen, aspirin), ACTH, corticosteroids (e.g., prednisone), drugs that cause kidney problem such as gentamicin or amphotericin, allergy or cough-and-cold products (e.g., pseudoephedrine).

Do not start or stop any medicine without first consulting your doctor or pharmacist.

Notes
Laboratory tests will be done periodically to check for metabolic adverse effects.

Learn to monitor your pulse and blood pressure. Talk to your health care professional about this.

Do not share this medication with others.

Missed Dose
If you miss a dose, take it as soon as you remember. If it is near the time of the next dose, skip the missed dose and resume your usual dosing schedule. Do not double the dose to catch up.

Storage
Store at room temperature below 86 degrees F (30 degrees C) away from light and moisture.

VENLAFAXINE

Common Brand Name: Effexor

Uses
This medication is used in the treatment of depression.

The extended release form of this medication (Effexor XR) is also used to treat anxiety.

How to Use
Take this medication by mouth exactly as prescribed.

During the first few days your doctor may gradually increase your dose to allow your body to adjust to the medication. Take this medication with food. Do not take this more often or increase your dose without consulting your doctor. Do not stop taking this drug suddenly without your doctor's approval. Your dose may need to be gradually reduced before it is stopped completely.

Side Effects
This medication may initially cause dizziness and nausea as your body adjusts to the medication. Other side effects reported include sweating, loss of appetite, dizziness, dry mouth, anxiety, tremor, blurred vision, constipation, sleepiness, weight loss, change in sexual ability. If any of these effects continue or become bothersome, inform your doctor.

Notify your doctor if you develop any of these serious effects: rapid or irregular heartbeat, chest pain, severe headache, trouble breathing, painful or difficult urination, skin rash. Venlafaxine may worsen conditions of high blood pressure.

This medication may cause drowsiness, dizziness, or clouded thinking. Use caution operating machinery or engaging in activities requiring alertness.

If you notice other effects not listed above, contact your doctor or pharmacist.

Precautions
Tell your doctor your medical history, especially if you have: kidney disease, liver disease, heart disease, high blood pressure, glaucoma, any allergies.

Drug Interactions

Tell your doctor of any over-the-counter or prescription medication you may take especially: monoamine oxidase inhibitors (e.g., tranylcypromine, phenelzine, isocarboxazid, selegiline, furazolidone), other antidepressants, cimetidine, lithium, sedatives, narcotic pain relievers (e.g., codeine, morphine), tramadol, seizure medication, tryptophan, selective serotonin reuptake inhibitor (SSRIs) (e.g., fluo-xetine, citalopram, paroxetine) sumatriptan, and medicine for weight control.

It is recommended to avoid alcohol while using this medication.

Do not start or stop any medicine without first consulting your doctor or pharmacist.

Missed Dose

If you miss a dose, take it as soon as you remember. If it is near the time of the next dose, skip the missed dose and resume your usual dosing schedule. Do not double the dose to catch up.

Storage

Store this medication at room temperature between 59 and 86 degrees F (between 15 and 30 degrees C) away from heat and light. Do not store in the bathroom. Keep this and all medications out of the reach of children.

VERAPAMIL

Common Brand Names: Verapamil HCI, Verelan, Calan, Isoptin, Covera-HS

Uses
This drug is a calcium channel blocker. Calcium is involved in blood vessel contraction and in controlling the electrical impulses within the heart. By blocking calcium, verapamil relaxes and widens blood vessels and can normalize heartbeats. Verapamil is used to treat chest pain (angina), high blood pressure or irregular heartbeats.

How to Use
This medication should be swallowed whole with a full glass of water unless your doctor directs you otherwise.

This medication must be taken as directed to prevent chest pain. It is not effective if taken only when chest pain occurs.

Do not stop taking this medication suddenly without your doctor's permission. Chest pain can occur if the medication is stopped too fast. Your dose may need to be gradually decreased before it is stopped completely.

Side Effects
This drug may cause dizziness and lightheadedness especially during the first few days. Avoid activities requiring alertness. When you sit or lie down for a while, get up slowly to allow your body to adjust and minimize dizziness.

You may also experience weakness, fatigue, nausea, muscle cramps, headache, flushing or constipation. These effects should disappear as your body adjusts to the medication. Inform your doctor if they become bothersome.

Notify your doctor if you develop: breathing difficulties, swelling of the hands or feet, irregular heartbeat.

If you notice other effects not listed above, contact your doctor or pharmacist.

Precautions
Before using this drug, tell your doctor your medical history, including: allergies (especially drug allergies), heart problems (e.g., heart rhythm disturbances, heart failure), liver or kidney disease, very low blood pressure, muscular dystrophy.

Before heart surgery, tell your doctor you use this medicine.

Limit alcohol intake.

Older adults may be more sensitive to the effects of this drug, especially side effects.

Drug Interactions

Tell your doctor of all prescription and nonprescription drugs you may use, especially if you have: beta-blockers, cimetidine, cyclosporine, digoxin.

Avoid any drugs that increase your heart-rate (the decongestants phenylephrine, pseudoephedrine and phenylpropanolamine are examples) especially if you are taking verapamil for high blood pressure. These drugs are commonly found in over-the-counter cough-and-cold products.

Do not eat grapefruit or drink grapefruit juice unless your doctor instructs you otherwise.

Do not start or stop any medicine without first consulting your doctor or pharmacist.

Notes

Do not share this medication with others.

Missed Dose

If you miss a dose, take it as soon as you remember. If it is near the time of the next dose, skip the missed dose and resume your usual dosing schedule. Do not double the dose to catch up.

Storage

Store at room temperature away from sunlight and moisture.

WARFARIN

Common Brand Name: Coumadin

Uses
This medication is a blood thinner used to keep blood flowing smoothly and prevent the formation of blood clots.

How to Use
Take this exactly as prescribed.
   Try to take this medication at the same time each day so you remember to take it.
   Your dose may be adjusted several times based on lab tests.
   Do not stop taking this without your doctor's approval.

Side Effects
Loss of appetite, nausea, diarrhea or blurred vision may occur at first as your body adjusts to the medication.
   Inform your doctor if you experience: unusual bleeding or bruising, blood in the urine, black stools, severe headache.
   In the unlikely event you have an allergic reaction to this drug, seek medical attention immediately. Symptoms of an allergic reaction include: rash, itching, swelling, dizziness, trouble breathing.
   If you notice other effects not listed above, contact your doctor or pharmacist.

Precautions
Before using this drug tell your doctor your medical history especially if you have: ulcers, diabetes, liver or kidney disease, high blood pressure, arthritis, thyroid problems, all recent infections, recent surgery, drug and food allergies.
   The FDA has stated that certain generic warfarin products are interchangeable. However, consult your doctor and pharmacist before switching warfarin products.
   Do not stop taking any medications that you are currently taking unless directed to do so by your doctor.
   If you have an illness that causes vomiting, diarrhea, or fever for more than a few days, contact your doctor as these problems can change the effect of this drug.

Limit your consumption of alcoholic beverages. Ask your doctor how much, if any, alcohol you may consume.

When receiving warfarin, avoid sudden changes in dietary habits. Avoid ingesting unusual increases or decreases of foods high in Vitamin K (liver, broccoli, cauliflower, cabbage, kale, spinach and other green leafy vegetables, green tea, certain vegetables, cheeses and certain vitamin supplements). It is best to avoid strictly vegetarian diets that consist of foods high in vitamin K.

While taking this medication, be extra careful to avoid injuries. This medication can cause heavy bleeding. Use an electric razor and be careful brushing your teeth.

Caution is advised when using this drug with older people because they may be more sensitive to the effects of the drug.

Drug Interactions
Many drugs interact with this medication.

Before using this drug, tell your doctor of all prescription and nonprescription drugs you may use especially any of the following: aspirin or aspirin-like drugs, anabolic steroids, barbiturates, clofibrate, phenylbutazone, disulfiram, cimetidine, sulfa-drugs, metronidazole, vitamin E, cholestyramine, phenytoin, erythromycin-like antibiotics, propylthiouracil, injectable antibiotics, griseofulvin, ethchlorvynol, quinidine, quinine, thyroid drugs, allopurinol, glucagon, rifamycins, glutethimide, aminoglutethimide, chloramphenicol, carbamazepine, vitamin K (or its derivatives), dextrothyroxine, anti-inflammatory medication used for arthritis or fever reduction, penicillin-type drugs, amiodarone, omeprazole, sulfinpyrazone, chloral hydrate, "statin" drugs (e.g., lovastatin), propranolol, tamoxifen, quinolone antibiotics (e.g., ciprofloxacin), SSRI antidepressants (e.g., fluoxetine), gemfibrozil, azole antifungals (e.g., fluconazole, miconazole, including vaginal dose forms), birth control pills, dong quai, ginkgo biloba, ginseng.

It is important that all doctors and dentists treating you know you take warfarin.

Do not start or stop any medicine without first consulting your doctor or pharmacist.

Notes
Do not share this medication with others.

Missed Dose
If you miss a dose, take it as soon as you remember. If it is near the time of the next dose, skip the missed dose and resume your usual dosing schedule. Do not double the dose to catch up.

Storage

Store at room temperature between 59 and 86 degrees F (between 15 and 30 degrees C) away from moisture and sunlight. Do not store in the bathroom.

ZOLPIDEM

Common Brand Name: Ambien

Uses
This medication is used to treat insomnia (sleeping disorders).

How to Use
Take this medication by mouth immediately before bedtime on an empty stomach or as directed.

This medication is usually taken for short periods of 7 to 10 days. Take this exactly as prescribed. Do not increase the dose or take this for longer than prescribed.

Side Effects
Daytime drowsiness, dizziness, headache, nausea, stomach upset, vomiting, diarrhea, lightheadedness, and dry mouth may occur. If any of these effects continue or become bothersome, inform your doctor.

Notify your doctor if you develop any of these serious side effects while taking this medication: chest pain, rapid heart rate, difficulty breathing, skin rash, fever, behavior changes, mental confusion, abnormal thinking, depression.

To avoid dizziness and lightheadedness when rising from a seated or lying position, get up slowly. Also avoid intake of alcoholic beverages which will aggravate these effects. Because this medication causes drowsiness, use caution engaging in activities requiring alertness.

If you notice other effects not listed above, contact your doctor or pharmacist.

Precautions
Tell your doctor your medical history, especially of kidney disease, liver disease, lung disease, drug dependency, depression, breathing problems, any allergies.

Drug Interactions
Tell your doctor of any over-the-counter or prescription medication you may take including: any medication for depression or seizures, narcotic pain relievers, sedatives, sleep medicines.

Avoid the use of alcohol while taking this medication.

Do not start or stop any medicine without first consulting your doctor or pharmacist.

Notes
Older adults are usually more sensitive to the effects of this medication, especially dizziness and confusion.

You may experience sleeping difficulties on the first few nights after stopping this medication. Be aware of this effect. If the problem continues, contact your doctor.

Missed Dose
If you miss a dose, take it as soon as you remember. If it is near the time of the next dose, skip the missed dose and resume your usual dosing schedule. Do not double the dose to catch up.

Storage
Store at room temperature between 59 and 86 degrees F (15 to 30 degrees C) away from heat and light. Do not store in the bathroom.